LET IT ROCK!

• • •

"Only the best" album & book reviews
by Rev. Keith A. Gordon
(written circa 2007 - 2015)

The Reverend's Archives, Volume 3

New York • Nashville

LET IT ROCK!
Album & book reviews by Rev. Keith A. Gordon

ISBN #978-0-9850084-9-9

Published by Excitable Press, a Conspiracy M.E.D.I.A company
35 Montclair Avenue • Batavia NY 14020

On the web: http://www.thatdevilmusic.com

•CONTENTS•

CD REVIEWS

• CONTENTS •

CD REVIEWS

• CONTENTS •

CD REVIEWS

BOOK REVIEWS

• CONTENTS •

BOOK REVIEWS

All these reviews have previously been published in both print magazines like *Blurt*, *Blues Revue*, and *Blues Music* magazine as well as online on the About.com Blues website and the Reverend's own music blog, That Devil Music (http://www.thatdevilmusic.com).

All cover artwork herein courtesy of the respective record labels and publishers

Much gratitude to all those who have helped support my humble literary efforts through the years, but particularly Fred Mills & *Blurt* magazine, Art Tipaldi & *Blues Music* magazine, Cary Baker, Bruce Iglauer & Marc Lipkin at Alligator Records, Mark Pucci, Tim Livingston at Sundazed Records, William James at Glass Onyon PR, Joe Grushecky, the Goose Creek guys & anybody I may have forgotten...

Thanks, as always, to Brother Willie Jemison, Steve Morley, Thom King, Threk Michaels, Sharon Underwood and, of course, my lovely wife Tracey!

Thanx also to 'Ranger' Rick Johnson and Lester Bangs for the inspiration and opportunity to take this wild rock 'n' roll ride for 44+ years!

• Introduction •

This, ostensibly, is the third volume culled from the Reverend's literary archives...whereas the first book in the series included mostly reviews from my late Trademark of Quality music blog (R.I.P. 2008), and the second tome featured blues and blues-rock related reviews – many of them written during my tenure as the 'Blues Guide' (i.e. Editor) for About.com circa 2008-2014 – lucky book number three focuses more intently on my rock 'n' roll obsessions, what we call 'classic rock' these days, i.e. the music I grew up listening to; tho' you'll also find a soupcon of prog-rock, heavy metal, blues, Americana, and maybe even a little jazz-fusion inside these pages...

I'm your distinguished host, the kindly Rev. Keith A. Gordon. For those of you who have asked, yes, I'm a fully ordained minister who found the attraction of the Devil's music to be greater than that of the Good Book, and I've been preaching about the sinfully delightful charms of rock 'n' roll since many of you were in short pants (and I'd yet to grow the luxurious beard which currently adorns my rugged but pleasant visage).

...but I digress. This collection of mostly album reviews was originally going to be called Let It Blurt! *in tribute to the late, legendary rock critic Lester Bangs, and because many of the 100+ reviews found herein were originally published by my friends at* Blurt *magazine (also named in honor of Mr. Bangs). Since my colleague Jim DeRogatis had already used that title for his most excellent biography of the aforementioned almighty Lester, I decided to instead go with the name of Chuck Berry's classic 1960 hit, which is a perfectly serviceable and descriptive title for the featured content.*

The Reverend contributed to Blurt *magazine from its founding in 2008 until I took my leave in 2012.* Blurt *editor Fred Mills, who grew up during the same era as I and also got his start writing in the trenches of the cultural wasteland of the small press, is a kindred spirit that allowed me to write about pretty much any damn thing that caught my*

• **Introduction** •

*attention in any given week, which I appreciated and enjoyed. Fred
and his crew do yeoman work at* Blurt, *keeping the rock 'n' roll flame
burning brightly by championing new artists while not ignoring the
trail-blazing oldsters that got us to where we are today. Check 'em out
online at* http://blurtonline.com.

*Somewhere along the way towards compiling these reviews for this
third book, however, I got a bit 'word-count crazy' and pumped up* Let
It Rock! *beyond its original concept to include reviews from my* That
Devil Music *website (www.thatdevilmusic.com) as well as the odd
item originally published in* Blues Revue, Blues Music *magazine, and
other long-forgotten zines. Herein you'll find around 90,000 words –
roughly the heft of a good-sized novel (and more than many books
from my idol Kurt Vonnegut, Jr. but, you know...without the
intelligence or literary gravitas).*

*These reviews are what we antique rockcrits call "long form,"
running 800 words or better – a stark contrast to much of what passes
for music criticism these days – and they're meant to inspire you to
discover the music that excites me as a fan and a writer, some of it
providing your humble scribe with cheap thrills for decades now. I've
been doing this gig a long time now, since I was an eager teenage rock
music fan and well into my current middle-age dotage. In trying to
share some great music, I hope that I entertain you readers with
enthusiasm and opinions formed over a lifetime of "letting it rock." So
get up from your couch and run down the street to your local indie
record store and buy some music, will ya!*

*Rev. Keith A. Gordon
September 2016
Somewhere outside of Buffalo, New York in the heart of the 'Rust Belt'*

CD/DVD REVIEWS

Johnny Winter
Still Alive And Well

Produced by Rick Derringer
On Columbia Records® and Tapes

BADLANDS
Badlands / Voodoo Highway
(Rock Candy Records)

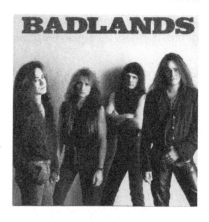

From the rather largish 'woulda, shoulda, coulda' file comes one of the great lost bands of rock 'n' roll, Badlands. Emerging from the 1980s nerf-metal scene, Badlands would be overshadowed first by the enormous success of L.A. sleaze contemporaries Guns N' Roses, a/k/a the luckiest bunch of Hollyrockin' droogs on the planet at the time, and then totally eclipsed by the grunge leviathan that steamrolled its way outta Seattle in 1991.

Badlands' lack of success remains a mystery almost two decades after the band's acrimonious break-up. The individual band members had the gutter-dwelling street rat look affected by Sunset Strip rockers like Motley Crue or the GN'R gang, lean and wiry with long hair and heroin chic. Badlands had an undeniable musical pedigree as well, guitarist Jake E. Lee making his bones as part of Ozzy Osbourne's post-Randy Rhodes band, vocalist Ray Gillen fresh off an ill-fated short stint with Black Sabbath. Future Kiss beat-blaster Eric Singer was another Sabbath alumnus, while Badlands bassist Greg Chaisson had clocked in with Ron Keel in Steeler.

Whether it was due to their lack of flamboyance when compared to even such notable second-and-third-tier glam-metal hellraisers as Love/Hate or Faster Pussycat, or because their blues-tinged hard rock sound drew more from Led Zeppelin than Hanoi Rocks, the guys in Badlands received little love from the City of Angels and, thus, were forever unable to break out of the L.A. rock ghetto.

Tis a shame, too, 'cause Badlands had found a strong creative team in Lee and Gillen, who had developed an uneasy songwriting relationship akin to Jagger and Richards, while the band's talents and electric chemistry allowed them to light up a stage wherever they toured. Badlands would manage to release just two great rock 'n' roll albums before burning out and breaking apart – their 1989 self-titled debut, and 1991's equally excellent *Voodoo Highway*.

Out-of-print almost from the date of its release, *Badlands* the album has long been ignored by U.S. reissue labels trying to mine gold from the major label archives, resulting in a seller's market charging collectors $50 or more for a first-gen CD copy. Originally released by Atlantic Records' Titanium imprint, *Badlands* has finally been reissued on CD by England's Rock Candy Records, the new release featuring re-mastered audio, a pretty cool bonus track on top of the ten original barn-burners, and a sixteen-page CD booklet with lengthy liner notes and a bunch of rare, unpublished band photos…undeniably a deluxe package that will have the band's international fan base foaming at the mouth.

As for the music? If you're unfamiliar with Badlands, don't cue up the CD expecting something along the lines of the Crue or Poison, or even Ozzy's bat-munching, 1980s-era Goth-metal Sturm und Drang. Nosirree, Badlands were unabashed Led Zeppelin acolytes, with maybe a dash of the Jeff Beck Group on the side of their plate, but definitely a boozy, blues-rock based gang o' houserockers. "High Wire" jumpstarts the album with a blast of white light/white heat, Gillen's voice teetering on the edge of the abyss as Lee's guitar slices-and-dices like some mutant six-string vegomatic. The rhythm section of Chaisson and Singer crashes with the best of 'em, delivering a blustery backbeat for the soaring vocals and guitar pyrotechnics. Call it Zeppelin mark II if you will, 'cause this is where the boys from Britain may have gone musically if not for Bonzo's unfortunate demise.

Badlands continues to singe your synapses with an unrelenting mix of mid-and-rapid-tempo firestarters that refuse to fall into flaccid power-ballad tropes. The label-dictated single "Dreams In The Dark" survived executive manhandling to become the band's calling card, garnering valuable MTV exposure (yeah, back when they used to play actual *music* videos) and inching into the *Billboard* Top 40.

The song itself is a pleasant enough lil' rocker with Gillen's voice sounding like Johnny Van Zandt on a wistful tale of romance and lust that could pass for a Southern rock number from a decade earlier if not for Lee's metallic riffing and the explosive rhythms behind Gillen's vocals.

The instrumental "Jade's Song" displays some of Lee's underrated fretwork, with dexterous acoustic-guitar strum serving as an extended intro to the deceptively benign "Winter's Call." The closest thing the album has to a ballad, "Winter's Call" starts out all gentle and sensitive and such before imploding like a deteriorating black star into another Zeppelin-esque pleasure wail of screaming vocals and guitars and TNT drumbeats.

The foreboding "Streets Cry Freedom" is drenched in dark malevolence, Lee's mesmerizing guitar lines matched by Gillen's muted vocals until the whole thing blows up in your face with a sonic howl colder and more powerful than any arctic wind. Gillen reaches Plant-like heights with a tortured and nuanced vocal performance delivered above sheer instrumental chaos. The band reaches for its inner Blackfoot with the bluesy, blustery "Rumblin' Train," which sports a fine set of Cajun-fried lyrics, a stomping rhythm, and Lee's best swamp-blues guitarwork.

"Devil's Stomp" offers up another understated intro that is randomly punctuated with sledgehammer blows of bass drum or wide slashes of wiry guitar. Lee's fretwork here is simply unbelievable, a pissed-off serpent that blindly strikes at anything within range while Gillen's black cat moan rides high above the fracas. A bonus track tacked on to the back end of this *Badlands* reissue, "Ball & Chain," is a rollicking blues-rock fever dream with a maddening recurring riff and enough cacophonic, cascading rhythms to make the most jaded of us wet our diapers in glee.

Reading through the liner notes in the deluxe sixteen-page booklet that accompanies this Rock Candy reissue of *Badlands*, it's amazing that the album was ever made in the first place. Label executives imagined a far different band than that which they signed, and kept trying to force them into the mold of washed-up hair-metal hacks rather than the young soul rebels they obviously were. The producer caused a split between the band's leads (Gillen and Lee) and the rhythm section, and at one point some damn fool suit wanted to toss Lee from the band that *he* started up in the first place.

Through all the madness and the tension, a classic album was created, however, and *Badlands* stands today as a pinnacle of the hard rock heights that were first explored by the Yardbirds, mapped by Eric Clapton and Cream, and explored by Zeppelin, Mountain, and other fellow travelers during the 1970s. Tossing aside the mindless hedonism and cretin worldview of other Hollywood street rats, and refusing to be bound by trends and expectations, Badlands aspired to more, and for a brief shining moment at the end of the 1980s, they achieved rock 'n' roll nirvana.

• • • • •

If their self-titled 1989 album had proven to be a difficult birth, with Badlands' manager usurping the producer's chair, and with Atlantic Records A&R "whiz" Jason Flom demanding a more commercial-sounding (i.e. trendy) sound from the band, *Voodoo Highway* would, in the end, be the band's undoing.

After touring for the better part of a year in the wake of *Badlands*, long-simmering tensions within the band would boil over at the end of the road. Singer Ray Gillen and guitarist Jake Lee were determined to eject drummer Eric Singer from the fold, with only bassist Greg Chaisson speaking on Singer's behalf...a strange turn of events as Singer and Chaisson had been at odds from day one.

Badlands found a new drummer in Jeff Martin, who had fronted L.A. speed-metal outfit Racer's X as their vocalist. Other changes were afoot, as the band kicked manager/producer Paul O'Neil to the curb, Lee taking over the controls for the production of *Voodoo Highway*.

With Lee at the helm, recording for *Voodoo Highway* started out better than the debut album, but would soon be undermined when Gillen went behind his band mates' backs to tattle to Flom that the band had more commercially-oriented songs that they were neglecting to record. It made for an uneasy vibe in the studio, production was eventually halted and then re-started, and by the time that *Voodoo Highway* actually hit the streets in 1991, Atlantic Records had officially washed its hands of the band.

Twas a shame, really, 'cause the label may have been able to bank a little dinero had they shown the slightest interest in the success of *Voodoo Highway*. The band's overt musical worship of Led Zeppelin was tempered in favor of a more streamlined metal-edged sound with just a bit of Southern-fried twang and a little good ol' fashioned rock 'n' roll funkiness.

Gillen's voice still soars menacingly like a hungry bird of prey, and the new rhythm section of Chaisson and Martin meshed nicely into a solid foundation that, while not as bombastic as Singer's eardrum assault, had enough big-beat bluster to shame any hard rock pretenders. As for Lee's guitar, the man remains one of the most underrated of guitar heroes, *Voodoo Highway* displaying a wide range of the man's talents.

Kicking off with chiming guitars and a swelling tsunami of rhythm, Gillen's leather-lunged wail opens "The Last Time" with a spark, the song's lyrics referencing, in passing, the Temptations/Rare Earth Motown gem "(I Know) I'm Losing You" in building an emotionally-draining performance. Gillen's tortured vox are complimented by Lee's raging fretwork, Badlands sounding more like a bluesy Guns N' Roses than a Zeppelin clone. Things quiet down somewhat for "Show Me The Way," the acoustic-strum intro leading into a muscular mid-tempo rocker with Gillen back into Robert Plant mode while Lee fills in around the edges of the bass/drums stomp with shards of razor-edged guitar.

The Mississippi funk of "Whiskey Dust" takes the band to its stripped-down, swamp-blues roots with a swaggering vocal performance by Gillen, an amped-up riff copped straight from Tony Joe White's "Poke Salad Annie" – perhaps the best since Jason & the Scorchers mangled the song a half-decade earlier. Lee's chicken-pickin' is the greasiest you'll hear outside of the Delta, each note lovingly covered in blood and mud. The instrumental "Joe's Blues" is a showcase for Lee's nimble-fingered fretwork, a lively country-blues number that is immediately steamrollered by the metal mastodon that is "Soul Stealer."

With a powerful vocal performance that cleverly blends Plant and Jim Morrison for a little grimy transcendence, "Soul Stealer" is the kind of evolved-in-a-straight-line-from-Zeppelin number that the Cult, Kingdom Come, or a dozen other clones would have liked to record. Lee's guitar shakes and rattles like a wild boar stuck with a hunter's arrows, while the rhythm section hits harder than a B-52 on a bombing run, the song's blues roots all but obliterated under an explosive rock 'n' roll sunburst.

A loud, taut guitar riff blasts the dust from your eardrums before Gillen's blustery vocals kick in on "Love Don't Mean A Thing," the song displaying a little o' that whiteboy foot shuffle that everybody from Humble Pie and Jo Jo Gunne to even GN'R had tried to perfect with varying success. Lee's riffing here is monster, blasting out of your speakers like that hungry alien facesucker leaping like a fiend from its host belly to attach itself to Sigourney Weaver's goodies. The title track lives up to its top-o-the-line billing with a dark-hued blues romp firmly rooted like cypress in some Louisiana swamp, Gillen's slinky vocals assisted by Lee's slithering Dobro pull.

Voodoo Highway contains the only cover song of Badlands' two albums, a spirited take of James Taylor's "Fire And Rain." While Gillen's voice lacks the warm sensitivity of Taylor's, he does a fine job of connecting with the material, bringing a little rock 'n' roll energy to the lyrics while the band's high-octane arrangement builds upon the original with emotional fretwork and a loose-knit rhythm track.

Lee, again, brings out the best in the song with a nervy solo that cuts to the quick. This performance is echoed again in the album-closing "In A Dream," an R&B-tinged ballad with gospel undertones, Gillen's soulful vocals carrying the song until Lee's subtle, high-lonesome guitar strum kicks in and underscores the emotion of the lyrics.

Like Icarus soaring too close to the sun, Badlands' defiant approach to their music would fly in the face of contemporary trends and eventually unravel the band's delicate chemistry. By the time that *Voodoo Highway* was released in 1991, the juggernaut that was grunge would dominate the charts. While Badlands' rootsy blues-metal would have creatively fit in perfectly between Pearl Jam's arena-rock dreams and Nirvana's complex punk-metal hybrid, label indifference and eventual hostility would put the band on the street within a year.

Ray Gillen would be sacked, then re-hired for an ill-fated U.K. tour when the band was unable to find a suitable replacement…in the end, Gillen was as essential to the Badlands' sound as guitarist Lee, and after recording a slate of demos for a possible Sony deal in late 1991, the band would break-up for good when Gillen seemingly sabotaged the deal by refusing a label-mandated physical exam. Gillen would be gone for good after dying of AIDS-related illness in December 1993.

Another casualty of label hijinx and the demanding rock star lifestyle, Badlands had its shot at the brass ring, only to see the rug pulled out from beneath them time after time. Between band in-fighting, creative tensions, and unrealistic label expectations, Badlands was doomed from day one…and still, they managed to deliver two classic albums of influential hard rock and blues-metal, all of the band's artistic battles and macho turf-fighting resulting in a rare and unique musical chemistry. With the long overdue re-release of both *Badlands* and *Voodoo Highway*, Badlands' often-overlooked musical legacy is ripe for rediscovery. (2011)

BIGELF
Cheat The Gallows   (Custard Records)

California rockers Bigelf have been embraced by the prog-rock crowd because…well, because they're just too damn weird to fit into any other critical or genre-based pigeonhole. This cosmic truth is both an albatross around the band's neck, and its most overwhelmingly appealing trait. A lot of times a rockcrit will tell you that "band X" doesn't sound like anybody else just 'cause they're unable to find any other noose-like adjective to throw around the artist's neck. In the case of Bigelf, when the Reverend tells you that "they don't sound like anybody else," you can bury that guarantee in the backyard because it's pure critical GOLD, kiddies!

It's not like Bigelf is any sort of flash-in-the-pan Pitchfork-approved indie band, either, considering that this motley bunch of psych-drenched, long-haired rock 'n' roll meanies have been kickin' the can since the early 1990s, mostly to little or no attention from you normal folks, only slightly more adoration from fellow musicians that respect both their dogged longevity as well as the hirsute qualities of their music.

Although these guys have probably been chased out of every major label office in the land by porcine security guards with pepper spray and hickory nightsticks, they managed to land on producer/songwriter Linda Perry's doorstep, and she agreed to capture their latest slab o' musical madness for posterity on her Custard Records label.

Cheat The Gallows is the most unusual album that you'll hear this year, an anarchic mix of hard rock, glam rock, and tongue-in-cheek Zappa-inspired irreverence with a decidedly '70s-styled classic rock aesthetic. There's some sort of conceptual construct going on here with the lyrics, tho' I'll be damned if I can figure it out. The songs here provide the listener a veritable roller-coaster ride from hell... "Gravest Show On Earth," the album-opener, is like a three-ring circus with Freddie Mercury as the ringmaster, and clowns that look like something out of a 1980s horror flick. The music dances and flits all over the place under the big top like some mutant lovechild of Queen and Marc Bolan, with a little symphonic elegance thrown in to really scare the bejeezus out of the listener.

The madcap antics are unrelenting on *Cheat The Gallows*, Bigelf displaying both a warped sense of humor, as well as an undeniable instrumental virtuosity that has endeared them to the aforementioned prog-rock crowd. Opening with a strained, scratchy vocal sunk deep in the mix like a radio broadcast from another planet, "Money, It's Pure Evil" swells with blasts of buzzsaw guitar and waves of lush instrumentation. With a creepy, semi-metallic horrorshow intro, "The Evils of Rock & Roll" is rife with razor-sharp psychedelic fretwork, shocks of odd instrumentation, and galloping drumbeats.

Yeah, it's an old rockcrit game to tell you that a band doesn't sound like anybody else, and then proceed to tell you who they kinda, sorta sound like, and the Reverend isn't one to buck the "music journalist" union and break with tradition. If you put your ear really close to the speaker while playing *Cheat The Gallows*, you'll hear scraps of early 1970s hard rock (Deep Purple, Black Sabbath), glam (Bowie, T-Rex, Queen), and prog-rock (Pink Floyd, King Crimson) among a thousand and one other sounds.

Most of all, Bigelf sounds exactly like Bigelf…the guitars soar with the precision of a hungry bird of prey, the bass rhythms are often syncopated and angular, the drumbeats hit your ears like a jackhammer, and the symphonic orchestration is confusing as hell, but works remarkably well. Too weird for the major labels, too scary for the indies, Bigelf continues to slug it out on their own terms, like a 70s-era acid-casualty biker bar band flung forward into the new century. Hell, what more could you ask for from a rock band? (2009)

BILL CHINNOCK
Badlands   (Collectors' Choice Music)

Long before CBS Records tried to remake him into the next Bruce Springsteen (no, I dunno why…maybe one wasn't enough?), Bill Chinnock was one of the last of the young soul rebels. Pursuing a houserockin' sound that was equally indebted to the Chicago blooze blast of Muddy Waters and Howlin' Wolf as it was to Chuck Berry's three-chord Sturm und Drang, Chinnock was a white bluesman – born in New Jersey, sure, but his heart was beating pure Delta grit.

One of John Hammond's many discoveries, Chinnock made his bones as part of the Asbury Park mafia, playing in various boardwalk bands with future and present E Streeters like Danny Federici, Gary Tallent, and Vini "Mad Dog" Lopez during the late 1960s and early '70s. At Hammond's recommendation, Chinnock exiled himself to Maine to work on his wordplay, later emerging as the East Coast poet laureate, his new songs matching intelligent lyrics to a raucous soundtrack that translated well to the stage and made him a bigger performance draw than the Boss during the mid-1970s.

Of Chinnock's 1975 debut album, *Blues*, Hammond said "listening to Bill Chinnock sing blues brings back the days of the old Paramount

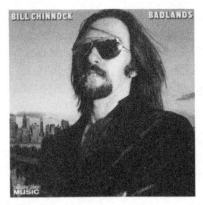

label with Ma Rainey," and he oughta know 'cause John Senior was there in person. Following a live set, *Badlands* was Chinnock's third album, originally self-released, and the one that finally caught the attention of the suite-sitters at Atlantic Records. The label signed B.C. to what seemed to be a creatively-advantageous deal, bought up all the copies of *Badlands* floating around the Northeast, and reissued the album with naught but a few additional flourishes.

Not that *Badlands* needed much tinkering, mind you, the album emerging from Chinnock's artistic psyche pretty much perfectly intact. The album-opening "Outlaw" is smoky big-band R&B revue stuff, with funky hornplay and Chinnock's soulful vox shouted out above a driving rhythm. Chinnock sounds like a cross between Tom Waits and David Clayton-Thomas on "Another Man Gone Down," the sound of heartbreak carved with tears into the grooves of the record.

Jazzy guitars and dancing synths sit atop a vaguely disco rhythm, but "Something For Everybody" is a bad-luck tale of homeless life in 1978 America that retains its optimism and hope in the face of desperation, stating "the streets are filled with money, the sidewalks paved in gold." Chinnock's "Crazy Ol' Rock 'N Roll Man" is a brilliantly-painted rock-n-soul anthem for every bar band and rock star hopeful that ever climbed onto a ramshackle stage while "Prisoner" is pure '70s-era R&B cheese, all soulman tease and ready-to-please with the Brecker Brothers holding down a funkified bottom end while Chinnock's lusty voice soars just below the clouds.

Chinnock's relationship with Atlantic went downhill fast after the label ignored *Badlands* in favor of a fresh album, one for which the singer felt they were trying to push his normally rhythmic, soul-driven sound into a more disco-oriented direction when all he wanted to do was RAWK! Slamming the door behind him on the way out, Chinnock returned to the indie hinterlands save for the mid-1980s travesty that was his CBS Records deal, enjoying a lengthy and productive career in music, video and graphic arts until his death in 2007.

Badlands remains a favorite with Chinnock's loyal fans, a soulful romp down the lost highway that separates rhythm & blues and rock 'n' roll, the album displaying the attitude of both. (2008)

BILL NELSON & THE GENTLEMEN ROCKETEERS
Recorded Live In Concert At Metropolis Studios, London
(Convexe Entertainment)

One of the best things to come about in the wake of the Internet isn't the availability of free music, it's the increased availability of music, period…and for a hardcore rock 'n' roll geek like the Reverend, jus' trying to get his collector's groove on, it's been a godsend! Back in the dark ol' pre-net daze, pinheads like yours truly had to thumb through well-worn back issue copies of music zines like *Trouser Press*, *Creem*, and *Bomp!* to finger hard-to-find albums from such far-flung locales as Canada and England to lust after.

If you were lucky, as I was for a short while, you lived near a collectors-oriented record establishment like Dearborn Music that stocked a healthy bunch of import singles and elpees; or maybe you had a monthly record show in town where you could put down your hard-earned coin on that limited edition 10" Clash EP or Italian Kate Bush 45 with the alternative studio version of "Wuthering Heights."

Otherwise, the demented rockist had to depend on wee mail order companies that advertised in the back pages of the aforementioned publications to carry that one shining stack 'o wax that you coveted. You would send a postal money order off to the advertiser and ask for a copy of THAT record for your slow-growing but oh-so-cool record collection, waiting patiently by the mail box for an official government employee to deliver your fab new tunes…

The Internet has rendered much of that dance moot, providing the hunter/gatherer/hoarder with abundant opportunities to find just about any recording ever made. It's also made the acquisition of formerly difficult import albums as easy as clicking a mouse on the right website. Case in point – Bill Nelson's *Recorded Live In Concert At Metropolis Studios, London* is a lush, deluxe set with two CDs and a DVD documenting an intimate, invitation-only March 2011 concert by Nelson and his band the Gentlemen Rocketeers. Nelson is a British artist, caught on film and tape in London, the album released by a Canadian record label, and available through the magic of the Internet for we rabid fans in the U.S. and elsewhere. For a diehard, lifelong rock 'n' roll fanatic, could life get any better?

Bill Nelson is a singular talent who has forged an amazing, albeit unique career that has spanned four decades now. He is best-known, perhaps, as the singer, songwriter, and guitarist for mid-1970s U.K. glam-metal band Be-Bop Deluxe. Formed at the height of England's glam-rock craze, Be-Bop Deluxe was more like Mott the Hoople in that they transcended glam to deliver five studio (and a live) albums of guitar-driven, proto-metal pop-rock tunes that served as a showcase for Nelson's intricate guitar textures.

After the demise of Be-Bop Deluxe, Nelson dawdled for a while with the experimental band Red Noise, eschewed the guitar entirely in favor of electronics for his frequently-misunderstood Orchestra Arcana, and quietly pieced together an impressive and prolific solo career that, while resulting in few commercial "hits" has nonetheless resulted in over 40 recordings that have earned the multi-instrumentalist a loyal following.

For the long-time Bill Nelson fan, *Recorded Live In Concert At Metropolis Studios, London* is a necessary addition to the ol' collection. The fourteen-track set list on CD one spans nearly the entirety of Nelson's lengthy career, including solo songs, a little Red Noise, and a handful of Be-Bop Deluxe favorites, all recorded with a full band that includes flautist/saxophonist Theo Travis (Gong).

The second CD is a good bit shorter, presenting a four-song solo acoustic "warm up" set that Nelson performed for the assembled crowd, including songs dedicated to his brother Ian ("A Dream For Ian") who played with Nelson in Red Noise, and one for his friend Stuart Adamson ("For Stuart") of Scottish rockers Big Country.

Recorded Live In Concert At Metropolis Studios, London starts with "October Man," from what was probably the closest that Nelson ever came to a hit album, 1982's *The Love That Whirls*. An engaging slice of new wave romanticism, the song reminds of Simple Minds or similar 1980s-era fare, with Goth-tinged vocals, mournful horn solos, doodling keyboards and synths, and shards

of angular guitars. The song has surprisingly aged fairly well, unburdened by the period clichés that hang like an albatross around the neck of a lot of the decade's early musical experiments. It doesn't take Nelson long to jump into the Be-Bop material, though, beginning with "Night Creatures," a somber mid-tempo dirge from the band's 1974 debut *Axe Victim*. Sounding more than a little like David Bowie in both his vocal phrasing and in the songwriting, the song's lush, swirling instrumentation serves to embrace and frame the lyrics nicely.

Switching gears, Nelson launches into the fluid 1992 solo track "God Man Slain," which oddly evokes late-period Bowie, but with a deceptive energy and zeal driving Nelson's hypnotic fretwork and Travis' random, soulful blasts of sax. By the time that Nelson returns from his solo trip to vintage Be-Bop fare, the audience is fully engaged, and the guitarist straps on his faithful Gibson ES-345, the same instrument he used on stage and to record with Be-Bop.

"Adventures In A Yorkshire Landscape," also from the band's debut, is a sumptuous musical showcase that displays not only Nelson's immense six-string skills, but those of the Gentlemen Rocketeers as well, the band erecting a magnificent instrumental backdrop against which Nelson embroiders his complex, elegant patterns. Travis's nuanced flute solo colors the instrumental passages and remind of jazz legend Herbie Mann.

The short-lived Red Noise period is represented by a pair of fine tunes, "Furniture Music" and "Do You Dream In Colour," both of which fall on the edgier side of late 1970s era new wave. The former is a martial, up-tempo construct with forceful, riffish instrumentation, and machinegun vocals – kind of like Gary Numan with fewer synths, bigger drum sounds, and tangled strands of wiry guitar. The latter opens with an oscillating synth buzz before devolving into an almost popish syncopated rhythm that reminds of Talking Heads, Nelson's oddball vocals surrounded by electronic dots and dashes. Some of my personal Be-Bop favorites come from the band's 1975 sophomore album *Futurama*, with which Nelson took a decidedly left-hand turn towards progressive-rock territory.

Evidently dissatisfied with the outcome of *Axe Victim*, Nelson fired everybody and got new musicians for *Futurama*, changing the band's sound immensely. While critics at the time questioned the prog-rock tendencies of *Futurama*, the album's best songs evince a sort of prototype pop-metal songwriting and performance that would influence the coming "New Wave of British Heavy Metal" bands. The larger-than-life "Maid In Heaven" offers up some of Nelson's most inspired guitarplay, the song's memorable riff and infectious melody matched by sing-a-long lyrics and the guitarist's great tone and energy. By contrast, "Sister Seagull" is a hauntingly beautiful performance with cascading instrumentation, judicious use of a melodic riff, and Nelson's high-flying solos. Performed beautifully here, the song's emotional lyrics are made all the more poignant by the powerful musical accompaniment, including the crying seagull guitar licks at the end.

As satisfying as the full-band performances may be, the four-song instrumental set provided by Nelson on the second disc is just as impressive. The shimmering guitarplay featured on "Beyond These Clouds The Sweetest Dream" is stunning in its scope and execution, while "Golden Dream Of Circus Horses" is just as powerful. The guitarist is accompanied on this one by Theo Travis, whose ethereal flute and saxophone flourishes meld perfectly with Nelson's exotic fretwork in providing a solid example of the artist's flirtation with a jazz-rock fusion sound. Nelson is accompanied on the two aforementioned tribute songs by a pre-recorded, almost orchestral soundtrack on synthesizer or a synclavier, but his live-wire guitar playing on both is simply sublime, the guitarist delivering pure emotion through his fingertips. The DVD part of the set includes a multi-camera shoot of both the full band and solo performances, and the sound on all of the discs is near-perfect, benefiting from the small studio venue and Nelson's firm hand in overseeing the final mix.

Listening to Bill Nelson is a lot like trying to tell a stranger about rock 'n' roll...the man's lifetime of music-making is far too intricate, varied, and uniquely personal to nail down firmly for more than a brief moment. Words fail in trying to describe the instrumental virtuosity and diverse artistic vision displayed by Nelson throughout 40 years and as many recordings.

The man makes music that is at once both frequently challenging and enormously entertaining, and *Recorded Live In Concert At Metropolis Studios, London* offers not only a career-spanning musical introduction to a one-of-a-kind artist, but also a rare visual document of Nelson's talents. For fans, this one is a no-brainer, while the curious newbie will certainly fall head-over-heels after checking out Nelson's *Recorded Live In Concert At Metropolis Studios, London.* (2012)

BILLY BRAGG
Life's A Riot With Spy Vs Spy   (Yep Roc Records)

When originally released in 1983, the seven-song EP *Life's A Riot With Spy Vs Spy* earned Billy Bragg a reputation as a historical curiosity. After all, punk rock was still hanging on while new wave and Goth had begun to excite U.K. audiences. Bragg, on the other hand, was a wandering English troubadour, singing of love and justice and freedom...definitely an anachronism in the modern, trend-driven, media-savvy world. At that time (as now), if you weren't a beautiful actor/model/coverboy-girl with a set of safe, bland, over-produced songs, you need not apply. Bragg didn't fit into that mold, relying instead on talent, attitude, and sheer guts in his attempt to make life-changing music.

Somehow, Bragg succeeded. Never a commercial artist, but always an influential one, his creative emphasis was on the lyrics, especially with his earliest work, which eschewed niceties such as production values and lush instrumentation in favor of the word, the voice, and a guitar. The result, on these seven songs, was simply devastating. A talented wordsmith with a taste for the bizarre turn of a phrase, Bragg had a sharp eye for the absurdities of modern life and relationships, and a satirical wit that sinks a razor-sharp rapier into the jugular of the subjects he aims at.

Bragg's political material voiced the most radical worldview since the early days of the Clash (Joe Strummer was a major influence on Bragg's songwriting), the songs made even more effective by the sparse musical accompaniment. Bragg's love songs are both emotional *and* bittersweet, never maudlin, and infected with a contagious romanticism more common to the folk genre than to punk rock.

In the thirty-three years since its original release, *Life's A Riot With Spy Vs Spy* has aged well, songs like "A New England" and "The Busy Girl Buys Beauty" benefiting from the timeless style of Bragg's writing and performances. The Yep Roc Records reissue of the EP features the original seven-song EP on one disc, and a second "bonus" disc of unreleased rarities, alternative versions and a great cover of John Cale's "Fear Is A Man's Best Friend."

Personally, I would have liked to have seen the label include the four songs from Bragg's *Between The Wars* EP here, to flesh out the first disc somewhat. However, this is a minor cavil, and since Bragg personally oversaw the Yep Roc reissue series, it was his choice, not mine...

In 1985, when the vinyl version of *Life's A Riot With Spy Vs Spy* hit these shores, I wrote that Bragg had "a great artistic future," and that although he would never become a "big star," he would always be an "interesting and dedicated performer." Through the years since, Bragg has never proved me wrong. (2006)

BILLY BRAGG
Talking With The Taxman About Poetry   (Yep Roc Records)

"But if you think all I do is press words other people use into my service Comrades, come here, let me give you my pen and you can yourselves write your own verses!" – Victor Mayakovsky, 1926

By the time of the 1986 release of *Talking With The Taxman About Poetry*, Billy Bragg's self-professed "difficult" third album, the artist had become the poet laureate of the musical left. A tireless troubadour with socialist leanings, Bragg places more fervor, energy, passion, and emotion in a single phrase or turn of a word than most artists are capable of mustering throughout an entire album.

After a couple of critically acclaimed British EPs and a full-length indie album, *Talking With The Taxman About Poetry* represented Bragg's major label debut in the United States. Although Bragg had softened some of the rough edges that endeared audiences to his early work, the lyrical arguments presented on Bragg's third album proved no less passionate, his penchant for radical polemics no less zealous.

Whereas Bragg's early songs featured only his thickly-accented vocals and an accompanying guitar, *Taxman* was fleshed out with a few additional strings, a horn or two, and even an occasional background harmony. The music remained stark, simple and effective, Bragg's folk-punk musical style serving to underline the importance of his lyrics. First and foremost, Bragg is a poet; a hopeless romantic with a revolutionary bent (not unlike Byron), whose lyrics deal almost exclusively with love and politics – not an entirely inappropriate combination, for one inevitably involves the other.

Bragg aims his pen mercilessly at the governments, institutions and the societies that would oppress the seemingly unflagging human spirit. Bragg champions the worker as a noble creature, envisions romantic love as the Holy Grail and, at times, jabs so deep in the heart with his lyrics and often times brutal lyrics that he is able to invoke the tears/passion he himself obviously feels.

The Yep Roc Records two-disc reissue of *Talking With The Taxman About Poetry* includes the entire album, re-mastered and spiffed up for the digital age, along with a bonus disc of rarities and inspired covers. Songs like Gram Parson's "Sin City," Woody Guthrie's "Deportees," and Smokey Robinson's "The Tracks Of My Tears" reveal the depth and scope of Bragg's musical influences and display the artist's charm and joy in music-making.

Even after 20 years and better than half a dozen album releases, Billy Bragg remains an acquired taste. His music has never been a commercial commodity, although he has enjoyed a hit song or two along the way. As this critic wrote at the time of this album's release, Bragg "is one of the most important artists to enter the rock arena in years – perhaps the most political folksinger since young Bobby Dylan strode into Greenwich Village with a guitar in hand."

Bragg remains a man with a message, a poet of uncanny vision and a socially concerned artist whose work remains as fresh and relevant today, in the days of Bush and Blair, as it was during the Reagan/ Thatcher era two decades ago. Much of today's "folk revival," the acid-folk music of artists like Devendra Banhart, owes a great debt to Bragg, an artist who, inspired by the music of Joe Strummer, would go on to create inspiring music of his own. (2006)

BILLY BRAGG
Worker's Playtime
(Yep Roc Records)

"If you've got a blacklist, I want to be on it…"

By the time of the 1989 stateside release of *Worker's Playtime*, punk-inspired folkie Billy Bragg had found an unlikely measure of commercial success in the U.K. and had developed a loyal cult audience in the United States. Whereas Bragg's early albums like *Brewing Up With Billy Bragg* (1984) and *Talking With The Taxman About Poetry* (1986) featured many politically-charged songs delivered from the singer's left-leaning perspective, they also offered up intelligent romantic commentary such as "Levi Stubb's Tears" and "Love Gets Dangerous." It is the tension of this dichotomy – the soapbox rabble-rouser shouting political rhetoric and the hopeless Celtic romantic singing love songs – that drives *Worker's Playtime*.

Working for the first time with noted producer Joe Boyd (Nick Drake, Fairport Convention), Bragg pretties up many of the songs on *Worker's Playtime* with finely tuned melodies and lush instrumentation, a stark contrast to his sparse previous work. The angry young man of Bragg's early EPs and debut album has, a half-decade later, mellowed somewhat, allowing the romantic songwriter to come to the

foreground. The result is a superb collection of material like "She's Got A New Spell," the melancholy "Valentine's Day Is Over" (featuring just Bragg's voice, guitar, and a piano) and the rollicking, self-effacing "Life With The Lions."

The most striking moment here, however, is "Waiting For The Great Leap Forwards," the song building from Bragg's lone piano-backed vocals to a swelling crescendo of choral voices and a grand finish. It's the defining moment of *Worker's Playtime*, an affirmation of the singer's social consciousness.

Even so, the song displays Bragg's growing disenchantment with politics as well as his wry sense of humor. Although proclaiming that "revolution is just a T-shirt away," Bragg asks, "will politics get me the sack?" In the end, Bragg surmises, "start your own revolution and cut out the middle man," evoking Dylan's "don't follow leaders, watch the parking meters..."

Worker's Playtime proved to be commercially questionable, fans and critics alike seemingly confused by the album's tentative nature and artistic contradictions between the "new" Billy Bragg (stronger production, more instrumentation) and the "old" (guitar and vocals). In reality, the album's sublime strength lies entirely in its uneasy nature, *Worker's Playtime* showcasing Bragg's evolution from street busker to self-aware musician. Somewhere between album number one and number three, Bragg realized that there might actually be a future to this music thing.

The material on the bonus disc of this excellent Yep Roc reissue – studio demos and outtakes – supports this critical perspective, showing Bragg experimenting with different ways to express his music. The demo of "She's Got A New Spell," with the Attractions' Bruce Thomas and the Jeff Beck Group's Mickey Waller, evinces a rock aesthetic while "The Short Answer" sounds like low-key Graham Parker, complete with the Rumour's Martin Belmont on guitar.

Other material, such as a stark, powerful cover of the Jam's "That's Entertainment" and an uncharacteristically soulful live reading of Tim Hardin's classic "Reason To Believe" display different facets of Bragg's talents.

In retrospect, *Worker's Playtime* is a solid collection of songs that served as an invaluable stepping stone to Bragg's work on albums like *Don't Try This At Home* as well as his collaboration with the band Wilco on *Mermaid Avenue*. It is in these grooves that you can hear Bragg becoming comfortable in his role as artist and musician, the album an important part of the artist's overall catalog and an influential release in its own right. (2006)

BLACK SABBATH
The Rules of Hell   (Rhino Records)

There are only two kinds of Black Sabbath fans on this cold, grey planet – Ozzy acolytes and Dio devotees. Forget about the fleeting tenures of singers Dave Walker, Dave Donato, and Ray Gillen, or those horrible records with Ian Gillan, Glen Hughes, and Tony Martin. And just who the heck is Jeff Fenholt? No, for the true Sab fanatic, it all boils down to the eight albums made with Osbourne circa 1970-79, or the four recorded with Ronnie James Dio between 1979 and 1982.

A couple of years ago, Black Sabbath guitarist Tony Iommi reunited the band's Dio-lead line-up under the banner Heaven & Hell, named for their 1980 album, as a way to promote 2006's *The Dio Years* set. The band recorded three new songs for that compilation, the collaboration resulting in a lengthy tour and a subsequent live recording. To satiate the tastes of those who have come around to Sabbath after experiencing Heaven & Hell, Rhino Records has done their 16-song *The Dio Years* one better by boxing up all four of the Dio-era Sabbath albums as the five-disc *The Rules of Hell* set.

Although the true believer already has most of this stuff, for the casual fan or newbie, *The Rules of Hell* captures the brief magic of the Dio-years Sabbath in an overflowing treasure chest, the four albums remastered and including newly-penned liner notes. The *Heaven and Hell* album is the cornerstone of the box, not so much a breath of fresh air after Ozzy as it was a hurricane-force blast, perfectly timed at the dawn of the "New Wave of British Heavy Metal." An influential album that yielded classic songs like "Neon Knights" and "Children of the Sea," *Heaven And Hell* masterfully paired Iommi's massive, doom-laden riffs with the former Rainbow vocalist's imaginative, fantastic lyrics and unique melodic sense.

Long-time Sabbath drummer Bill Ward left the band due to personal problems, to be replaced for 1981's *Mob Rules* by former Rick Derringer skin-basher Vinny Appice. The foursome recorded a suitable follow-up to the Platinum™-selling *Heaven And Hell*, following much the same blueprint, i.e. heavy riffing, scorching fretboard runs, and bombastic rhythms. The album-opening "Turn Up The Night" is a dark, rumbling rocker with histrionic vox, while "The Sign of the Southern Cross" is a Goth-tinged molten doom-stomp that starts life on gossamer wings before emerging from its chrysalis as a light-chewing, flesh-rending carnivore. For Sabbath, *Mob Rules* was the right album at the right time: capital-H Heavy with plenty of metallic theatrics.

There has always been a lot of discussion among fans over *Live Evil*, the two-disc concert set unabashedly mixing songs from the two previous studio albums with vintage Ozzy-era gems like "Paranoid" and "War Pigs." The dichotomy was not lost on listeners, and *Live Evil* retains a muddied reputation among the faithful to this day. Still, there is some quality noggin-knocking to be found on *Live Evil*.

Whether you're grooving to the speeding two-wheeled hog that is "E5150," its tailpipe belching fire as Iommi marks the pavement with his scorched-asphalt six-string garroting, or genuflecting towards the temple of doom that is "Black Sabbath," the band's original signature song, the album delivers enough bone-deep chills and plodding thrills to satisfy even the most couch-bound hesher. There are fourteen songs total on *Live Evil*, each performance a sign of the impending apocalypse.

When the smoke had cleared after the release of *Live Evil*, Dio would bolt from the Sabbath ranks in '82 to form his own band; bassist Geezer Butler would depart a couple of years later. A decade passed, heavy metal was seemingly on the ropes, and as both Dio's self-titled band and the Sabs were floundering in the tidal wave emerging from Seattle, the original *Heaven And Hell* crew reunited for the middling *Dehumanizer* in 1992.

An attempt to re-imagine Sabbath for the confusing alt-rock daze of the '90s, *Dehumanizer* turned away from the swords-and-sorcery imagery of Dio's earlier work in favor of a Voivod-like struggle between humanity and technology. Although the dour collection illustrates Sabbath at its darkest, and songs like "TV Crime" or "Time Machine" (from the movie *Wayne's World*) are rife with Appice's cannonball drumbeats, Dio's soaring vocals, and Iommi's 12-gauge blunderbuss approach to riff-playing, the truth is that a dozen other bands did this sort of thing much better at the time, and *Dehumanizer* sank like a stone, suffering from the same tensions that broke up this incarnation of the band a decade previous.

Dio would return to his solo career, while Iommi continued to carry Black Sabbath on his shoulders throughout the '90s and into the new millennium – even reuniting with Ozzy once upon a time – until the band's current reincarnation. For the crazed and the curious, *The Rules of Hell* captures every note of the often-overlooked Dio-era Sabbath, taking the listener back to the storied roots of Heaven & Hell, warts and all... (2008)

BLUE CHEER
Vincebus Eruptum / Outsideinside   (Sundazed Records)

Back in the primordial stew that was mid-to-late 1960s era rock 'n' roll, record label execs were literally clueless about the music, and were just as likely to chase trends as they were to discover new talent.

With their collective ears to the ground, they listened for the buzz, and in 1966 and '67, nowhere was the howling louder than in the San Francisco Bay area. The region was home to a virtual buffet of bands and styles, from the electrified blues-rock of Big Brother & the Holding Company (featuring Janis Joplin) and the folk-influenced psychedelia of Jefferson Airplane to the Grateful Dead's original roots-rock stew.

What was missing from the San Francisco sound was a true hard rock band...and into the breach would step the almighty Blue Cheer. Louder, bolder, and brasher than any other band on the scene, Blue Cheer evolved...or some would say mutated...from a six-piece blues-rock outfit complete with dueling guitarists and a harmonica player, into a nasty, turbocharged power trio in the image of the Jimi Hendrix Experience. Signed to Dutch-based Phillips Records, noted mostly for its success in the classical music field, Blue Cheer represented the label's attempt to capitalize on the growing garage-rock side of pop music.

Phillips had no idea what they were getting themselves in for, however. Blue Cheer was brought to their attention by fledgling producer and popular S.F. radio deejay Abe "Voco" Kesh, an Armenian blues fan who would also discover guitarist Harvey Mandel. The band was managed by a Hell's Angel member nicknamed "Gut" and, well, Blue Cheer had a tendency to play every bit as loud in the studio as they did on stage, redlining the equipment and freaking out the recording engineer.

While Phillips may have thought that they were getting an American version of Eric Clapton and Cream, or maybe even Led Zeppelin, what they got was *Vincebus Eruptum*, a debut album completely devoid of melody, bruising songs performed by sonic thugs who mangled the blues-rock equation with squalls of piercing guitar and spine-bashing rhythmic overkill.

Blue Cheer's *Vincebus Eruptum* roared out of the gate, literally, with bluster and ferocity that wouldn't be matched for almost a decade...or until Motörhead released *its* ground-breaking, earth-shaking 1977 debut album. Released in early 1968 and riding on the back of the band's first Top 20 single – a grungy, fuzztone, feedback-ridden reading of Eddie Cochran's "Summertime Blues" (also successfully covered by the Who) – the album would peak at number eleven on the *Billboard* Top 200 albums chart, and rock 'n' roll would never be the same again. This Sundazed Records label CD reissue restores the album to its glorious, bulldozer mono mix.

"Summertime Blues" still sounds pretty damn hot today, although Blue Cheer's performance of the song has long since been overshadowed by the Sturm and Drang of thousands of bands that followed the same blueprint to musical notoriety in the decades to follow. In its day, though, the song sounded like nothing and nobody else – not for Blue Cheer the fey moptop harmonies of the British Invasion bands, or even the niceties of polite, boy-next-door garage-band America. Blue Cheer's "Summertime Blues" sounded like the Four Horsemen of the Apocalypse straddling their iron steeds, belching fire and shrouded in smoke, filthy rock 'n' roll bikers coming for your daughters with phallic guitars and amps set on eleven.

Guitarist Leigh Stephens' fretwork on the song broke new ground, establishing the framework for what would eventually become heavy metal, ringing with reckless abandon, the performance itself riff-happy, druggy, feedback-drenched psychedelic-blues with the heaviest bass line the recording tape could capture, and drums that sounded like the soundtrack to a short boat ride down the River Styx. That "Summertime Blues" became a hit single is a testament to the musical anarchy that ruled the 1960s, as well as an indicator of the madness creeping into rock 'n' roll.

Much of *Vincebus Eruptum* follows along the same darkened path towards insanity, the band forever corrupting traditional blues in a haphazard and amphetamine-fueled haze of which Eric Clapton and Cream, or even John Mayall's Bluesbreakers could never conceive. A cover of B.B. King's classic "Rock Me Baby" is warped beyond even the low standards the band set with "Summertime Blues," the song's sludge-like dino-stomp pacing matched by Stephens' razor-sharp, demented fretwork (a mutant approximation of King's unique single-note leads), bassist Dickie Peterson's husky voice lacking all pretense of nuance as he mauls the lyrics…only drummer Paul Whaley manages to come anywhere near a standard blues rhythm, but even that is lost come the bridge as chaos reigns, Stephens' axe flies off the planet, and the once-subtle percussion explodes like a brick of C4.

Even Peterson's original songs evince the same sort of dirty, greasy signature as the band's much-beloved cover tunes. "Doctor Please" sounds like Humble Pie thrown down a deep, dark well, the bass-drums rhythm track creating an enormously claustrophobic vibe while Stephens' manic mangling of his guitar bludgeons the listener with sound and fury. "Out Of Focus" isn't much different, although it does allow Stephens to show off a few more chops than his previous stammer-and-stun, and the band strikes a sort of slippery groove as Peterson's quicksand vocals barely project above the din of the instrumental soundtrack.

Vincebus Eruptum closes out with a particularly-inspired cover of Mose Allison's classic "Parchman Farm" (notoriously listed on the album cover as "Parchment Farm"). Performed as a sequel, of sorts, to "Summertime Blues," the band cops an almost identical melodic arrangement as their hit single upon which to unravel Allison's lyrical tale of betrayal. Stephens' solos bob and weave like a punch-drunk prizefighter throughout the five-minute jam, Whaley's drumwork slips and slides from light-fingered, jazzy brushes to jackhammer blasts of white light, while Peterson's leaden bass technique clearly opens the door for Black Sabbath's Geezer Butler to stagger through a year later.

Whaley's tribal drumming intros the blast furnace that is "Second Time Around," the song teetering on the edge as it balances a semblance of garage-rock innocence and melody with the freefalling musical cacophony that characterized the most adventurous of the era's psychedelic acid rock explorers.

Although the song won't open your third eye, its overall oozing instrumental mud is certain to bongo-beat your eardrums even as it carelessly slaps your medulla oblongata into submission. And that's it for Blue Cheer's debut album…six tarpit tapestries, roughly half-an-hour in length, which will take you days to recuperate from…

• • • • •

How do you follow up a hit album, as unlikely as its success may have been? For Blue Cheer, whose debut disc *Vincebus Eruptum* hit number eleven on the albums chart, spawning a Top 20 hit single with a cover of "Summertime Blues," you basically follow the words yet spoken by drive-in movie critic Joe Bob Briggs. Sayeth the beloved B-movie scribe, "if you're gonna make a sequel, *make a sequel*. Bring the dead people back to life and *do it all over again*."

And that's pretty much what Blue Cheer did with their sophomore effort *Outsideinside*…resurrect all the bodies they'd buried with their blunt-edged, riff-driven musical attack while refining their sound with an even *muddier* mix and a bunch of new, but no less dull and rust-flaked, production tools.

Whereas Blue Cheer's debut was louder than the ass-end of a fighter jet, and denser than a room full of politicians, the album's production was ultimately designed…if, indeed, much thought went into it at all…to mimic the band's incendiary live shows. With *Outsideinside*, however, they were seemingly inspired by all of the psychedelic outlaws that made up their hometown music scene, bands like the Jefferson Airplane and Quicksilver Messenger Service who were using the full capabilities of contemporary recording technology to create a multi-textured, head-tripping sound.

In the hands of Blue Cheer and heavy-handed producer Abe "Voco" Kesh, these advances in studio tech smoothed out some, but not all of the band's jagged edges, and further reinforced the smothering wall-of-noise that was the Blue Cheer trademark. It seems that while their first album had been recorded under the influence of whiskey and amphetamines, *Outsideinside* displayed a definite hallucinogenic influence.

As such, Leigh Stephens' guitar was multi-tracked and multiplied in the mix, his free-riffing technique flying straight out of your speakers like a pissed-off honey badger. Dickie Peterson's already heavier-than-uranium bass style was reduced to a thick, migraine-inducing throb while Paul Whaley's drums were frequently downplayed to a mere eardrum-shredding sledgehammer rather than the head-bashing wrecking ball that had almost dominated *Vincebus Eruptum*. While *Outsideinside* lacked the casual menace and amateurish, bang-a-gong mentality of its predecessor, that's not to say that it  was lacking in velocity or ferocity. The band still pursued a louder-than-God, blues-infused psychedelic-rock sound, albeit with a few more vintage R&B and boogie-blues elements thrown into the boiling brew this time around.

For instance, the album-opening original "Feathers From Your Tree" starts out like your typical hippie hash, with a few folkie strings and odd vocal harmonies, Peterson's voice almost lost in the chorus until the nut breaks open and Stephens' six-string begins screaming and Whaley's percussion stirs up a lazy cyclone comprised of flurries of drumbeats and raffish whacks on the old cymbal. Altogether, the song is somewhat more claustrophobic and schizophrenic than much of the era's psych-rock and clearly foreshadows the coming flood of doom-minded fellow travelers like Sir Lord Baltimore, Black Sabbath, and Pentagram.

Peterson's "Just A Little Bit" breaths a little fire-and-brimstone into the album's grooves, picking up the pace with a mid-tempo yet undeniably muddy performance where the vocals are sinking quick in the song's quicksand arrangement, Whaley's drums blast away like a chattering machinegun, and Stephens' multi-tracked guitars stun in their fuzzy magnificence with both a fluid tone and imaginative phrasing. The group-written "Come And Get It" is a flashback to the band's debut, a muscular, Cro-Mag composition that offers up raging fretwork, hurricane-strength blast-beats, and Peterson's speed king vocals shouting up from the darkness of the mix.

Whereas a full half of the songs on the Blue Cheer's debut had been covers, *Outsideinside* offers up only two significant departures from the band's new internal songwriting dynamic. The Rolling Stones' "(I Can't Get No) Satisfaction" is revved-up and amped-up beyond the original's heart-attack pace, Blue Cheer stripping down the instrumentation at times to just Stephens' humming, buzzing guitar, the entire thing racing past your ears like a bad dream. Whaley's locomotive drumbeats drive the performance to a manic crescendo as Stephens' solos sting like a knife-cut behind Peterson's speedfreak vox.

By contrast, the band's cover of Albert King's "The Hunter" (also done nicely by British blues-rockers Free) is about as straight a performance as the trio could muster with this short-lived line-up. Peterson's vocals are edgy, but the groove is fat and swings hard, and Stephens' guitarwork is uncharacteristically subdued. The Stephens-Peterson collaboration "Magnolia Caboose Babyfinger," later covered (appropriately) by Seattle tricksters Mudhoney during the grungy 1990s, is a short, sharp shock of an instrumental, hitting a quick lick and quitting in favor of the album-closing musical strokefest that is "Babylon." Pulling out all the stops, Blue Cheer crowbar every psychedelic cliché and hard rock sleight-of-hand they can imagine into slightly less than four-and-a-half minutes, thus giving birth to both Iron Butterfly, Kyuss, *and* therefore, Queens of the Stone Age.

Lacking both the ear-shattering charisma and the shocking element of surprise that made *Vincebus Eruptum* an unexpected hit, *Outsideinside* fared much less well commercially, the album barely scraping its way into the Top 100 and failing to yield even a moderately-successful single. The tide had quickly turned for Blue Cheer, and guitarist Leigh Stephens would become the band's first – although nowhere near its last – casualty, leaving before the recording of 1969's *New! Improved! Blue Cheer* to pursue a solo career with the release of his future cult fave album *Red Weather*.

Meanwhile, Dickie Peterson would carry the torch as Blue Cheer's original founding member, leading various band line-ups well into the 21st century with a number of album releases and sporadic touring, the band's 2007 swansong *What Doesn't Kill You...* a welcome return to the caveman-dumb dinosaur rock that built Blue Cheer's reputation in the first place. Sadly, the band's return to rock would be sidetracked when Peterson, the prototype hard rock bassist, passed away in 2009. Still, there's no underestimating the band's influence on the evolution of rock 'n' roll, and its status as one of a handful of true originators of heavy, heavy music. (2012)

BLUE MOUNTAIN
Midnight In Mississippi / Omnibus   (Broadmoor Records)

Let's face the brutal facts, shall we? Mississippi roots rockers Blue Mountain had a couple of strikes against them from the very beginning. Formed by singer/guitarist Cary Hudson, bassist/vocalist Laurie Stirrat, and drummer Frank Coutch in 1993, the band's seminal mid-to-late 1990s work was released by Roadrunner Records, a label better known for extreme heavy metal and piddlin' hard rock in the Nickelback vein…wooosh, there goes the ball! Strike two: Blue Mountain's intelligent blend of rootsy rock, folk, country, and country-blues was, perhaps, too smart for a room that was just beginning to embrace the concept of "alternative country" when the band broke-up in 2001. One more swing and yer outta here…

To Blue Mountain's credit, the band kept on choogling right until the end, when hiccups in the relationship between Hudson and wife Stirrat resulted in the break-up of the band. Before they went their separate ways, however, Blue Mountain released both a live album and a collection of covers of good old timey "mountain music." During Blue Mountain's hiatus, Hudson recorded three solo albums while alt-country inched a little closer to the mainstream during the ensuing years. The trio reformed in 2007, their handful of live performances garnering widespread acclaim. As a result, Blue Mountain has launched its own independent record label, and released two new albums – *Midnight In Mississippi* and *Omnibus*.

Midnight In Mississippi is an all-new collection of Blue Mountain songs, the band's first in almost ten years and, really, it's like they never really went anywhere at all. The band's timeless sound of crickets chirping, coyotes howling, and kudzu growing is faithfully reproduced in the jangly Southern charm of "She's A Wild One" or the hoedown stomp-and-roll of "Free State of Jones," which includes some mighty fine fingerpickin' courtesy of Mr. Hudson. "Groove Me" has a distinctive jam-band quality with a slight funky lilt and twangy charm, while the title track is a forceful, grungy Neil Young rocker with a big sound and bluesy roots that name checks Junior Kimbrough's juke joint. Hudson's lyrical skills remain amazing throughout *Midnight In Mississippi*, the chemistry between he and Stirrat is simply stunning, and the contributions of drummer Coutch are often overlooked due to their powerful subtlety.

• • • • •

If *Midnight In Mississippi* is forward-leaning, Blue Mountain looking intently into the future, then that album's companion, the retrospective *Omnibus*, is a fond gaze backwards into the band's past. A fourteen-song collection of re-recorded material from the band's three Roadrunner albums, money has to be the main reason for this exercise. Knowing the music biz as I do, I'd wager that the band sees little or nothing in the way of substantial monies from their Roadrunner days – even with the recent label reissue of *Dog Days* – and by re-recording these songs, and releasing them on their own label, maybe…just maybe…the good folks in Blue Mountain might make a dime or two of their own here.

Regardless of their reasons (and I'm sure that they had good 'uns), *Omnibus* isn't just some tedious studio play date or a crass attempt to wring a few dollars out of past glories (Eric Burdon, call home!). The arrangements of these new renditions are leaner and meaner than previous, and by cherry-picking the best fruits of their labors, Blue Mountain has assembled a sort of "greatest hits" collection for a band that never did have anything resembling a hit, but sure as hell should have! *Dog Days*, the band's erstwhile 1995 debut, is heavily represented here, with six strong songs; three are culled from 1997's *Homegrown*; and the last five were chosen from 1999's *Tales of A Traveler*.

The songs on *Omnibus* are not only some of Blue Mountain's best, but they're long-time fan favorites, too. "Blue Canoe" is a mid-tempo country-rock gem with a gentle guitar strum, brilliant lyrical imagery, a slightly yodeled chorus, and loads of charm. "Soul Sister" sounds like another Neil Young outtake, with lush tumbleweed instrumentation, solid vocal harmonies, and wistful memories. The spry, acoustic-guitar-driven "Bloody 98" hits your ears like Woody

Guthrie chugging a blast o' white lightning, while the upbeat "Poppa" displays Hudson's vocal chops with lyrical gymnastics and a honky-tonk Friday night arrangement.

It's good to have Blue Mountain back, if only because true reckless country soul is a hard-to-find commodity. If *Midnight In Mississippi* and *Omnibus* are any indication, Blue Mountain hasn't lost a single step during their absence from our lives... (2008)

BLUES MAGOOS
Psychedelic Lollipop / Electric Comic Book   (Sundazed Records)

The decade of the 1960s was a truly magical time for rock 'n' roll music. It began in the '50s with Bill Haley dancin' around his timepiece and Elvis singing about a hound dog, and jumped quickly into the new decade with the Beatles wanting to hold your hand and the explosion of the whole British Invasion thing (i.e. the Stones, the Who, the Kinks, et al).

Independent and major record labels alike cashed in on the seemingly-endless "Baby Boomer" youth movement, and if a lot of people in positions of authority didn't really understand the whole rock 'n' roll thing, they were not nearly as risk adverse as their corporate cousins of today.

During the 1960s, labels often signed artists and threw records out into the marketplace to see what trends they could create or, more often than not, ride on the coattails of until the fad was thoroughly played out. Yeah, this mindset resulted in a lot of crap singles *and* albums being released, and your local Salvation Army or Goodwill store are probably stacked to the rafters with some of them. But this marketing philosophy also meant that a lot of interesting, entertaining, and imaginative music hit the streets during the 1960s and early '70s, a lot of it subsequently disappearing into the rabbit hole of obscurity.

"One hit wonder" is the phrase often used to describe a lot of these obscure bands and artists of the 1960s, musicians that were able to put their finger on the pulse of the teen zeitgeist for one brief, all-too-quickly-gone moment of success. This moment was usually

represented by a single song that dominated AM radio for the space of three or four weeks before consigning the artist to a life of performances at potting sheds, teen dance clubs, and county fairs until they threw in the towel. The Bronx, New York based Blues Magoos were the literal definition of the "one hit wonder," the lead-off track on their 1966 debut album *Psychedelic Lollipop* a number five hit single with the infectious sing-along "(We Ain't Got) Nothin' Yet." It was a height they'd never reach again.

The song's prominent bass line, chiming keyboards, escalating guitar solos, and vocal harmonies successfully combined a psychedelic-pop soul with a garage-rock heartbeat, driving "(We Ain't Got) Nothin' Yet" into the upper reaches of the charts. Unlike many one hit wonders of the era, however, the remainder of *Psychedelic Lollipop* isn't mere chaff. The haunting "Love Seems Doomed" might have been an unlikely pop hit, the song's melancholy vocals matched by swirling instrumentation, eerie keyboards, and an altogether depressing vibe that is all the more impressive given the buoyant nature of the band's big hit single.

The band's inspired reading of J.D. Loudermilk's white-trash classic "Tobacco Road" is more indicative of their garage-blues roots. Delivered with appropriate soul and snarling instrumentation, the song's familiar riffs are extended to a radio unfriendly four-and-a-half minutes with a psychedelic jam more worthy of Iron Butterfly than a Top 40 pop band. Mike Esposito's lead guitar squeals like a trapped animal, while vocalist Ralph Scala's keyboard waxes and wanes ominously like the soundtrack to a Hammer horror film. The rest of the band chimes in with a clash of instrumentation before they march back into the song's more comfortable territory. Everything that would follow after this raucous cover of "Tobacco Road" might seem tame by comparison, but *Psychedelic Lollipop* offers a few other fine moments.

The bluesy "I'll Go Crazy" mutes Scala's vocals beneath the instrumentation, his soulful delivery accented by the syncopated harmonies and scraps of twangy guitar.  The band's original "Sometimes I Think About" is a rather sophisticated (for the era) rock song with a dark ambiance that is helped along by dirge-like vocals and arcane keyboard fills that borderline on feedback. The guitarwork here is quite nice, provocative even, displaying a cool tone and timbre that plays well off the organ riffing. "She's Coming Home" is another great rocker, with plenty of guitar and screaming keyboards, rowdy harmonies, and an overall steely resolve that eschews psychedelic frippery in favor of muscular blues-rock.

• • • • •

Less than six months passed between the release of *Psychedelic Lollipop* and the band's sophomore effort, *Electric Comic Book*, but the resulting recordings sound years apart. The band had spent much of the time in-between the two albums touring, tightening up the chemistry between the individual players.

Plus, the world had changed rapidly during the ensuing days and weeks, and the songs on *Electric Comic Book* evince more of the psychedelic flavor hinted at by the band's debut. While the Blues Magoos' label obviously tried to position the band to take advantage of this "flower power" imagery, they just as obviously had some other ideas.

While *Electric Comic Book* didn't yield any hit singles – the closest it came was with the #60 chart spot achieved by "Pipe Dream" – the album offers up an engaging mix of psychedelic rock and blue-eyed soul nonetheless. Scala's raging keyboards dominate "Pipe Dream," an up-tempo rocker that displays a punkish intensity, Scala's low-key vocals overshadowed by the song's intricate arrangement and the complex interplay of Mike Esposito and Emil "Peppy" Thielhelm's guitars. The dreamy "There's A Chance We Can Make It" is stone-washed in a veritable wall of sound, the sharp guitarplay and solid rhythms spinning around the spacey vocal harmonies, creating a sort of discordant and disconcerting edge to the performance.

The less said about the ridiculous "Life Is Just A Cher O' Bowlies" the better, the song a bad example of psych-pop with dreary guitars, a claustrophobic mix, and a ridiculously inane sing-along chorus that a six-year-old would know better than to blurt aloud. Better is the Blues Magoos' reading of the garage-rock classic "Gloria," the band breathing new life into Van Morrison's too-frequently covered gem by mixing in some chaotic instrumentation and gang vocals (not harmony, really), scraps of Esposito's guitar clashing with Scala's keys while the overall instrumental anarchy drives the song to new (punkish) heights. While the CD cover shows "Gloria" at a mere 2:12, the stereo clocks it in at a delightfully pumped-up six-minutes of savvy, street-smart rock 'n' roll cheap thrills.

Much the rest of *Electric Comic Book* alternates between muscular, grungy rock and psych-pop. One stand-out is the British-sounding "Albert Common Is Dead," a brief treatise on 1960s conformity and consumerism that mixes Syd Barrett-era psychedelic Pink Floyd with fast-and-furious instrumentation often delivered at Ramones-level intensity. A cover of Jimmy Reed's "Let's Get Together" highlights the band's R&B roots with slippery guitarplay, a funky beat, gruff vocals, and honky-tonk piano-pounding while "Take My Love" treads close to Young Rascals' turf with a soulful keyboard riff, a shuffling rhythm, and raucous harmonies. "Rush Hour" is a flat-out rocker with snarling vocals, tightwire guitar, and a steady locomotive heartbeat.

With the benefit of better than 40 years of hindsight, the performances on *Electric Comic Book* sound a bit more rushed, the songs less fully-formed than those on *Psychedelic Lollipop*. Listening to the two albums together (clocking in just slightly more than an hour total), however, with updated digital sound, the contrast between them isn't so apparent as to be distracting. Instead, these two albums sound like different sides of the same coin.

The Blues Magoos may have been the result of a certain time and place in pop culture history, when record labels were more willing to experiment, but these albums are more than mere relics of the 1960s, Blues Magoos much more than a mere "one hit wonder." These albums are the sound of a band trying to find itself while adrift in the constantly-changing cultural rapids which, when you think of it, is the story of rock 'n' roll itself. (2011)

BOB SEGER & THE SILVER BULLET BAND
'Live' Bullet / Nine Tonight   (Hideout Records/Capitol Records)

By 1980, Detroit rock 'n' roll legend Bob Seger was finally beginning to see some payoff in a career that had crawled along slowly for almost 20 years. His *Against The Wind* album quickly vaulted to the top of the charts on its way to multi-Platinum™ sales status and would yield a handful of hit singles, earning the artist his first Grammy® Award. Seger would later ride this rocket of popularity for the next decade and a half, chalking up seven straight Platinum™ albums on his way to induction in the Rock & Roll Hall of Fame in 2004.

Back in '76, however, Seger was just another heartland rocker with his career in the balance. After a four-year/four-album stint with Capitol Records in the late 1960s/early 1970s, Seger struggled following a single indie label release and a pair of albums for Warner/Reprise Records, none of which sold in significant numbers even as Seger's live audience continued to grow.

Looking for one last shot at the brass ring, Seger and his long-time manager Punch Andrews formed the Silver Bullet Band with local musicians like former Third Power guitarist Drew Abbott and sax player Alto Reed, both of whom Seger had previously worked with.

It was as Bob Seger & the Silver Bullet Band that this new crew would record 1975's *Beautiful Loser* album, Seger re-signing with Capitol for one last chance at fame and fortune. The band dutifully hit the road in the wake of the album's release, even scoring an opening slot for Kiss, only to get kicked off the high-profile 1976 tour after a dozen or so shows for upstaging the headliners. Somewhere along the way, they performed for hometown fans at Cobo Hall in Detroit, the 1975 show recorded for posterity and released the following year as *'Live' Bullet*.

Contrary to conventional wisdom, it wasn't *'Live' Bullet* that broke Bob Seger to national audiences. Released in early 1976, the two-LP set would slow burn its way to number 34 on the *Billboard* Top 200 albums chart, with most of its sales success coming in the wake of the release of Seger's 10th studio album, *Night Moves*, later that year.

Seger's career breakthrough with *Night Moves* would motivate fans to check out *'Live' Bullet*, which built word-of-mouth and prompted further sales of *Night Moves* and *Beautiful Loser* in a self-fulfilling cycle that would push all three albums to millions of copies in sales.

The reason behind the eventual success of *'Live' Bullet* is quite simple – in a decade littered with live albums from bands that often had no business climbing on a stage, the performance by Seger and the Silver Bullet Band that was captured by *'Live' Bullet* crackles with a raw energy and electricity forged by a couple hundred nights on the road. Drawing on material from *Beautiful Loser*, as well as songs from Seger's first seven albums and a handful of choice covers, *'Live' Bullet* represented the best of 1970s rock 'n' roll and it would become one of the best-selling live albums of all time.

Recorded in front of an enthusiastic hometown crowd at the Motor City's legendary Cobo Hall in the heart of downtown Detroit, *'Live' Bullet* kicks off with a scorching cover of the Ike & Tina Turner classic "Nutbush City Limits." With drummer Charlie Allen Martin kicking away at the bass drum, accompanied by Drew Abbott's scorching fretwork, Seger pulls out all the stops in providing the song a high-octane performance with a spoken word nod to the audience, the song cresting to a frenzied finish.

The retrospective, semi-ballad "Travelin' Man" is a literate tale of life on the road that has long been a fan favorite. While, in time, Seger's ballads would become more polished in delivery, in 1976 even his mid-tempo material could suddenly explode into a cacophony of guitar, keyboards, bass, and drums; Seger's soul-drenched vocals pulled inspiration from influences like Otis Redding and James Brown. "Travelin' Man" cranks along for a few minutes before reaching its instrumental peak, then segueing seamlessly into "Beautiful Loser," the song both an audience favorite and a sorely

overlooked gem in the Seger songwriting catalog. Sporting a nifty set of Van Morrison-styled lyrics that firmly place the singer in the role of the misunderstood loner, Abbott's bluesy albeit understated guitar licks and Robyn Robbins' gospel-tinged keyboards perfectly frame Seger's elegant vocals. Seger and the band lend an undeniably funky slant to Morrison's "I've Been Working,"
alternating between soft and hard, the performance peppered with Abbott's imaginative six-string play and icy blasts from Alto Reed's ever-present saxophone. Seger channels his inner James Brown on the vocals, swaggering and swooning like a vintage soul-shouter, taking the song to new heights.

Seger turned to his rich and deep back catalog for many of the performances on *'Live' Bullet*, often with astounding results. The classic rock radio staple "Turn The Page," a great lament on the weariness of life as a rock 'n' roll road warrior, was first recorded for Seger's criminally-out-of-print *Back In '72* album, one of the best hard rock records of the era.Seger's high lonesome vocals here are accompanied by a truly sparse, smothering arrangement with Reed's ethereal saxwork providing a nice edge to Martin's brushes and Abbott's muted guitar.

From this point, the gloves come off and *'Live' Bullet* achieves the terminal velocity that would make rock 'n' roll history. "U.M.C. (Upper Middle Class)" is a funky, R&B tinged rocker from Seger's 1974 album *Seven*, a bit of social commentary with a slippery groove and twangy fretwork.

Early blues/rock legend Bo Diddley's signature tune, "Bo Diddley," is fuel-injected with an amped-up reading of Diddley's namesake staggered rhythm, Seger shouting out the lyrics above Reed's rockin' sax and the hard-driving instrumental bedrock built by bassist Chris Campbell and drummer Martin.

From his 1968 album of the same name with the Bob Seger System, "Ramblin' Gamblin' Man" was his first regional hit back in the day, establishing the artist as a hard rock favorite in the narrow band of the Northeast U.S. "rust belt" that runs in a line from Detroit to Buffalo, New York. Delivered here, the song is seen as both a triumph and a desperate last shot at fame. Seger spits out the lyrics rapid-fire, with a swaggering certainty as the band lends harmony vocals above the houserockin' rhythmic chaos, which itself is carpet-bombed with Abbott's razor-sharp leads.

The crowd-favorite "Heavy Music" is Seger covering himself, the song a mid-1960s original by Bob Seger & the Last Heard that appeared on his excellent 1972 collection of covers, *Smokin' O.P.'s*. While generally an up-tempo number, it's really designed as a breather for the band as the singer engages in a little call-and-response with the audience as various band members throw down brief solos before jumping in for a big finish. Campbell's underlying bass line here is particularly strong, menacing and, well, heavy with just a taste of funk.

"Heavy Music" leads directly into the barn-burner "Katmandu," then a new track from *Beautiful Loser* but a live staple ever since, and as close to a hit single as that album would enjoy. Abbot walks the song in with a few raucous guitar licks as Seger does a spoken word intro that jumps into the fast-paced and now-familiar rocker. A rollicking lyrical flight-of-fancy with shout outs to various regions of the country, "Katmandu" allows the band to show off its chops, with Martin's locomotive drumbeats and Reed's soulful sax notes rising to the surface.

'Live' Bullet closes out with the two-fisted knockout punch of "Get Out Of Denver" and a cover of Chuck Berry's "Let It Rock." The former is a frantic, fast-paced, Chuck Berry-inspired rocker from *Seven* while the latter is an equally up-tempo Berry track from *Smokin' O.P.'s*.

While delivered with a street-punkish ferocity and intensity, "Get Out Of Denver" is a hilarious story-song with scorched-earth guitar, honky-tonk piano-pounding, and crashing drumbeats. "Let It Rock," a garage-rock standard, is performed entirely in the spirit of the original, with a driving beat and blistering guitar.

A lone bonus track has been attached to the end of *'Live' Bullet* for this 2011 reissue, a 1976 recording from a Pontiac, Michigan performance – not quite Seger's backyard, but definitely in his neighborhood, a show that reportedly drew 80,000 fans from across the state years before Seger was a star anywhere else.

A cover of the blues classic "I Feel Like Breaking Up Somebody's Home," a song that has been sung by everybody from Etta James and Albert King to Ann Peebles, it adds an appropriate coda to the original album. Showcasing one of Seger's finest soulful vocal turns and Abbott's stinging, emotional fretwork, the song reaches back into the artist's deep blues and R&B roots, displaying a rootsy edge that would largely be worn down by Seger's 1980s-era commercial peak.

• • • • •

In the summer of 1980, Bob Seger & the Silver Bullet Band accomplished something that no artist before or since has done, selling out nine consecutive shows at Detroit's Cobo Hall, and then adding another half-dozen or so sold-out performances at the nearby Pine Knob Amphitheatre a couple of months later.

Pre-Internet, tickets were sold on a lottery basis – you sent in your money order with a self-addressed, stamped envelope and, if you were lucky and the gods smiled upon you, the postman would ring later with your tickets. The Reverend would be lucky enough to grab four pairs of tickets for the Detroit shows, which featured local legend Mitch Ryder coming out of retirement to open for Seger.

Some of the performances from those nine legendary nights in Detroit would be mixed with portions of a Boston show from later in 1980 to comprise the tracklist of 1981's *Nine Tonight*, Seger's second live album in a little more than five years. A lot had happened during the four year interim after the release of the 'Live' Bullet album that had cemented his success in the wake of that year's commercial and critical breakthrough, Night Moves. Seger's 1978 follow-up, Stranger In Town, would build upon his earlier popularity and reach number four on the Billboard magazine albums chart, while 1980's Against The Wind would hit number one.

Considering the successes of the previous few years, and the enormous demand for Bob Seger & the Silver Bullet Band as a touring entity, it made sense for Capitol to release another live collection so soon after the previous album. It should come as no surprise that Nine Tonight draws more heavily from Seger's late 1970s albums rather than his earlier work, and features live versions of the big hits of the previous five years like "Night Moves," "Fire Lake," and "Against The Wind," among others.

The Silver Bullet Band itself had changed by the time of the shows documented by Nine Tonight, drummer Charlie Allen Martin replaced by former Seger sidekick David Teegarden after a tragic accident, and keyboardist Craig Frost brought on board from Grand Funk Railroad. With guitarist Drew Abbott and saxophonist Alto Reed still in the spotlight, though, the Silver Bullet Band roared on without missing a beat, and Nine Tonight would rapidly hit number three on the Billboard albums chart on its way to selling over three million copies.

Nine Tonight opens with the title track, a song originally recorded for the soundtrack of the movie Urban Cowboy; here the song takes on a greater immediacy. An up-tempo rocker with thick instrumentation, with Abbott's guitar set on stun and Reed's sax blasting wildly, Seger's vocals seem strained, the song seemingly not part of his and the band's normal rotation.

Their cover of Otis Clay's Memphis soul classic "Tryin' To Live My Life Without You" fares much better; released as a single, it hit number five on the charts. Atop the band's Southern-fried groove, Seger again turns to James Brown for inspiration, sweating and strutting across the stage as he delivers a pitch-perfect reading of the original's heartbreak lyrics.

A large part of Seger's success was built upon his finely-crafted ballads, with "You'll Accomp'ny Me," from *Against The Wind*, a perfect example. Seger's ability to take his sentimental, often heart-wrenching lyrics and imbue them with no little soul while retaining a gruff, masculine demeanor allowed both men and women to embrace the songs. "You'll Accomp'ny Me" is a mid-tempo romantic plea with simple but imaginative lyrics, Seger's smooth vocal performance assisted by a steady soundtrack with dashes of piano and guitar.

While his ballads are what grabbed the lion's share of radio airplay and put money in the bank, it was the rockers that sold concert tickets, and *Nine Tonight* has its share of both. "Hollywood Nights" is a glitzy, revved-up story-song, a romantic tale of the type that John Mellencamp would later ride to success. With a driving rhythm and plenty of guitar and piano threaded throughout, Seger's considerable vocals are almost swallowed up by the instrumental crescendo.

"Old Time Rock And Roll" was an obscure track from *Stranger In Town* until it was used in a memorable scene in the movie *Risky Business*; its subsequent release as a single would barely scrape the Top Thirty, however its longevity and consistent radio airplay over the following 30 years would make it a pop culture touchstone.

Here, "Old Time Rock And Roll" is delivered as a blustery, swaggering rave-up complete with female backing vocals and an undeniable bluesy undercurrent that is guaranteed to get your toes tapping. Reed's sax blows like an inspired cross between King Curtis and Clarence Clemons while Abbott's guitar, nearly overshadowed by the claustrophobic instrumental track, gets down to a lil' funky chicken-picking.

"Against The Wind" is one of Seger's more recognizable ballads, a character-driven (autobiographical?) lament with some great lyrical lines and brilliant imagery. Seger nails the vocals here with a beautiful wistfulness, the world-weary perspective of the romantic soul looking backwards at what might have been before accepting his fate.

Frost's piano here provides elegant accompaniment, but it's Seger's plaintive voice that drives the performance.

The rocking "Feel Like A Number" is another sadly overlooked selection from the Seger songbook, neither fish nor fowl as it ventures into uncertain social commentary, something the artist had seldom done since the early 1970s and "U.M.C." Seger's outrage is just as appropriate today as it was in 1980, the song dripping with working class angst and assembly-line alienation.

Seger's vocals are slung low in the mix, Abbott's riffs riding the wind alongside Teegarden's gale-force drumbeats before exploding into an incendiary solo as Seger nearly screams the lyrics, exclaiming "dammit, I'm a man!" above the cluster of instrumentation. This is the one truly exemplary performance from the album that would have been worthy of *'Live' Bullet.*

Another big hit from *Against The Wind*, "Fire Lake" is a Springsteen-styled, character-driven tale with a bit of country twang mixed with R&B uproar that would become another classic rock radio staple and hit the top of the charts. The career-building "Night Moves," another classic Seger ballad, is where the artist's talent finally caught up with his ambition, delivering a near-mystical account of teenage lust and romance that struck a chord with audiences from coast to coast. Seger's live 1980 rendition of the song differs little in substance from the 1975 original save for maybe a little more passion, a little more dynamics in the sound, and a richer instrumental backdrop.

The rambunctious "Rock And Roll Never Forgets," also from *Night Moves*, is one of several Seger odes to the rock 'n' roll aesthetic; in the hands of a lesser artist it would sound pandering and silly, but Seger always brought a street-savvy regal air to such performances. The reading here is a guitar-driven party with a blue-collar vibe, Abbott's six-string ringing like a bell as Frost's piano tinkles away in the background and Teegarden's drums lurk nearby delivering the big beat. It's the kind of bar-band-made-good storytelling that much of Seger's legacy was built on, and he does it proud.

An equally raucous, road-tested cover of Chuck Berry's "Let It Rock" is a long-time feature of the band's live set, and although the version for *Nine Tonight* was (sadly) edited by several minutes to cram it on the CD, the unbridled energy and reckless spirit of the song shines through nonetheless. For this 2011 reissue, "Brave Strangers," from *Stranger In Town*, has been tacked on the end of the album as a bonus track, and while the song is an effective, introspective mid-tempo rocker, it's too much in the vein of "Night Moves" or "Against The Wind" to stand out. They'd have been better off including the full edit of "Let It Rock" and let the album truly blow down the doors.

Bob Seger would go on to achieve greater heights of success in the 1980s and, to a lesser extent, the 1990s, even while cutting back on both touring and recording after his prolific creative streak during the 1970s. In 1995, Seger would effectively retire from the business for better than a decade while raising his family, returning to the spotlight with 2006's *Face The Promise*, which would take him back to the top of the charts and Platinum™ sales status. A sold-out tour would follow the album's release, and prompt the possibility of a new Seger album in 2012.

One of the last major artists to resist the lure of digital music sales, Seger finally acquiesced with the reissue releases of *Nine Tonight* and *'Live' Bullet*, both albums available on CD and from iTunes and other online retailers for downloading. The re-mastered sound of both reissues is vastly improved from the original CD releases, and even the cover artwork of *'Live' Bullet* is crisper and clearer than the fuzzy crap they used for the 1999 CD reissue I'm looking at.

'Live' Bullet is arguably the better of the two albums, with more rock and less squawk, and the performances are, by and large, more stripped-down, raw and rockin' than the lushly-orchestrated arrangements you'll find on *Nine Tonight*. Still, for fans that discovered Seger in the late 1970s or early 1980s rather than with "Ramblin' Gamblin' Man" and "Lucifer," *Nine Tonight* is a fine artifact of the artist's commercial peak.

Now that you're a bona fide rock 'n' roll legend, Bob, can you get over your embarrassment of those early albums and reissue CD versions of such long out-of-print 1970s-era albums as *Mongrel*, *Ramblin' Gamblin' Man* and, for Pete's sake, *Back In '72*? Really, Bob, it's about time… (2011)

BRIAN ROBERTSON
Diamonds and Dirt   (SPV Records)

As one-half of the fierce twin-guitar knockout punch that fueled much of Thin Lizzy's mid-to-late '70s-era material, Scotland-born Brian Robertson – "Robbo" to his friends – helped write the instruction manual for a unique hard rock/heavy metal guitar sound that would, in turn, inspire and influence folks like Iron Maiden, Def Leppard, and a legion of 1980s-era "New Wave of British Heavy Metal" bands.

Robertson left Thin Lizzy when his relationship with frontman Phil Lynott fell apart due to various disagreements, and he subsequently formed the hard-rocking Wild Horses with former Rainbow bassist Jimmy Bain. That band drifted apart after a pair of albums that achieved moderate success in the UK, and Robertson moved on to Motörhead, an ill-fated fit that quickly spit the guitarist back out on the street. Through the ensuing years, Robertson would perform with Swedish rockers Lotus, and with artists like Pat Travers, Frankie Miller, and Graham Parker.

Missing from Robertson's resume is a proper solo album, something that, these days, every 20-year-old fretburner in a band considers their ticket out of obscurity. Robertson released a six-song EP, *The Clan*, in 1995, but he'd never thought of a full-length solo album until a friend, listening to some old songwriting demo tapes, convinced the guitarist that he had some gems amongst those old songs. Robertson got together with some friends like bassist Nalley Pahlsson (from the Swedish band Treat) and drummer Ian Haugland (Europe) as well as vocalists Leif Sundin (ex-Michael Schenker Group) and Liny Wood, and recorded *Diamonds and Dirt* in Stockholm.

Robertson's solo debut is a rollicking collection of energetic, guitar-driven original tunes and inspired, well-chosen, close-to-the-heart covers of songs by friends Thin Lizzy and Frankie Miller. While some of the performances sound a wee bit dated, most of 'em just sound timeless, capturing the same reckless spirit that the 18-year-old Robertson brought to his first Thin Lizzy performances nearly 40 years ago. *Diamonds and Dirt* kicks off with the title track, a melodic rocker with big roots, Foreigner-styled larger-than-life riffing, and

Sundin's classic AOR vocals. As Robertson freely tugs at the strings like a convict seeing the light of day for the first time in years, Sundin's vocals are complimented by Wood's soaring backing harmonies, her voice adding a wonderful counterpoint to Sundin's vox.

"Diamonds and Dirt," the song, could be a big radio hit if FM still played rock 'n' roll instead of a facsimile and too-many commercials, and in 1981 it would have been huge. It's a solidly-written and constructed song, and a clear sign that Robertson learned a thing or two at Phil Lynott's knee all those years ago.

Ditto for "Passion," another hard rock styled throwback with scorching guitarplay, a funky rhythm that would make Prince blush with envy, and an infectious chorus. The Thin Lizzy obscurity "It's Only Money" (circa *Night Life*) is a staggering metallic stomp with heavy riffs, Haugland's monster drumbeats, and a gymnastic vocal take from Sundin. Robertson's solos here are simply stunning, underscoring the vocals and explosive rhythms with fierce finality.

A slightly better-known Lizzy cover, "Running Back" (from *Jailbreak*, for all of you keeping score at home) is provided both "fast" and "slow" versions; the former is a joyful reading that reminds of Frankie Miller's best blue-eyed soul moments, with honky-tonk piano and a rolling rhythm to carry the song along at a fair pace, while the latter is a mid-tempo strut with Chicago blues roots and crunchy fretwork, and a dash of the exotic via Ola Gustafsson's elegant Dobro. Neither version sounds like the original, and that's cool with this rabid Lizzy fan 'cause both sizzle and burn like white phosphorus, proving both Phil Lynott's timeless talents as a songwriter and Robertson's impressive skills as an arranger and bandleader.

Speaking of ol' Frankie, Robertson does his pal a large favor on *Diamonds and Dirt* by covering not one, but *three* Miller songs.

The first, "Mail Box," is a bluesy rocker with a swinging rhythm, big screaming guitars, and jackhammer drums, tho' to be entirely honest it's hard not hearing the incredible, underrated Miller singing the words (the Scottish singer/songwriter largely sitting on the sidelines since a life-threatening brain hemorrhage in '94).

"Do It Till We (Drop It)" is an unabashed hard rock journey with roots in the 1970s, but would be comfortable in any era with nimble guitarplay and a buoyant rhythmic soundtrack. Both pale next to one of Miller's most treasured songs, "Ain't Got No Money" (a minor hit back in the day for Bob Seger). Robbo brought in singer Rob Lamothe (Riverdogs) for this "bonus track," and Lamothe clearly nails Miller's original intent with a gruff, rolling vocal performance that is further colored by Robertson's wiry, fiery guitar licks. No, it won't replace Miller's considerable original, but it's a hot 'un nonetheless!

Robertson's original material sits well between that of his highly-considered friends, and displays a myriad of influences and styles. The engaging "Texas Wind" features buzzing, rattling guitars that play like Jeff Beck, and powerful locomotive rhythms that flow beneath Sundin's vocals like a tsunami. Robertson's solos are at once both metal-edged and jazzy, combining the best of both worlds in creating some sort of invigorating jazz-metal fusion.

The previously-unrecorded "Blues Boy" was a co-write by the guitarist with former bandmate Lynott, the song a red-hot, mid-tempo British blues-rocker with arid Texas roots and guitar that sounds like a cross between Stevie Ray Vaughan and Gary Moore (another Thin Lizzy alumnus).

Robertson's lone vocal performance comes via a performance of Jim White's "10 Miles To Go On A 9 Mile Road," an odd choice from an otherwise overlooked songwriter. The intro is Middle East raga with psychedelic flavor, Robertson's growling vocals spoken as much as sung, not entirely unpleasant but obviously lacking in tone and nuance. Still, they work here, especially given the lyrical construct, the song fleshed out by piercing guitar licks and vocal harmonies that echo and fatten Robertson's voice. The exotic feel of the raging raga passages is balanced by shards of serpentine fretwork.

Robertson's *Diamonds and Dirt* is an overall engaging debut, delivered some 30 years late, perhaps, but better late than never, eh? The guitarist clearly has his heart in the right place, still bangs and mangles his chunk of wood and steel with as much fire as he did in his teens, and has a fine way with the words.

There remains a large market for this sort of guitar-driven melodic rock, especially in Europe, and I suspect that a largely-hidden stateside audience exists as well. Make no mistake, Robertson's sound *is* a throwback to an earlier, simpler musical era and that's a good thing. We have enough angst and alienation and darkness in rock music these days…with *Diamonds and Dirt*, Brian Robertson drops a little sunshine on our heads. (2011)

BURNING SPEAR
Marcus Garvey / Garvey's Ghost   (Hip-O Select)

To the casual reggae fan, the sun rises and sets with Bob Marley. From his earliest work with the original Wailers (Peter Tosh and Bunny Wailer) during the late 1960s and early '70s, to the international stardom afforded his late '70s albums (which, to be honest, were really solo albums by Marley with an assorted, albeit talented backing crew), Rasta Bob is the name and face associated with reggae for many.

Truth is, the island of Jamaica has shared many musical wonders with music lovers through the years, from the soulful Heptones, Toots and the Maytals, and the charismatic Jimmy Cliff to lesser-known, but no less talented artists like Steel Pulse and Black Uhuru. In terms of importance and popularity on the small island nation, however, perhaps none of the above-named artists personifies the pride and hope of the Rastafarian ideal better than Winston Rodney, a/k/a Burning Spear.

During a chance late 1960s meeting with the already-legendary Bob Marley in their shared hometown, Marley pointed the young, ambitious Rodney towards Kingston and producer "Sir Coxson" Dodd's Studio One. Rodney spent around five years with Dodd, recording better than two dozen songs, and honing his craft as a singer and songwriter. It was when Rodney hooked up with sound system operator Lawrence "Jack Ruby" Lindo during the mid-'70s, however, that he became the Burning Spear.

Sound systems, for those of you not in the know, were an important part of Jamaican musical culture, and the impetus for the development of both ska and reggae music. Starting in the late 1950s, sound system operators would hold large street parties in the ghettos of Kingston, with music provided by huge, turntable-driven sound systems powered by portable generators. The operators would charge admission and sell food and drink as DJs played the hottest American R&B sides for the hundreds, sometimes thousands of partiers.

These events brought in a lot of cash for the operator, and a sort of "arms war" started as they built larger and louder sound systems to compete with other operators. Eventually, as the demand for new music grew faster than American labels could supply records, operators like Sir Coxson became producers and studio owners. Enlisting Jamaican musicians, a steady stream of new music was created, and the styles of ska and reggae developed as the island's artists tried to approximate American R&B music.

Often times, the songs recorded by artists like the Wailers would be "exclusive" to the producing operator, who played it at parties and would release it on 45rpm single only if demand warranted it. Jamaican immigrant DJ Kool Herc would bring the sound system to America in the late 1970s, which led to the rise of hip-hop in NYC…but that's really a story for another time.

It was from this sound system culture that Jack Ruby emerged, the owner of Jack Ruby's Hi Fi and one of the most popular "roots reggae" DJs in the country. In Rodney and Burning Spear he found his cash cow, much as Dodd had with Marley in the 1960s. The first collaboration in the studio between Ruby and Burning Spear – now a trio that included Rodney, Delroy Hines, and Rupert Willington – resulted in the scorching single "Marcus Garvey."

A mesmerizing track with Rodney's lyrics paying homage to the Black nationalist hero Garvey, the three men's deep enchanting vocals are backed by the seasoned studio outfit the Black Disciples, which included bassists Robbie Shakespeare and Aston "Family Man" Barrett, drummer Leroy Wallace, and guitarists Earl "Chinna" Smith and Valentine "Tony" Chin.

"Marcus Garvey" was originally used by Ruby as a sound system exclusive, but the song's popularity led to its eventual vinyl release, and it became a best-seller. Burning Spear followed up this initial success with the blistering commentary of "Slavery Days," a hypnotizing rhythm threaded, snakelike, beneath Rodney's outraged vocals and condemning lyrics. It, too, would become a big hit and Ruby put Burning Spear in the studio with the Black Disciples to record a full-length album, resulting in *Marcus Garvey*, a powerful collection of roots reggae with often politically explosive lyrics.

When the album started selling by the truckload on the island, and sensing that he was holding commercial dynamite in his hands, Ruby took *Marcus Garvey* to England and Chris Blackwell, where it was released by Island Records in 1975. Fueled by Rodney's socially-conscious lyrics, Burning Spear's infectious vocal harmonies, and an inspired reggae soundtrack, the album blew up almost immediately.

Aside from the two aforementioned singles, *Marcus Garvey* included some of the darkest, scariest, and most potent reggae music then put to wax, songs like "The Invasion," with its deep dub soundtrack and trancelike vocals; the horn-driven "Old Marcus Garvey," another tribute to the Jamaican legend; and the up-tempo "Jordan River," with its Biblical references and rapid-fire (almost rapped) vocals.

Given the popularity of *Marcus Garvey* in both Jamaica and England (and, to a lesser extent, America), it seemed for a while that Burning Spear might challenge Bob Marley & the Wailers as the champions of reggae. Rodney was angered by Island's remix of the album's tracks, however, which changed the speed of many songs to appeal to white audiences…a situation not assuaged by the subsequent "dub mix" of *Marcus Garvey* that was released by Island as *Garvey's Ghost* in 1976.

Garvey's Ghost downplayed Rodney's intelligent lyricism and haunting vocals in favor of instrumental mixes of the original songs that placed the emphasis on the Black Disciples' amazing musical skills. With just scattershot vocals rising above the fray, the music is free to dart and jump throughout the mix, and while ten songs of mostly-instrumental dub may seem like overkill to the casual fan, it's worth the investment in time and attention to catch the subtle nuances and the immense talent poured into the performances on *Garvey's Ghost*.

Burning Spear would release *Man In The Hills*, its proper follow-up to *Marcus Garvey*, in late 1976. Again working with producer Ruby and the Black Disciples, the album offered up another ten politically-charged tunes, including a re-make of Burning Spear's original Dodd-produced single "Door Peep." Still chafing at his treatment by Island Records, however, Rodney would break away from producer Ruby, dump Hines and Willington, and take on the Burning Spear mantle as his own, wearing it proudly for almost thirty-five years now.

Rodney launched his own Burning Spear label to ensure control over his music, and has produced or co-produced every album since. During the ensuing years, Burning Spear has become one of Jamaica's most legendary artists; a status reinforced by the recognition afforded Rodney by his Grammy® Award win in 1999.

This Hip-O Select reissue of *Marcus Garvey* and *Garvey's Ghost* pairs the two albums back together again, and brings both of these essential slabs of reggae history back into print after years of neglect. While other reissue versions have drawn from the Island Records albums, this reissue package was digitally re-mastered from the original analog tapes. While I don't know how much of Ruby's initial production was restored here – it's been over three decades since the Reverend heard the original albums in their explosive Jamaican vinyl versions, courtesy of my old Rasta friend Earl – these new 21st century versions of *Marcus Garvey* and its dub companion sound pretty esoteric to these ears.

Regardless, it's good to have an album of the importance of *Marcus Garvey* back in print, even if for a little while. If all you know of reggae music is Bob Marley, you owe it to yourself to check out Burning Spear. You'll never think of reggae in the same way again... (2010)

CAPTAIN BEEFHEART & THE MAGIC BAND
Live From Harpos 1980
(Gonzo Multimedia)

Don Van Vliet, better known by his stage name Captain Beefheart, is one of those hipster musical icons that a lot of people have *heard of,* but far fewer have actually *heard.* A talented multi-instrumentalist (harmonica, saxophone, clarinet) and dynamic singer, Vliet was influenced by the blues and jazz music of his youth, taking his cue from artists like Howlin' Wolf, Robert Johnson, and John Coltrane.

As a teenager, he would become friends with like-minded musical oddball Frank Zappa, a contentious relationship that began in the 1950s and was on/off until Zappa's death in 1993. The collaboration resulted in several recordings over the years, including one fine full-length album, 1975's *Bongo Fury.*

Taking on the stage name Captain Beefheart, Van Vliet hooked up with the Magic Band, a Los Angeles-based R&B outfit. Captain Beefheart & His Magic Band (as they were originally billed) recorded a couple of bluesy but unconventional singles for A&M Records that got them dumped by the label. After the Captain shook up the band's line-up and brought in guitarist Ry Cooder (then of blues-rock outfit Rising Sons), they recorded the *Safe As Milk* album for Buddah Records in 1967.

Displaying a heavy blues influence, the album would nonetheless offer signs of Beefheart's future musical amalgam of psychedelic rock, blues, improvisational jazz, and avant-garde experimentation that would result in 1969's *Trout Mask Replica*, an album of such enduring weirdness and timelessness that it has influenced countless songwriters and musicians to follow, from Tom Waits to Sonic Youth and beyond.

Beefheart recorded thirteen albums with the Magic Band between 1965 and 1982, when he hung up his microphone for a life of creative contemplation and visual art, a rare case of an influential musician making the leap into the art world, where Van Vliet's drawings and paintings demanded premium pricing and were exhibited in galleries and museums worldwide. During his tenure at the head of the Magic Band, however, Beefheart's artistic temperament earned him the reputation of being a real asshole. A strict bandleader and notorious cheapskate, Beefheart kept his band mates in perpetual poverty and frequently abused them verbally and, sometimes, physically.

Still, due to his recognized genius, Beefheart was able to recruit and keep a number of extremely talented musicians in his Magic Band through the years. Such was the case as illustrated by *Live From Harpos 1980*, an invaluable document that captures a remarkable performance by Beefheart & the Magic Band at Harpos, a longstanding Detroit concert venue, in December 1980.

Touring in support of the *Doc at the Radar Station* album, which was released in August 1980, the Magic Band that backed up Beefheart in the Motor City included guitarist Jeff Moris Tepper, bassist Eric Drew Feldman, and drummer Robert Arthur Williams, all of which had also appeared on 1978's *Shiny Beast (Bat Chain Puller)* album. The line-up on this cold night in Detroit was rounded out by guitarists Richard Snyder and Jeff Tapir/White.

The Reverend attended this show at Harpos; I frequently haunted the club (as well as the New Miami) after getting off work from the Trailways bus station in downtown Detroit. Since it began hosting rock 'n' roll shows in 1973, Harpos had become a worthy heir to Russ Gibbs' legendary Grande Ballroom, hosting shows by artists as diverse as Ted Nugent, Mitch Ryder, Johnny Winter, Cheap Trick and, yes, Captain Beefheart.

The club moved more towards heavy metal in the 1980s, and rap/hip-hop in the 1990s (including legendary Goth rapper Esham, the real "Motor City Madman"); best I can tell, they're still rockin' at Harpos today. I probably got to the club late; as I wouldn't have left downtown until midnight, but I wasn't going to pass up the rare opportunity to catch Captain Beefheart & the Magic Band perform live, even if I don't remember much of it today (so long after the beer-fueled decade of the '80s).

The set list for *Live From Harpos 1980* is appropriately heavy on material from *Radar Station*, comprising six of that album's twelve songs, including a growling, snarling performance of "Hot Head" that features some stellar guitarplay with shotgun solos, and Beefheart's mesmerizing vocals dancing sloppily atop a fractured, circular rhythm. "Ashtray Heart" is of a similar construct, with Beefheart's scatting vocals be-bopping alongside a syncopated soundtrack and squalls of razor-sharp guitar. The sagely-titled "A Carrot Is As Close As A Rabbit Gets To A Diamond" is an enchanting, all too brief instrumental with guitars intertwining to create an elegant, classically-oriented soundscape that is atypical for the Captain and his band.

Among its 17 songs, *Live From Harpos 1980* also includes several choice cuts from across the band's storied career. The Delta blues-influenced "Abba Zabba" is a throwback from the *Safe As Milk* album, a dark-hued stomper with tribal rhythms and the Captain's best raspy, Howlin' Wolf styled sandpaper vocals. "My Human Gets Me Blues" dates back to *Trout Mask Replica*, the song a nifty lil' slice o' jump 'n' jive with surreal, seemingly stream-of-consciousness lyrics and a cacophonic symphony as a backdrop. Originally recorded to appear on an unreleased (until 2012) album of the same name, "Bat Chain Puller" landed on *Shiny Beast (Bat Chain Puller)*; its performance here is all right angles, with raw, primal, often-screamed vocals and jumbled instrumentation that often works at cross purposes with itself.

Also from *Shiny Beast*, "Suction Prints" is the sound of collapsing buildings, with Beefheart's tortured saxophone up front, barely escaping from the instrumental barrage of squealing guitars, madcap drumbeats, and thunderous rhythms. In the best Beefheart tradition, it sounds like it was created by a brace of insane criminals who broke out of the asylum and found refuge in a recording studio, each inmate taking out their hostilities and fractured obsessions on the innocent instruments.

The sound on *Live From Harpos 1980* is a notch above bootleg quality – hollow, muddy, slightly distorted, and with a bit of echo – most of which is par for the era in which it was recorded, some of which is due to the provenance of the original tape, no doubt (sounds to my ears like a good audience recording).

Since Captain Beefheart & the Magic Band never released a live album during the nearly two decades of their existence, however, and as there are only a handful of readily available live Beefheart albums to be found, *Live From Harpos 1980* is a welcome addition to the artist's canon. The performances are singularly abrasive, and thoroughly entertaining, if you're of a similar mindset (and evidently a small number of us fellow travelers are in that odd position). Captain Beefheart isn't for everybody, but he might just be for you! (2014)

CHOCOLATE WATCH BAND
No Way Out / The Inner Mystique   (Sundazed Records)

As far as 1960s-era garage-rock goes, the Chocolate Watch Band was influential far beyond the band's meager commercial reach. Although they would become West Coast musical heroes during the mid-to-late 1960s, with a handful of red-hot (and, later, highly collectible) 45rpm singles to their credit, culminating in a series of well-received full-length albums, the band suffered from a serious personality crisis.

Their management and producers would frequently bring in studio players to overdub the band's recordings, material would be released under their name that had little or no connection to the band itself…not entirely heard of in mid-'60s L.A. but not something that helped define a band's identity, either.

Regardless, on the basis of a trio of odd studio albums and a reputation for holding their own on stage with the likes of the Mothers of Invention and the Yardbirds, by the mid-'80s, the Chocolate Watch

Band (later changed to one word, "Watchband") would become bona fide *Nuggets*-approved garage-rock legends.

Formed by a group of junior college students in Los Altos, California in 1965, the original Chocolate Watch Band was heavily influenced by the British Invasion sound of bands like the Rolling Stones, the Kinks and, later, by the Pretty Things. They were one of the first wave of what esteemed critic Lester Bangs would call "punk rockers," Vox-yielding young hoodlums roaring out of their garage practice space and into the high school gyms and community centers of California to make teenage girls swoon at the front of the stage.

After the usual shuffling of band members, the Chocolate Watch Band as known and adored by collectors of 1960s-era garage-rock treasures included vocalist Dave Aguilar, guitarists Mike Loomis and Sean Tolby, bassist Bill Flores, and drummer Gary Andrijasevich.It was with this line-up that the Chocolate Watch Band recorded its initial singles – four red-hot slabs o' R&B-styled proto-rock cheap thrills – as well as appearing and performing as themselves in the teen exploitation movie *Riot on Sunset Strip*.

With all of this high-profile activity to hype the band, you'd think that their debut album would basically record itself and roll off the retail shelves and into the hands of eager fans. In an era when the "serious adults" in the room (i.e. managers & producers) often messed around with a young band's sound (see: Strawberry Alarm Clock, Electric Prunes, etc), producer Ed Cobb, with engineers Richard Podolor and Bill Cooper, just couldn't help but impose their own agenda on top of the band's considerably fresh and highly-rocking original sound.

As such, Chocolate Watch Band's 1967 debut album, *No Way Out*, although considered by many to be a classic of the garage-rock era, is not nearly as great as it might have been. The band's early singles would have provided a solid foundation on which to build a debut album, but the production staff saw fit to include only two of these performances – "Are You Gonna Be There (At The Love In)" and "No Way Out" – in the final mix. The former is a down-n-dirty R&B-tinged rocker with gang vocals, an infectious rhythm track, and greasy overdriven guitars that only bolster Aguilar's Jaggeresque vocals, the latter is a rock 'n' soul hybrid with wiry fretwork, a slight psychedelic edge (mimicking the fledgling San Francisco sound), cool snarling vox lost beneath droning, hypnotic instrumentation, and an overall dangerous vibe that was too cool for school in '67.

The full band line-up only appears on two other tracks on *No Way Out*, a meager representation on record that was curious even by then-current standards. An inspired cover of Chuck Berry's rollicking "Come On" is a revved-up hot-rod of mid-'60s rock, with echoed, haunting guitar notes lingering like storm clouds above Aguilar's rapid-paced, 1950s rockabilly-styled reading of the lyrics. The singer's original "Gone And Passes By" offers up exotic instrumental flourishes alongside a bouncy Bo Diddley beat, Aguilar's emotional vocals overshadowed by a lush mix that includes squalls of guitar, bass, and drums creating a maelstrom of sound.

Of the other material on *No Way Out*, there are a few gems that emerge in spite of the producer's interference. "Let's Talk About Girls" is a stone cold R&B romp a la early Stones that would have benefited from Aguilar's energetic vocal style; for whatever reason, studio pro Don Bennett's voice was dubbed over the band frontman's vocals.

The band's instrumental track rides low in the mix and features some tasty jolts of Mark Loomis's guitar, helping to rescue the song from disaster. Ditto for a cover of Steve Cropper's "Midnight Hour," which succeeds regardless of Bennett's flaccid vocals, as the band cleverly injects a soul-drenched Booker T & the M.G.'s sound with livewire rock 'n' roll electricity.

Much of the rest of *No Way Out* is suspect, however, as two instrumental songs – the clumsy attempt at a psychedelic mindtrip that was "Dark Side of the Mushroom" and the equally spacey pastiche of styles (rockabilly, surf, psychedelic) that was "Expo 2000" – were written by engineer and future uber-producer Richard Podolor and recorded with session players. These songs are "Chocolate Watch Band" in name only, as they lack the band's input and just provide a songwriting royalty for an interfering studio engineer. Another track, "Gossamer Wings," was written by singer Bennett, and uses the basic instrumental track from the band's 1966 B-side "Loose Lip Sync Ship" as a backdrop for Bennett's dull-as-dirt, soft-psych performance.

In spite of its flaws, *No Way Out* offers around 60% of the cheap thrills one could expect from a recording of its era, maybe a C+ or B-grade that could have been a solid B+ had singer Aguilar's charismatic voice not been removed from the aforementioned tracks in favor of the less-talented vocalist. At the heart of the problem was the fact that producer Ed Cobb had never even seen Chocolate Watch Band perform live, and didn't realize the assortment of talents that he had in the studio. An otherwise talented songwriter and producer that would go on to work with artists like Fleetwood Mac and Steely Dan, Cobb imposed his own vision on the band to mixed effect.

• • • • •

Although the Chocolate Watch Band's debut album *No Way Out* suffered from excessive studio tinkering by producer Ed Cobb, their sophomore effort – 1968's effervescent *The Inner Mystique* – was mostly created out of the ether in the studio by engineer Richard Podolor. The band itself had literally imploded in mid-'67, guitarist Mark Loomis leaving first to pursue his drug-fueled dreams of creating psychedelic-folk music with the Tingle Guild, which featured original Watch Band vocalist Danny Phay.

Drummer Gary Andrijasevich would follow Loomis out the door, with singer Dave Aguilar right behind him, leaving guitarist Sean Tolby and bassist Bill Flores as the remaining members. The pair recruited new band mates to fulfill live bookings, but by the end of 1967 the band was essentially dead in the water. That didn't stop Ed Cobb and Richard Podolor, though, neither of whom wanted to leave money on the table; they literally pieced together *The Inner Mystique* from whatever odds 'n' ends they found in the studio, creating the rest, branding it "Chocolate Watch Band" and slipping it past an unsophisticated, pre-Internet audience that didn't know any better.

The first side of *The Inner Mystique* – three of the album's meager eight-song tracklist – was entirely Podolor's show. Using un-credited studio pros, along with singer Don Bennett, whose unremarkable vocals had been shoehorned into the grooves of *No Way Out* without the band's knowledge or approval, Podolor approximates the R&B-drenched psychedelic roots of the Chocolate Watch Band with mixed results. The album-opening "Voyage of the Trieste," credited to producer Cobb, is a swirling, raga-touched psychedelic instrumental that stirs a bit of jazz-rock fusion into the grooves…not entirely uninviting, but it has nothing to do with the band whatsoever. The same goes for the Cobb-approved five-minute psych jam "Inner Mystique," which offers up some inspired playing, just not by any real Chocolate Watch Band members, and almost a year too late to catch the initial wave of psychedelic rock fervor.

The stand-out of side one is a torrid cover of "In The Past," originally by fellow garage-rock pioneers We The People. Although Bennett's vocals are soft-pedaled in favor of the song's jangly instrumentation, the result is pleasant enough and would have been a solid single release at the time. Side two, however, offers up some prized authentic Watch Band treasures, most notably in the band's wired cover of Ray Davies' "I'm Not Like Everybody Else." With Aguilar's snarling vocals right up front with Loomis's taut fretwork, and with the rhythm section providing a big beat backdrop, the song's defiant edge stands among the best performances of the era.

The album-closing "I Ain't No Miracle Worker" showcases the band's immense talents, Aguilar coming on strong like an American Eric Burdon on a slow-burning, R&B-seared mid-tempo rocker with sneering, emotional vocals matched by some elegant, Spanish-flavored Loomis fretwork and a solid rock 'n' roll soundtrack with large drumbeats and heavy bass lines.

Two studio outtakes – the soulful "Medication" and "Let's Go, Let's Go, Let's Go" – offer Bennett's vocals overdubbed atop Aguilar's voice. As for the former, we should begrudgingly offer Bennett his due for not fudging up the basic vocal track and delivering as strong a performance as he ever would under the Watch Band name. He was helped, no doubt, by the spiky, punkish guitar lines provided the song by Loomis, as well as a rolling rhythm track.

The less said of "Let's Go, Let's Go, Let's Go" the better…Bennett's hoarse, charmless vocals are thankfully hidden low in the mix while the band slogs away lazily behind him. The listener is never sure whether this is supposed to be a traditional blues song, with Otis Spann-styled piano in the background, a big beat R&B rave-up, or a rockabilly romp, and it fails on every level. Better is the band's cover of Bob Dylan's "It's All Over Now Baby Blue," a former B-side that seems to include vocals by both Aguilar (appropriately *Memo From Turner* period Jagger) and Bennett (eh) riding atop a busy psychedelic swirl of instruments that reminds of *Flowers* era Rolling Stones.

Although neither the Chocolate Watch Band's *No Way Out* or *The Inner Mystique* sold in remarkable quantities, and were anything but representative of the band's high-voltage live sound, the two albums would continue to increase interest in the band. In late 1968, the Chocolate Watchband would reform with the first recorded line-up mostly intact, Aguilar replaced by Phay, and with original Watch Band guitarist Ned Torney brought back into the fold after his stint with the Army.

This version, now known as the Chocolate Watchband, would record 1969's *One Step Beyond*, eschewing their earlier Stones-inspired R&B vibe for a more mellow folk-rock sound similar to Moby Grape or the Charlatans. Still, it represented the most original Watchband music caught on tape, even if the band had evolved beyond recognition, and by 1970 even this version of the band was done.

Still, Chocolate Watch Band's reputation as flamethrower live performers, along with reissues of their first two albums, would find a new audience in the post-*Nuggets* and *Pebbles* '80s, influencing a new generation of throwback garage-rockers like the Lyres, the Chesterfield Kings, and others, while original vinyl copies of *No Way Out* and *The Inner Mystique* would trade on the collector's market for premium prices. As a result, several band members, including singer Aguilar, second line-up replacement guitarist Tim Abbott, and the rhythm section of bassist Bill Flores and drummer Gary Andrijasevich would reunite in the late 1990s and begin playing again.

This re-formed Chocolate Watchband recorded a live collection of their original material, *At The Love-In Live!* in 1999, followed by an all-new album of mostly Aguilar originals titled *Get Away* in 2000.

They would continue touring well into the 2000s, and in 2010 the band re-recorded a number of songs from the first three albums, releasing it as *Greatest Hits*, the Chocolate Watchband story coming full circle and providing a happy ending to a saga that began in 1965... (2012)

CLUTCH
Blast Tyrant   (Weathermaker Records)

Clutch has been banging around on the fringes of the hard rock and heavy metal realms for two decades now, achieving a certain notoriety and a modicum of success. Formed in 1991, the Maryland band attracted major label attention due to the buzz surrounding their jammy, intense live performances.

Clutch would spend much of the decade of the 1990s bouncing back and forth between labels, all of which tried in vain to get lead madman Neil Fallon and the band to adhere to some sort of (commercially-viable) alt-nu-metal aesthetic, like those good boys in Korn or Incubus.

Truth is, whether you consider him a madman or a genius, or maybe a little of both, Fallon and his band of merry pranksters have always been a square peg resisting placement into any sort of round hole. Through the years, Clutch has earned begrudging respect from metal fanboys and savvy, clued-in hard rock hipsters alike by pursuing an eclectic musical vision that includes slippery, groove-laden metallic funk (not unlike Faith No More); slow-drone doom (think Sabbath, or maybe contemporaries Kyuss); 1970s-era "classic" rock; and ramshackle electric blues (years before Jack White got his stripes).

By 2004, though, after better than a decade spent hanging around the lower rungs of the major label machine, Clutch went the indie route and signed with DRT Records, a label founded by former Gentle Giant member Derek Shulman. The artist-friendly label seemed like a good fit, and with like-minded fellow travelers such as Fu Manchu calling DRT home, the original line-up of Clutch – vocalist/guitarist Fallon, guitarist Tim Sult, bassist Dan Maines, and drummer Jean-Paul Gaster – made themselves comfortable and recorded what many consider the band's best album, *Blast Tyrant*. Out-of-print these past few years, Clutch has reissued *Blast Tyrant* as a deluxe, two-disc set on the band's own brand-spankin'-new label, Weathermaker Records.

What makes *Blast Tyrant* so beguiling is the reckless abandon of the band's performances. The album opens with, well, a blast of sound and fury in "Mercury," Fallon's splintered guitarplay evoking both Tony Iommi and Ritchie Blackmore with a blistering intro that is chaotic and pure blinding white light before the singer's growling, menacing vocals kick in above a slingshot rhythm, the song's brief mythological-based lyrics flashing by in a heartbeat before the song devolves into pure electronic buzz.

"Profits of Doom" is a more traditional heavy metal song, sounding slightly like Ted Nugent's "Great White Buffalo" around the edges, Fallon's beard-puller vocals wrapped around lyrics that read like a Biblical tempest. As the swirl of clashing guitar, bass, and galloping drumbeats swells ever greater behind him, Fallon's voice rises and falls in tandem like a Primitive Baptist preacher slinging fire and brimstone at the heathens at some backwoods Mississippi tent revival. As the song reaches an unsustainable fervor, it breaks down into pure glossolalia, Fallon spitting lyrics about "John the Revelator" and how you should never "trust the white man driving the black van, he's just saving all his voodoo for you" in what seems to be a lyrical damning of the Pharisees of modern finance.

Not that "The Mob Goes Wild" is any less frenetic, starting out with a nonsensical rap by Fallon about his pants and some dance before the song launches into what seems to be an anti-war rant delivered above a guitar-driven, fierce-as-a-rabid-wolverine soundtrack that runs like a runaway train fast, fast, fast through your consciousness as suddenly the singer recommends that we all move to Canada and smoke "lots of pot" and proposes that we "bum rush the border guard before he and his dog ever knew it." The insanity spirals out of control, ending with amplifier buzz and ear-ringing drumbeats. "Cypress Grove" is a bit of malevolent Southern-fried funk, the song's redneck tale warning of seriously mean women and dangerous games, referencing both Ronnie James Dio and bluesman Bukka White, perhaps, as Fallon and Sult's twin-guitar thuggery bruises and beats you into submission.

Whew…just when you think that Clutch couldn't deliver anything more maddening with *Blast Tyrant*, you discover that they were just warming up, getting us ready, you see, for the radioactive activity to follow the nearly-perfect first four tracks. The lyrics of "Promoter (of earthbound causes)" sound like something from the mouth of Norse myth's evil trickster Loki, the song bouncing from ancient Egypt to Ragnarok (the Viking apocalypse), playing like some sort of acid-etched fever-dream, the protagonist stating "A little bit of Ritalin goes a long way" and that he's "ready to rock if you wanna roll." You can bet that heads are gonna roll before this trip is over, Fallon and crew grooving on a rock-rap trip reminiscent of Kid Rock but with a lysergic fountain of youth at their left hand, the entire emotional anguish of the words not coming to any conclusion but sounding so cool as the song tilts out of control.

By contrast, the metallic-blues of "The Regulator" harkens back to the Mississippi Delta, sliding in on the wings of a finely-strummed acoustic intro that is soon joined by swirling psychedelic electric. Fallon's slightly off-register vocals display a gospel fervor as they rise with the instrument's amplification, foreshadowing the band's great 2007 blues album *From Beale Street To Oblivion*. Pounding out a muscular riff and featuring the band's now-trademark smothering instrumentation, "The Regulator" seems to be some sort of morality play, but it's hard to tell for sure, the song ending with a pleading "how many times have I prayed that the angels would speed me away?" above a suddenly-changing, Faith No More-styled electric funk conclusion.

And thus rolls *Blast Tyrant*, Fallon's individually oblique lyrical vision applied to the band's increasingly and delightfully noisy, metal-edged, funky, and fleet-footed surrealistic musical landscape. "Worm Juice" seems to be about some sort of hallucinogenic liquor, "Army of Bono" gleefully skewers politics and celebrity by satirizing everybody's favorite bonehead Irish rock star; I know who it is, and you too. The muscle-bound "Spleen Merchant" is a riffy rocker with more mind-bending lyrics and a guitar squeal that would have made Jimi move over while "Ghost" toasts the dearly departed, Fallon once again calling up an Old Testament fury while death stalks us all in the form of the syncopated rhythms and elegant acoustic fretwork. The instrumental "WYSIWYG" closes out *Blast Tyrant* with classic rock dignity, the bleating bass-n-drums framework complimented by Gaster's broken-glass cymbal crashes and shards of jagged guitar.

The bonus disc provided this reissue of *Blast Tyrant* is called "Basket of Eggs," an odds 'n' sods collection of demos and acoustic alternate takes that often move in an entirely different direction from the main album. "Box Car Shorty's Confession" is a rollicking blues number with scraps of spry harpwork and a storyline fitting of Leadbelly or Skip James. An acoustic version of "The Regulator" frames the song in a somewhat different light, adding a little more mud and grit to the original's Delta influence, slowing it down to a mean-spirited crawl.

"Tight Like That" is another dark, bluesy acoustic bonfire with gruff, almost spoken-word vocals and "Drink to the Dead" combines a jazzy undercurrent with a shuffling beat and muted vocals to great effect. Of the demo tracks, "Cattle Car" stands out for its unabashed use of cowbell, its undeniable infectious circular riffs, and its blustery vocals while "Steve Doocy" provides a not-so-subtle commentary on Fox news morality above a bed of screaming guitars and scraping rhythms.

Clutch was, and is, a creative entity entirely its own, painting with a palette of the band's unique creation. *Blast Tyrant* successfully blends 1970s-inspired hard rock with heavy metal, blues, jazz, and 1990s-styled alt-metal influences, throws in a jam band's love of lengthy improvisation and literate, sometimes absurdist, and frequently incoherent lyrics.

Neil Fallon makes you work for your pleasure, and there's no doubt that this can be challenging music to wrap your brain around. The destination is worth the sojourn, however, *Blast Tyrant* displaying the band's one-of-a-kind vision with white light clarity. (2012)

DAVE DAVIES
Rippin' Up Time   (Red River Entertainment)

Guitarist Dave Davies has had the good – or bad, depending on your perspective – fortune to be a talented songwriter in a legendary band with a great wordsmith in his brother Ray. The younger Davies brother's imaginative and influential fretwork over the decades was as integral a part of the Kinks sound as were Ray's words and vocals, and the occasional Dave song recorded by the band during its commercial run ("Love Me Till The Sun Shines," "Funny Face," and "Trust Your Heart" among them) proved that he had the goods.

Davies has also enjoyed a sporadic but modestly successful career as a solo artist apart from the band, notably 1980's *AFL1-3603* and 1983's *Chosen People*, but the guitarist put aside his own efforts for 20 years to contribute to the Kinks, reappearing as a solo artist with 2002's *Bug*. He's since made up for lost time, releasing a string of five critically-acclaimed studio and live albums during the new millennium that culminates in 2014's *Rippin' Up Time*. Much like the previous year's *I Will Be Me*, Davies explores a mix of romanticized nostalgia and contemporary storytelling with an undeniable rock 'n' roll soundtrack.

Rippin' Up Time is a guitar-driven album, and nowhere is this more apparent than on the album-opening title track. With his six-string vibrating with a grungy energy every bit the equal of, say, *Rust*-era Neil Young, Davies' gruff vocals tread water above the feedback-drenched, distorted, squealing, entirely delightful instrumentation that smothers any hint of nuance in pure sonic overkill. Davies' lyrics are poetically dense, something about reality and madness and sadness that could only be penned by somebody that's been there, lived the life, and triumphed in the long run. It's a monster of a performance, the song setting the stage for the rockin' leviathan to follow.

Much like its predecessor, "Semblance of Sanity" delves into the question of sanity/insanity, understandable, perhaps, for an artist a decade down the road from a life-threatening stroke. Still coming to grips with his altered brain chemistry, Davies surrounds the dark Goth vibe of his lyrics with a heavy, discordant soundtrack from which sharp-edged, angular guitar licks emerge like frenzied laser beams. "King of Karaoke" is a more traditional, Kinks-styled rock tune with a discernible melody providing a foundation for Davies' reminiscence-tinged lyrics, which reference everybody from the Kinks and the Beatles to Elvis, Jimi Hendrix, and even the Knack (!). With a slight flamenco guitar

styling and exotic rhythms, the song is somewhat wistful, but Davies really imbues the performance with heart and soul, and the instrumentation is pure elegance.

"Front Room" may be the beating heart of *Rippin' Up Time*, a nostalgic remembrance of growing up in post-war England. With folkish lyrics blanketed by whimsical instrumentation, Davies fondly recalls time spent with his family, the early days of the Kinks, even favored music like Lonnie Donegan and Howlin' Wolf, the memories joyously delivered with nicely crunchy guitar solos. If "Front Room" evinces a pastoral vibe, "Nosey Neighbors" is the B-side of those particular memories. With a slicing, riff-driven arrangement, "Nosey Neighbors" buries its scornful lyrics amidst a clamor of guitar and percussion, creating a cyclone of chaos that pairs perfectly with the song's sentiments.

The dino-stomp "Mindwash" neatly sidesteps spite with clever lyrics that tackle advertising, the media, even big business and their attempt to, well, "mindwash" us with smoke and mirrors and corporate propaganda. Davies delivers the lyrics above explosive percussion and deadly guitar licks, his guttural vocals perfectly suited to the task.

By contrast, "In The Old Days" is another walk down memory lane, but this is a humorous stroll with fast-paced vocals, crashing rhythms, searing fretwork, and lyrics that tell the tale, warts and all, with Davies refusing to sugar-coat the missteps that life often brings. "Through My Window" ends *Rippin' Up Time* with another Kinks-styled melodic rocker, this one displaying a bit more melancholy in

Davies' vocals than anything else on the album. But the song also stamps 'paid' on the past, all debts erased, Davies expressing a sentiment that clearly looks forward rather than backwards.

Dave Davies' *Rippin' Up Time* is a solid collection that will appeal not only to the long-suffering Kinks fan desperately dreaming of a reunion that may never happen, but also to any classic rock fan looking for some primo-grade ear candy that sounds contemporary and edgy but retains the cherished rock 'n' roll traditions of slashing guitars, rhythmic bass lines, and heavy-handed drum play.

Nothing in the grooves here is going to replace *Sleepwalker*, *Misfits*, or *Low Budget* in the mind of the late-period Kinks fanatic, but *Rippin' Up Time* is a snortin', stompin', hard-rockin' record that entertains, Dave Davies' earnest muse evincing more heart than nearly any other album released this year. Davies is a bona fide talent enjoying a second (or third) chapter in a lengthy and storied career. (2014)

DAVE MASON
Certified Live / Let It Flow   (BGO Records)

Singer, songwriter, and guitarist Dave Mason first came to prominence as a valuable member of the late 1960s British rock band Traffic, formed with drummer Jim Capaldi and Spencer Davis Group alumni Steve Winwood. Mason's on-again/off-again status with that band would be represented by Traffic's first two albums, after which Mason would begin an extended period of roaming that would see him record with Jimi Hendrix on "All Along The Watchtower," perform with Eric Clapton as part of Delaney & Bonnie & Friends, and appear on George Harrison's *All Things Must Pass* before jumping back into Traffic for the 1971 tour that resulted in the live album *Welcome To The Canteen*.

Mason launched his solo career proper with 1970's *Alone Together*, a collection of rock 'n' soul similar to the ground that Delaney & Bonnie were then plowing, even going so far as to share a hit song with his friends in "Only You Know And I Know." The artist's relationship with his label, Blue Thumb Records, was as poor as that with Traffic, however, and it wasn't until Mason jumped ship to Columbia Records that he'd begin to regain the ground lost with poorly-conceived Blue Thumb releases. After a pair of studio albums for Columbia that received varying critical and commercial reception, Mason went the live route with 1976's *Certified Live*, reissued by British archival label BGO Records as a two-disc set with 1977's *Let It Flow* album.

The performance captured on Mason's *Certified Live* has often been downplayed or outright shunned by critics in the past, but listened to with fresh ears some 35 years later, the collection holds up remarkably well. Mason delivers a solid, often times inspired performance of both early originals and well-placed cover songs. Released as a then-trendy double-album, *Certified Live* was the result of years of steady touring by Mason and crew, a chore that was only beginning to pay off in record sales and chart position.

The set opens with what would become Mason's signature song, Traffic's "Feelin' Alright." Although not as fluid or claustrophobic as the performance he delivered with the legendary British band in 1968, this version displays a sly, funky undercurrent. Mason picks up the pace a little and infuses the song with some nice chicken-scratched fretwork in front of drummer Rick Jaeger's lively beats and Mike Finnigan's energetic keyboard flourishes. The muscular "Pearly Queen," a Mason co-write with former bandmate Steve Winwood during their Traffic partnership, is more indicative of Mason's early solo work. Mason's guitar flows and ebbs with certainty, his growling vocals riding atop a solid wave of stabbing keyboards and rolling drumbeats.

Culled from his 1974 self-titled Columbia debut, "Show Me Some Affection" is the sort of blue-eyed soul that Mason played as part of Delaney & Bonnie & Friends, the song a foreshadowing of the sort of commercial material that would drive 1977's *Let It Flow* up the charts. Mason's nimble vocals are combined with Finnigan's Southern soul-tinged keys and scraps of melodic guitar. A cover of Dylan's "All Along The Watchtower" is a clever combination of the scribe's folkish original reading and Jimi Hendrix's explosive re-interpretation; while Mason's vocals lack the soulful gravitas and excitement of Hendrix's, his fretwork here is delightfully explosive, and when combined with rhythm player Jim Krueger's solid instrumental backdrop and Jaeger's big beat drums, it makes for an electric performance.

The remainder of *Certified Live* runs the gamut from solid to dynamic rock 'n' roll. A cover of the Eagles' "Take It To The Limit" is an odd choice by any standard, but I guess that Mason liked the song, although he has a difficult time re-creating that band's Canyon-bred, high lonesome sound. Mason's original "World In Changes" offers a much more complex and interesting performance, acoustic guitar strum threaded alongside Mason's gruff vocals while bassist Gerald Johnson and drummer Jaeger keep a rhythm flowing beneath Finnigan's chiming keyboards. The song offers some exciting signature changes that veer dangerously close to prog-rock turf while Mason's vox are a fine British approximation of Southern soul.

The Muscle Shoals sound of "Only You Know And I Know," from Mason's 1970 solo debut, was a Top 20 hit for both Delaney & Bonnie and for Mason, and for good reason. The song's energetic flow is provided by Krueger's nimble rhythm guitar, Finnigan's gospel-tinged keyboards, and constant heartbeat drums riding above a funky bass line. A cover of the Spencer Davis Group gem "Gimme Some Lovin'" sorely lacks Steve Winwood's blessed vocals, but is provided a mid-tempo re-imagining here with waves of keyboards, swinging rhythms, and backing harmony vocals, all delivered with an indomitable rock 'n' roll spirit.

• • • • •

While *Certified Live* didn't provide Mason and Columbia Records the career boost they both hoped for, the album only slowly inching its way up the charts to number 78, it did provide the perfect breather from the road that Mason needed to re-charge his creative batteries. The result was 1977's studio effort *Let It Flow*, which would prove to be his best-selling album for Columbia, yielding the biggest hit single of his career in the classic rock standard "We Just Disagree," which rose to #12 on the charts as it drove *Let It Flow* to Platinum™ sales status.

While *Let It Flow* isn't widely considered to be Mason's best studio album – that honor would go to *Alone Together*, with his self-titled 1974 set a close runner-up – it stands solidly in the artist's top five efforts. The LP opens with the lofty "So High (Rock Me Baby And Roll Me Away)," the second single from the album evincing a new "soft rock" aesthetic with imaginative acoustic guitar, harmony vocals that sit in a deep melodic groove, bits of subtle hornplay, and solid, tho' not overpowering rhythms.

Written by guitarist Jim Krueger, "We Just Disagree" is the loss-leader here, the hit driving a million copies of *Let It Flow* out the door. It's a good song, too, with an infectious chorus, a truly melancholy vibe, sparse instrumentation, and fleeting, nuanced fretwork. Krueger's lyrics are nifty, too, memorable and emotional, sticking in your head much the same way a frozen burrito sticks in your gut hours after eating.

Let It Flow has plenty to offer aside from the obvious 800-pound chart-topper; Mason's original "Mystic Traveler" is the sort of folkish, ethereal hippie construct that was the foundation of much of Traffic's catalog. Mason's vocals here are appropriately wistful, the song's lush instrumentation creating a cool, cosmic, out-of-body outer-space ambiance. The Southern-fried funk of "Takin' The Time To Find" sounds hopelessly out-of-date in 1977, but Mason imbues the song with a soulful quality with smooth vocal chops, a can't miss chorus, some jazzy fretwork, and Finnigan's spacey keyboard riffing. If it had been released as a single, "Takin' The Time To Find" might have followed "We Just Disagree" up the charts.

As it was, "Let It Go, Let It Flow" was the third minor hit single from *Let It Flow*, crawling and scratching its way up to #45 on the charts. Built in the same vein as "We Just Disagree," the song offers up an energetic vocal performance and a hook-laden chorus bolstered by an inventive guitar riff, spry keyboards, and rambling drumbeats. The forceful "Seasons" might have made another good single, the radio-friendly mid-tempo rocker featuring vocal harmonies courtesy of Stephen Stills and the angelic Yvonne Elliman, wide slashing guitar solos, chiming keys, and bits of well-placed horn. Another Krueger composition, "What Do We Got Here?," is a sprawling slab of blue-eyed soul with Krueger's understated vocals and fanciful orchestration not unlike some of Isaac Hayes' work at the time.

Dave Mason would spend much of the 1980s trying to duplicate the modest success that he enjoyed during the previous decade. He would jump on various trend-driven bandwagons; try his hand at synth-pop; even going so far as to record a duet with Michael Jackson, all to no avail. A brief stint with Fleetwood Mac during the 1990s only tarnished his good name, and it wouldn't be until his 2008 "back to basics" effort *26 Letters 12 Notes*, his first album in over a decade, that Mason would grab back some of his creative mojo.

For a while, though, coming off his often-tumultuous relationship with Traffic, Dave Mason sat atop the 1970s-era classic rock mountain. *Certified Live* and *Let It Flow* are welcome reminders of the artist's talents and vision. (2011)

DAVID OLNEY
The Stone   (Deadbeet Records)

Nashville's David Olney is one of the city's truly underrated musical treasures…forget Kenny Chesney and Tim McGraw and all that Music Row pap, 'cause while they may be selling more records they're not, at heart, true storytellers. They simply take clichéd words cranked out by some Music City songwriting assembly line and imbue the material with a modicum of personality. By contrast, Olney is an old-school wordsmith in the Townes Van Zandt tradition, mixing folk and blues with roots-rock in spinning tales that shoot straight for the heart of the human condition.

Olney's second mini-album, *The Stone* – following last year's *Film Noir* EP and released in time for the Easter holiday – is a six-song EP providing a unique accounting of the death and resurrection of Jesus. Olney revisits three older songs on *The Stone*, providing his previous creations with new interpretations, adding three new songs to complete his insightful personal take on "the greatest story ever told." What makes Olney's version here so mesmerizing is that each song takes a different lyrical view of Christ's resurrection, the story told, in turn, by a con man, a donkey, a murderer, and a soldier.

The Stone opens with "Jerusalem Tomorrow," Sergio Webb's classical-styled guitarplay weaving a beautiful tapestry of sound behind Olney's rich, sonorous spoken word vocals. This is the con man's tale, originally appearing on Olney's 1989 album *Deeper Well* and later recorded by Emmylou Harris. An intricate first-hand tale of Christ's ministry, it's a prelude, of sorts, of the story to follow. Another older song, the largely-forgotten "Brays" from Olney's 1995 album *High, Wide and Lonesome*, offers the perspective of a lowly donkey who feels like a stallion after carrying a humble Jesus on his back. "Blessed am I of all creatures, blessed am I of all beasts," sings the donkey in Olney's haunting voice, the lyrics accompanied by producer Jack Irwin's ethereal orchestration, which creates a fascinating musical atmosphere.

One of the EP's new compositions, "Brains" is a funky blues romp fueled by Olney's growling vocals and fluid harmonica playing. Told from the perspective of a policeman looking to find out "the brains of the operation" behind Jesus and his disciples, with a sly reference to Judas on the side, it's an unlikely but effective way to recount the story, and probably the most playful song on the EP. David Roe's subtle bass lines and Irwin's nuanced percussion lay down a solid foundation beneath Olney's voice, the lyrics calling to mind every cop-show cliché you've ever seen on TV, delivered with tongue only partly in cheek. Seemingly referring to the last supper, "Flesh and Blood" is a more traditionally folk-oriented performance, with Olney's droning guitar-strum providing a counterpoint to his warm vocals, a bit of Woody Guthrie-styled harmonica complimented by Webb's piercing guitar tones.

The last of the old tracks, the amazing "Barabbas," originally appeared on Olney's 1999 album *Through A Glass Darkly*. A central character in the Christ narrative, the thief Barabbas had his death sentence commuted by Pontius Pilate while Jesus of Nazareth was crucified. Astride Webb's strident classical fretwork, Olney tells his rambling tale of Barabbas's imprisonment with Jesus and subsequent freedom, the thief later questioning his release and traveling across the land to tell his tale which, in itself, represents a form of spiritual redemption. Irwin lays in mariachi-styled horns in places, their odd dissonance adding nicely to the overall vibe of the story while Webb's intricate and beautiful guitar playing is simply breathtaking.

The Stone ends with "A Soldier's Report," the tale of Christ's resurrection told in the somber voice of a confused and troubled soldier present at the crucifixion and charged with guarding the tomb of Jesus. Above Webb's insistent and sometimes discordant fretwork, with a few cacophonic blasts of horn thrown in, Olney unfolds the soldier's shame at discovering that Christ's body had disappeared, and his subsequent misgivings about the future that the mysterious event portends. It's a powerful performance, Olney closing out *The Stone* with an open ending that invites further musical examination.

David Olney is not a Christian songwriter, per se, nor does he frequent religious themes often, but when he does address matters of faith, he does so with the same intelligence and in the same thought-provoking manner as every song he pens. With *The Stone*, Olney has successfully wrestled with difficult religious mythology, adding his artistic voice to the history of the tale with no little majesty and grace. (2012)

DEVON ALLMAN
Ragged & Dirty
(Ruf Records)

Devon Allman – Greg Allman's son – has kicked around the blues-rock scene for a decade and a half now, first as frontman of Devon Allman's Honeytribe, and later as one of the main creative voices in the roots 'n' blues supergroup Royal Southern Brotherhood. It's been obvious from the start, however, that Allman has long been searching for his own sound – whereas the Honeytribe album *Space Age Blues* evoked more of a jam-band vibe, his proper solo debut, 2013's *Turquoise*, was a tasty gumbo pot full of Southern soul, blues, funk, and rock that showcased Allman's talents as a songwriter.

With his sophomore solo effort, *Ragged & Dirty*, Allman takes another all-important step towards crafting his own unique musical vision, the guitarist setting aside his Southern roots for a moment and sojourning to Chicago along a well-worn path traveled by so many bluesmen before him. Working with seasoned veterans from the bands of Charlie Musselwhite, Billy Branch, and Buddy Guy, Allman and producer/musician/songwriter Tom Hambridge have put together an electrifying collection of songs that dredge up half-forgotten memories of 1960s-era Chi-town soul and blues and vintage '70s rock riffs while somehow retaining a contemporary essence.

Ragged & Dirty kicks off with the stomp 'n' stammer of "Half The Truth," a Foghat styled dinosaur that offers big rhythms, slippery guitarwork, and an infectious groove. Hambridge plays the drums, hitting the cans with an effect like a machine gun's recoil while Allman gets funky with the git and keyboardist Marty Sammon adds background flourishes from his Hammond B3. It's an energizing song, and probably goes over gangbusters in a live setting 'cause it simply jumps off the turntable, grabs you by the ears, and demands that you pay attention.

Penned by Hambridge and country-rocker Lee Roy Parnell, "Can't Lose Them All" is probably the closest that Allman comes here to his legendary father, not so much in his vocal delivery but rather in the overall sound and texture of the song, which simply glows with heart and soul. Allman's stinging fretwork here is fluid, almost jazzy, but provides many shades of blue while his vocals are similarly sultry as the band delivers a subtle groove in the background. Hambridge custom-wrote several songs for *Ragged & Dirty*, and "Leavin'" is one of the best, a twang 'n' bang roots-rocker that features Allman's acoustic strum and Bobby Schneck Jr.'s leads, the two players' guitars intertwined to create a mesmerizing effect.

Allman proves himself a fine interpreter of other artist's work here, beginning with a loving cover of the Spinners' R&B classic "I'll Be There." Allman's taut, soulful guitarplay here is surpassed only by his emotional vocals, which manage to capture the feeling of the original while adding a few tears to the lyrics; Wendy Moten's background vocals offer a nice counterpoint while Sammon's keyboards bring an air of elegance to the arrangement. Allman tackles bluesman Otis Taylor's difficult "Ten Million Slaves" with reverence and authority, his vocals dropped an octave to properly capture the serious story told by the lyrics. With Felton Crews' heavy bass line throbbing in unison with Hambridge's tribal percussion, Allman's somber vocals relate the tragic tale of African slaves being brought to America. The anguish of the lyrics is underlined by Allman's scorching fretwork, which offers a thinly-veiled menace throughout the song.

The title track of *Ragged & Dirty* is an old Luther Allison cut, and Allman does it proud here. He and the band develop a funky groove for the tune, Allman's slightly electronically-altered vocals adding a nasty edge to the words, his high-flying guitar perfectly welding psychedelic-rock and blues together for a powerful rendition of a classic Allison performance.

Allman penned a few original tunes himself for the album, the best of these being his ode to the Windy City, "Midnight Lake Michigan." A late-night blues jam with a rock 'n' roll heart, just about everything on this instrumental – from Allman's imaginative, scorched-earth guitarplay to Sammon's moody keyboard fills to Hambridge's explosive drumwork, and everything in between – is simply perfect, the performance telling a story without uttering a word.

Allman's other originals also excite, from the funky rocker "Blackjack Heartattack" to the traditionally-styled "Back To You." The former is a rapid-fire, foot-shuffling blues-rock Godzilla with an undeniable groove, monster fretwork, and a feedback-tinged wall of sound while the latter is a throwback to the Chicago blues sound of the 1970s with strong vocals, expressive guitar licks, humming keyboards, and a solid, if subtle rhythmic backbone. The album closes with the acoustic blues tune "Leave The City," Allman's "back to the country" screed offering nuanced vocals, supple resonator guitar pickin', and Hambridge's minimal percussion. It's a fine closer, with a strong albeit gentle vibe that displays another side of Allman's multi-faceted musical personality.

There's no doubting Devon Allman's enormous talents, which are frequently overlooked in discussions in favor of his familial pedigree. Sit down and give *Ragged & Dirty* a spin, though, and you'll discover a young artist that is blazing his own musical path, not necessarily following in his famous father's footsteps but rather creating his own intoxicating blend of blues, soul, and rock 'n' roll. *Ragged & Dirty* is Allman's best album to date, but given the road he's walking, my guess is that the best is yet to come. (2014)

DWIGHT TWILLEY
Green Blimp   (Big Oak Records)

Along with such hallowed rock 'n' roll icons as Alex Chilton, Todd Rundgren, and those guys in Badfinger, singer/songwriter Dwight Twilley is one of the godfathers of power pop, influencing a generation of artists that includes Paul Collins, Peter Case, and Matthew Sweet. Sadly, label mismanagement, poor distribution, and pure bad luck conspired to keep the Dwight Twilley Band – really, just Twilley and partner Phil Seymour – from achieving the level of success they deserved for their whipsmart lyrics and Sun-Records-meets-Liverpool pop-rock sound.

Twilley's first single, the white-hot "I'm On Fire," cracked the Top 30 at #16 in 1975, but when it took over a year for his label to release his debut album *Sincerely*, a true power pop gem, any commercial momentum was seemingly forever lost. A full length album recorded during this delay was subsequently shelved and went unreleased. Still, Twilley and Seymour soldiered on, creating the equally awesome *Twilley Don't Mind* album in 1977, but although it rode loud and proud alongside the likes of Big Star, Badfinger, and the Raspberries, it sold poorly with the typical label lack of support for a style they just didn't understand. Twilley and Seymour went their separate ways after almost a decade together, and Seymour tragically died young in 1993 after a brief solo career and a stint with the Textones. To this day, Twilley honors his late friend by not performing those early songs originally sung by Seymour.

Twilley has forged a meager solo career during the ensuing years, critics heaping effusive praise on his half-dozen studio albums and various odds 'n' sods collections and live sets, while the artist himself has experienced trials and tribulations that no musician should suffer. *Blueprint*, a 1980 album recorded for Arista, was shelved by the label and remains unreleased, and although Twilley's 1984 album for EMI, *Jungle*, yielded a Top 20 hit in the song "Girls" – a collaboration with friend Tom Petty – within a couple of years Twilley would find himself without a label deal. The new millennium has been kinder to the artist as the Internet has helped him build a new fan base, and a slew of archival releases have cemented Twilley's genius status as a power pop songwriter and performer.

It's against this backdrop of struggle that Dwight Twilley releases *Green Blimp*, his first collection of new studio material since 2005's wonderful *47 Moons*. While Twilley may have found more than his share of obstacles during a career that has now spanned four decades, his skills as a wordsmith and crafter of power pop magic remain marvelously intact.

By way of example, check out the album-opening track "Get Up" from *Green Blimp*. An incredibly fluid slow-grinder with a low-slung groove and slightly echoed vocals, the song injects itself into your consciousness with the persistence of a tick and the power of a tornado. If "Get Up" doesn't make you want to shimmy-n-shake like a hound dog, then it's safe to assume that you've reached room temperature, bubbie!

While the rest of *Green Blimp* doesn't exactly replicate the deep-seated swagger of "Get Up," is doesn't disappoint, either. The jangly "Speed of Light" features chiming guitarplay, delicious backing harmonies from Twilley's buds Susan Cowsill and Rocky Burnette, and an overall shimmering musical vibe that doesn't fail to mesmerize. It's just a damn enchanting song, but then again, so is "Me and Melanie." Sounding like a long-lost mid-'60s Beatles outtake, Twilley's lofty vocals and bittersweet lyrics evoke a thoroughly charming romantic soundscape while the lush instrumentation makes one wonder what may have happened had Twilley first broken through a decade earlier than '75, when this sort of intelligently-crafted pop-rock had a better chance to succeed.

The title track opens with a little nifty guitar-strum and wan instrumentation before Twilley's sing-song vocals come bouncing in. The song's fantasia-colored lyrics are akin to the Beatles' "Yellow Submarine," but the instrumental accompaniment is full and multi-textured while the guitars work at odd angles against the whimsy, providing an edge to the lyrical sentiments.

"You Were Always There" is vintage Twilley, just a hauntingly lovely romantic ballad with a disarming mid-tempo beat and vocals to melt the cold, cold heart of even the most diehard rock 'n' roller. With a fat opening bass line and a jangle worthy of T-Rex, "It Ends" is a dense glammy construct, with Twilley's vocals nearly lost in the mix, the guitars – Twilley and/or original bandmate Bill Pitcock IV – riding high above the rhythm with a stunning resonance.

The artistic apex of *Green Blimp*, however, can be found in the defiant sentimentality of "It's Never Coming Back." More than just another shiny, shimmering power pop gem that rides on white-capped waves of chaos, Twilley says "good bye" to the missteps, mistakes, and miscues of the past decades with "It's Never Coming Back." Above a gorgeous, radiating clash of sounds and emotions, Twilley sings "The choices were made, for good or for bad; Things that you reach for, the dreams that you had; We all wanted it all to last, but only fools can wish for that, 'cause it's never ever coming back…the past is in the past."

With these couple of lines, Twilley dismisses the heartaches that he didn't have much control over anyway, and sets the course straight for a future so bright the man should buy a new pair of sunglasses. Comfortable, maybe for the first time, with the albatross of fleeting fame, Twilley seems happy just making music and to hell with the star-making machinery.

Don't think for a moment that the half-dozen or so tracks from *Green Blimp* that aren't mentioned here are mere filler unworthy of our attention...songs like the guitar-driven, energetic "Stop" or the lilting "Let It Rain," which is as beautiful a ballad as you're ever going to hear with your jaded 21st century ears, are as carefully-crafted and full of life as everything else on *Green Blimp*.

It's clear with this wonderful collection of songs that Twilley still shares a special relationship with his individual muse, and although "justice" as a concept seems to be woefully obsolete in these cynical times, if indeed true justice did exist, then Dwight Twilley would be recognized and rewarded for his contributions to rock 'n' roll. The man deserves no more and no less than everything...

(For those power pop fans wanting to know what all the fuss over Dwight Twilley Band is about, Australia's esteemed archive label Raven Records has recently released *On Fire! The Best Of Dwight Twilley, 1975-1984*. This 24-track compilation includes such Twilley faves as "I'm On Fire," "Sincerely," "Twilley Don't Mind," "Girls," and many more! There's not a duff track in the bunch, and the album receives the Reverend's official seal of approval.) (2010)

ELLIOTT MURPHY
Notes From The Underground   (Elliott Murphy Music)

Before Bruce was "The Boss," before Little Stevie Forbert haunted the doors of Manhattan's nightclubs, before anybody had even heard of Johnny Cougar, the Long Island-bred Elliott Murphy was the best-and-brightest of those necklaced with the "new Dylan" albatross. A literate scribe with a penchant for observational, poetic lyrics set to an undeniably rocking soundtrack, Murphy's '70s-era albums – gems like

Aquashow, *Lost Generation*, and *Night Lights* – went nowhere and sold few copies.

To his credit, Murphy never attempted to change his spirited blend of rock and folk; he merely sharpened his pen and recorded intelligent, destined-for-obscurity works like 1986's *Milwaukee*. Although American record buyers ignored the talented wordsmith in favor of hair-metal and grunge, European audiences loved Murphy's sophisticated wordplay.

Moving his family to Paris, Murphy continued to work throughout the '90s, cranking out classics like 1993's *Unreal City*. His steadfast refusal to bow to musical trends or industry expectations has earned Murphy a solid reputation as a songwriter's songwriter as well as the friendship of folks like Bruce Springsteen, Billy Joel, Sonny Landreth, and others.

Murphy's best work is always filled with brilliant imagery, and *Notes From The Underground*, the artist's latest, is certainly no exception. The album-opening, mid-tempo rocker "And General Robert E. Lee" begins with a strongly strummed guitar before launching into a storm of cinematic lyricism, a tale of romance gone wrong with references to James Cagney, Charlie Chaplin, and other cultural touchstones, Murphy's vocals supported by a mournful, weeping lead guitar.

The subdued, Dylanesque "The Valley Below" matches Murphy's best low-register, croaking vocal performance with sparse instrumentation that builds from a silent buzz to a resounding rattle-and-hum, the song's romantic lyrics delivered with no little passion. "What's That" is a spry rocker, Murphy's rapid-fire vocals spitting out stream-of-consciousness wisdom, organized A to Z, the song delivering essential knowledge on everything from love to tea to personal hygiene.

The beautiful "Ophelia" is pure, trademark Murphy…rough-hewn vocals caressing delicate, carefully-crafted vocals above a stunning blend of acoustic guitar and lush rhythms. The dark, discordant "Frankenstein's Daughter" features Murphy's son Gaspard on guitar, supporting his father's fractured, atmospheric vocals with intriguing, off-kilter fretwork. The haunting "Crying Creatures of the Universe" offers an almost spiritual vocal delivery, with sorrowful harmonica and folkish guitar supporting the singer's wistful remembrances.

The lyrical themes visited by Murphy on *Notes From The Underground* are familiar favorites of the songwriter: the cost of love and loss on the human soul; the intrusion of the past on the present and future; the long shadow cast by the places we've been and the people we've known. No other songwriter provides these themes with more thought and vitality than Elliott Murphy, the finely-drawn protagonists of his songs standing on the outside of life, looking in. They're life's misfits and outlaws, men literally without countries, their homelessness as much a state of mind as it is a physical absence.

Notes From The Underground is a perfect showcase for Murphy's uncanny ability to spin words into emotional landscapes. Supported by a talented band that has developed a special musical chemistry with Murphy – especially the phenomenal guitarist Oliver Durand – the expat rocker has created his best album since 1998's *Beauregard*, a late-career triumph that proves that Elliott Murphy remains the poet laureate of rock 'n' roll. (2009)

EMERSON, LAKE & PALMER
A Time and A Place   (Shout! Factory Records)

Formed in 1970 by keyboardist Keith Emerson (The Nice), guitarist/ vocalist Greg Lake (King Crimson), and drummer Carl Palmer (Atomic Rooster), the trio known worldwide as Emerson, Lake & Palmer wasn't the "supergroup" that it was heralded as at the time so much as a collaboration of disgruntled musicians looking for new artistic opportunities.

Commercially, ELP exploded onto the U.S. charts with a 1970 self-titled debut album that cleverly fused classically-oriented art-rock with the growing progressive rock trend to create a genre-smashing set of songs. Displaying a heretofore "Gothic" edge to their music that reminded (some) listeners of Atomic Rooster's darkest hues, and easily displaying the instrumental virtuosity of rivals like King Crimson, Yes, or the Moody Blues, the album showcased the three members' talents in the best possible light.

Subsequent albums would tumble quickly from the band's creative efforts: 1971's *Tarkus*, 1972's live *Pictures At An Exhibition* and *Trilogy*, and 1973's *Brain Salad Surgery* – considered by many fans to be the band's best – would propel ELP to worldwide superstar status. The band burned too brightly, perhaps, and by the end of the 1970s, ELP experienced an acrimonious break-up that kept the three musicians from performing together until the early 1990s...and make no mistake, it was the band's raucous live performances that fueled its record sales.

While Palmer would flail at his drum kit like he was bludgeoning it into submission, Emerson's impressive array of electronics gear allowed the musician to stab recklessly at piano, keyboards, or synthesizers with the tact and subtlety of a rabid badger. In turn, Lake's six-string gymnastics were positively sane when compared to the instrumental madness of his band mates.

The band released three live albums during its first decade together, but even the several hours of music represented by those multiple-disc sets pales next to the band's total commitment to live performances. The recently-released four-CD box set *A Time and A Place* balances out the band's too-brief catalog, presenting a career-spanning oversight of the best of Emerson, Lake and Palmer live.

A Time and A Place is divided neatly into three distinct eras, the first representing the band's early 1970s origins. The first CD in the set opens with "The Barbarian," a lengthy piece adapted by the band from Bela Bartak's "Allegro Barbaro." While not quite as involved as some of their other performances here, "The Barbarian" manages to cram a lot into its five-plus minutes nonetheless.

Recorded at ELP's first major concert performance at the 1970 Isle of Wight Festival in the U.K., the band rages across the sonic landscape with fierce determination, seemingly wedging classical piano, psychedelic guitar, bombastic drumplay, and proggish keyboard riffs into the mix with a figurative crowbar. It's a chaotic, powerful performance made all the more impressive by the band's instrumental virtuosity and total lack of guile.

You'll find several ELP fan favorites amidst the 72-minutes-and-change worth of music on disc one. Emerson's "High Level Fugue" brings the band indoors to London's Lyceum Ballroom in late 1970 for a spirited romp. Fueled by the pianist's manic pounding of the 88s, Emerson solos for approximately 2/3s of the song before Palmer's jazzy drumbeats come crashing in, and Lake's serpentine fretwork weaves its way through the maddening syncopation. The band's re-imagining of composer Aaron Copland's "Hoedown," captured live at the legendary 1972 Mar Y Sol Festival in Puerto Rico, is an energetic, measured performance that strays very little from the recorded version familiar to many in attendance, tho' Emerson manages to wrangle a little space-noise from his trusty Moog synthesizer.

Performances of two of ELP's best-known and beloved songs, "Still…You Turn Me On" and "Lucky Man," are taken from a 1974 show at the Civic Center in Tulsa, Oklahoma. Both songs were written by Greg Lake, and both are fine examples of the best that progressive rock has to offer. The former is a moody, provocative tone poem with whimsical lyrics and imaginative instrumentation that perfectly melds each of the three musician's strengths in the creation of a magical moment. The latter features a fine vocal performance by Lake, accompanied by folkish guitar-strum that places an emphasis on the lyrics. Shorn of its studio trappings, offering just Lake and his instrument, the song takes on a different vibe altogether. Disc one finishes up with a bang, a thirty-four minute jam on "Karn Evil 9" from 1974 that features more prog-rock raging at the machine than you may care to swallow in one sitting.

The second CD of *A Time and A Place* documents the band's late 1970s work, basically 1977 and '78, really, before the big break-up that would send the band members in different directions for over a decade. Cranking to a stylish opening with a lively, synth-driven cover of the classic, menacing "Peter Gunn Theme," the disc jumps immediately into the extended madness that was "Pictures At An

Exhibition." Performed here in a severely-condensed sixteen-minute version taken from a Memphis 1977 show, the song loses none of its power due to brevity, the band's melding of the work of composer Modest Mussorgsky with mid-'70s prog-rock instrumentation audacious even by ELP standards, a breathless roller-coaster ride across an art-rock horizon.

Although featuring few songs as well known as those on the first disc, tunes like "Tank" (from the self-titled 1970 debut LP) and "Tarkus" (from the 1971 album of the same name) are important entries in the ELP canon. This 1978 performance of "Tank" is a frenetic, nearly breathtaking tightrope sprint that condenses the original six-minute song into a two-minute race against time that provides urgency to Palmer's drumbeats and an electrifying shock to Emerson's stabbing synthesizer riffs, eventually leading into a lengthy and explosive drum solo. On the other hand, "Tarkus" is afforded an only slightly reduced running time, although the pace is no less frantic as the band plays its lines with alarming madness, the listener wondering what sort of hellhounds were on their trail.

Still, it's with their more obscure material that ELP often surprises. The band was never afraid to kick up a bit of kitsch now and then, and their breakneck take on Scott Joplin's 1899 ragtime hit "Maple Leaf Rag" is no exception. A 1978 performance of Prokofiev's "The Enemy God Dances With The Black Spirits" is exhilarating and illuminating in its fusion of the classical and progressive worlds, while Lake's beautiful "Watching Over You," from *Works, Vol. 2*, is as close as the band ever came to creating a conventional British folk-rock ballad.

Emerson's inspired, jazzy piano play is perfectly married to Lake's fluid vocals on the 1920s British folk standard "Show Me The Way To Go Home." Not surprisingly, there's nothing on the second CD from ELP's ill-fated "break up" album, 1978's *Love Beach*, which is for the better, really. By 1979, the rigors of the road and the pitfalls of the business had clearly gotten to Emerson, Lake & Palmer, and the trio was at creative odds with each other after cranking out seven studio and two live albums in a mere eight years. More than the result of mere artistic fatigue, hundreds of nights on the road in close proximity to one another had created tensions beyond ego, and the band broke up at the end of the decade with the member's allegedly unable to stand one another.

Lake would forge a moderately successful solo career during the 1980s, and Palmer would fall into the accidental goldmine that was the supergroup Asia, while Emerson wrote film scores. Lake and Emerson would briefly reunite for an album and tour in 1985, recruiting journeyman drummer Cozy Powell (Rainbow, Whitesnake) to replace the hesitant Palmer (who was making bank with Asia). This new "ELP" trio recorded a single unremarkable album that somehow still managed to place in the Top 40 in America, showing that a lot of original ELP nostalgia remained among the band's fans. Suspecting that he had been chosen for the drum seat because his name began with a 'P', the prickly Powell scooted out of the ELP universe before the end of '86, leaving his band mates high and dry. Things would pick up in 1991, however, as Asia met its inevitable end and Palmer rejoined his mates in a properly-reunited Emerson, Lakes and Palmer.

The third CD in *A Time and A Place* documents the '90s-era Emerson, Lake and Palmer reunion with performances taken from 1993 through 1997. While not quite as bombastic as their 1970s-era shows could become; the 1990s version of ELP shows a talented, mature band that hasn't lost a step, merely learned that you don't have to end every musical sentence with exclamation marks. The band's 1992 *Black Moon* album, its first collection of new material in over a decade, is represented here by three inspired performances.

While Greg Lake's voice shows a distinct lessening of it warmth and richness a couple of decades on, his vocals on this 1993 performance of "Paper Blood" take on a timbre closer to Dave Cousins' of Strawbs than his old ELP work. Backed by harmony vocals, the song is a stampeding rocker that benefits from Emerson's heavy hand on the keyboards and Palmer's heavier sticks on the drums. "Black Moon" sounds like vintage King Crimson, but with nastier six-string work, a heavier-than-lead bass line, imploding drumbeats, and lightning-bolts of synthesizer. The third song here from *Black Moon*, the album's first single "Affairs of The Heart," is an engaging ballad with a warm vocal track and intricate fretwork by Lake and some nice keyboard flourishes by Emerson.

Sadly, disc three includes nothing from the band's ill-fated and final (so far) studio album, 1994's *In The Hot Seat*, an under-recorded and unsympathetic recording whose songs may have fared better in the live setting. Instead, we get a smattering of old-school ELP (an acoustic guitar-oriented reading of "From The Beginning" from *Trilogy* with some fine, nuanced Palmer drumwork; a full-bore prog assault on "A Time and A Place," from *Tarkus*) mixed with rare odds 'n' sods like the surprising ragtime-styled piano instrumental "Honky Tonk Train Blues," or the edgy art-rock instrumental "Creole Dance." A 1993 performance of the dark-hued "Knife Edge," from ELP's long-ago debut, stands out for its malevolent voodoo vibe, Emerson's restrained keyboard-bashing, and some great drumming by Palmer alongside Lake's mesmerizing vocals.

The fourth and final disc of *A Time and A Place* takes a surprising and welcome tack, providing listeners with a collection of a dozen tracks culled from various fan-recorded bootlegs that span the entire 20-year career of the band. Admittedly, the sound quality lessens considerably on these covertly-recorded performances, but they stand out in contrast mostly because the rest of the live material in the box set sounds so damn good. Still, designed with the fan in mind, what true ELP follower is going to quibble with a 1972 performance of the art-rock/space-rock epic "The Endless Enigma" or a romp through "Abaddon's Bolero" from the same year? ELP fanatics can sink their teeth into a haunting version of "Jerusalem" from 1974, or an enchanting reading of the hit "I Believe In Father Christmas" from 1993.

If it seems like *A Time and A Place* is geared towards the ELP fanatic, well, yeah it is. While much of the material here was previously released on various collections, many long out-of-print, this four-disc set is a cost-effective way for the collector to gather up 43 fine and entertaining performances by one of prog-rock's most exciting and dynamic live bands. While the success of Emerson, Lake & Palmer never matched that of contemporaries Yes or Genesis, and they seldom received the critical acclaim afforded King Crimson, their place in the prog-rock galaxy is safe and secure, ELP one of the most influential and ground-breaking bands in the genre. (2010)

EMERSON, LAKE & PALMER
Live At Nassau Coliseum '78   (Shout! Factory Records)

By 1978, the progressive-rock supergroup Emerson, Lake & Palmer were definitely on their last legs, the trio's new album, *Love Beach*, coasting mid-way up the *Billboard* album chart with momentum created entirely by the band's increasingly tarnished reputation. The two previous ELP albums were no more than collections of solo works and studio outtakes by keyboardist Keith Emerson, guitarist Greg Lake, and drummer Carl Palmer, released to "get something out" after a four-year band hiatus (and, to some extent, the ploy worked, as the two-album set *Works, Volume One* would climb to number 12 on the charts and sell better than a half-million copies).

ELP was clearly a band just "going through the motions" when they climbed on the stage at the Nassau Veteran's Memorial Coliseum in February 1978, the individual members collecting a paycheck with an eye towards some indeterminate musical future that, sadly, didn't include any of their other mates. It's telling that *Live At Nassau Coliseum '78*, a two-disc set documenting the band's performance that night, doesn't include a single song from *Love Beach*, as clear a sign of ELP's lack of confidence in the new material as you'll ever see from a band. Instead, they people this live set with mostly well-known and well-traveled material, sometimes diving over the top with their instrumental zeal in an attempt to flog another dollar from the prog-rock punters that comprised their shrinking audience.

Disc one of *Live At Nassau Coliseum '78* opens well enough, the band's synth-dominated take on Aaron Copland's "Hoedown" featuring Emerson's lively keyboard-banging and Palmer's thundering drumbeats. The time signature changes, offbeat rhythms, and general discordance of this 17-minute version of "Tarkus" provide plenty of space for the three band members to stretch out and do their thing, from Lake's tortured vocals and dark fretwork to Emerson's imaginative keyboard play and Palmer's Latin-influenced percussion. The more measured (and shorter) "Take A Pebble" creates a fantasia vibe with Lake's ethereal vocals, Palmer's flurries of drumbeats and cymbal-brushes, and Emerson's rolling, and often jazz-tinged piano notes.

However, the five-minute-and-twenty-one-second performance of Emerson's "Piano Concerto #1 (1st Movement)" is pure musical masturbation, a "look at me Ma! See what I can do!" moment that breaks the mood and mystery of the previous two songs with a disconcerting crash that hits your ears much as a root canal tickles your mouth. It shows how much Emerson had come to dominate the band's sound, and not for the better, as it puts the chemistry of the three band members badly out of balance.

Luckily, the jaunty and almost hysterical "Maple Leaf Rag" shakes the audience back into reality, while a pair of Lake compositions – "C'est La Vie" and the hit "Lucky Man" – salvage the remainder of the set. Lake's lofty vocals and filigree guitarwork, with just a hint of synth near the end, help create an enigmatic atmosphere for the former; while the latter's well-worn familiarity is complimented by Lake's haunting voice and beautiful fretwork. The disc closes out with "Pictures At An Exhibition," another fine example of the band's chemistry when they're at their best, the fifteen-minute-plus performance a carnival funhouse of varying moods and textures, Emerson creating some downright odd sounds with his wall of synthesizers, Palmer's syncopated drumbeats sounding more like King Crimson than even Bill Bruford's work for that band, and Lake's soaring guitar lines helping form an interesting musical ambiance.

The second disc of *Live At Nassau Coliseum '78* opens with the lightweight "Tiger In A Spotlight," an outtake first included on *Works, Volume Two* that sounds a little out-of-place here as Lake tries an ill-fated attempt at a hard rock vocal style above a rinky-dink piano and drum accompaniment. Safe to say that it's not ELP's best musical moment, but it's easily redeemed by the shimmering beauty of Lake's heartfelt "lullaby," "Watching Over You," his emotional vocals complimented by a wonderful guitar construct and Emerson's gently humming keyboards. The refreshingly chaotic "Tank," from the band's 1970 self-titled debut, is a short, sharp shock of blazing synthesizers, blasting drumbeats, and taut bass lines that, unfortunately, leads directly into Palmer's extended drum solo, which sucks the oxygen and enthusiasm out of the room faster than you can say "1970s cliché."

The brief, blistering "The Enemy God Dances With The Black Spirits," adapted by composer Sergei Prokofiev's "The Scythian Suite," is actually a much better showcase for Palmer's rhythmic talents than his meandering drum solo. Placed in context with Emerson's own percussive keyboard-bashing, Palmer's carpet-bombing of beats and cymbal crashes vie admirably with the keyboards as the song's lead instrument. *Live At Nassau Coliseum '78* closes with two extended performances that, together, run nearly half-an-hour; "Pirates" certainly has its moments, but mostly it just illustrates the oft-criticized excesses of the prog-rock genre, with a little too-much instrumental noodling even for this died-in-the-wool, prog-lovin' rockcrit.

By contrast, the band dips back into the Copland songbook for an extended look at the composer's "Fanfare For The Common Man," Palmer's explosive percussion and the epic sweep of Emerson's keyboards setting the stage for a perfect blend of technical virtuosity and creative imagination. The song's driving rhythms are cleverly punctuated by Emerson's constant riffing, while Palmer's workout on the skins is both massive and impressive, with jazzy licks and Latin rhythms flying under the radar. Lake's rhythmic fretwork rides low in the mix, providing a solid foundation for Emerson's rampaging synth-mania.

Tally up those invigorating musical moments on *Live At Nassau Coliseum '78* and compare them with the all-too-frequent infuriating interludes and you'll come up about 50/50 – good enough for any major league B-baller, but kind of shabby for talents the scope of Messrs. Emerson, Lake *and* Palmer. While the band has several live albums in its catalog, including the three-disc *Ladies and Gentlemen*, there has yet to be a really stellar document of the band's performance art captured at its best…and that includes *Live At Nassau Coliseum '78*, where the band comes up with too little, too late in the game.

Definitely designed for the hardcore fan in mind, the curious would be better served introducing themselves to ELP through one of the band's first four acclaimed studio albums. As for the rabid prog-lovin' droog, check out the uniformly excellent *A Time And A Place* four-disc collection of live ELP from Shout! Factory. The set not only includes several of the most thrilling performances from *Live At Nassau Coliseum '78*, but also provides a career-spanning overview of the best of Emerson, Lake & Palmer in a live setting. (2011)

FAIRPORT CONVENTION
What We Did On Our Holiday / *Unhalfbricking*   (Water Music)

While American folk singers were still trying to capture the spirit of Woody Guthrie in song with their battered Martin guitars, across the pond in England outfits like the Strawbs, the Incredible String Band, and Fairport Convention were trying to take traditional folk music in different directions.

With the benefit of hindsight, it's been rightly concluded that Fairport Convention was the best of breed, the band's brightest line-up including possibly the best folk-rock singer ever in Sandy Denny, the serviceable pipes of vocalist Ian Matthews, and the incredible fretwork of Richard Thompson. The band's second and third albums – *What We Did On Our Holiday* and *Unhalfbricking*, both released in 1969 – are timeless collections of elegant British folk-rock music.

Fairport Convention poached Sandy Denny from the Strawbs to replace departing vocalist Judy Dyble just in time to record the band's sophomore effort, *What We Did On Our Holiday*. The change in the band's sound was remarkable, Denny bringing an ethereal quality to the music that was absent from the debut album. A mix of originals penned by band members, with a smattering of well-chosen, unlikely covers, the album was more pastoral than the band's debut, but no less ambitious.

Denny's angelic vocals soar across songs like the ethereal "Fotheringay," while the bluesy "Mr. Lacey" displays Thompson's growing guitar skills. The Joni Mitchell cover "Eastern Rain" is an atmospheric piece with rumbling percussion and swells of

instrumentation, while the traditional "She Moves Through The Fair" melds all of the band's talents into a haunting performance wherein voices and music achieve perfect balance. It is amazing to consider, nearly 40-years after the release of *What We Did On Our Holiday*, the fact that none of the band members were older than 23, and three (including Thompson) were still in their teens.

• • • • •

Matthews left Fairport Convention in late 1969 to form Matthews Southern Comfort, necessitating another change in the band's sound. More than just a male counterbalance to Denny's powerful vocals, Matthews also provided songwriting support. With Matthews largely absent from the making of *Unhalfbricking*, the band would edge closer to the 'folk' side of the folk-rock equation. As such, *Unhalfbricking* is a strong, if not spectacular collection, weighing heavier on covers and traditional tunes (including three – count 'em! – three Dylan songs) than previously.

The album nevertheless offers its share of whimsy, such as a Cajun remake of Dylan's "If You Gotta Go, Go Now" as "Si Tu Dois Partir," sung in French, and an unlikely British chart hit. Denny's beautiful, gossamer "Who Knows Where The Time Goes?" is, perhaps, the singer's best-known song, but Fairport's eleven-minute romp through the traditional "A Sailor's Life," featuring future band member Dave Swarbrick's fiddle, is a breathtaking ride on the waves of the band's future. (2008)

GARLAND JEFFREYS
The King of In Between   (Luna Park Records)

When he is remembered – if he is remembered at all – Brooklyn, New York born-and-bred singer/songwriter Garland Jeffreys is fondly recalled for either his 1973 FM radio hit "Wild In The Streets" and/or his lively remake of the garage-rock classic "96 Tears," which brought

Jeffreys his highest chart position and best-selling album in 1981's *Escape Artist*.

Part of Jeffreys' obscurity is due to his intelligent, challenging lyrics, which often deal with urban life, racial strife, and other heady subjects set to music that cleverly welds streetwise rock 'n' roll with elements of blues, jazz, folk, and reggae.

After recording ten albums between 1970 and 1997, Jeffreys literally disappeared from the U.S. music landscape, instead traveling frequently to Europe where much of his back catalog remains in print, performing for a growing and appreciative audience. With *The King of In Between*, the 67-year-old musician has released his first album in better than 13 years, picking up almost exactly where he left off in the late 1990s. Jeffreys' whipsmart lyrical observations on life in the Big Apple and beyond lack none of the bite of his earlier work, while the music on *The King of In Between* is every bit as eclectic and entertaining as ever.

"Coney Island Winter" opens with shimmering guitar and a deep rhythmic groove, Jeffreys' half-spoken/half-sung words mesmerizing in their impact and intellectual depth. The funky "Streetwise" offers up haunting vocals, lush strings, and Larry Campbell's imaginative fretwork while the rollicking "The Contortionist" features Lou Reed providing doo wop vocals behind Jeffreys' pleading voice. The bluesy "'Til John Lee Hooker Calls Me" is a sprawling boogie-rock tune that name checks Hooker, Bo Diddley, and James Brown while also evoking Elmore James.

While not a conventional blues album per se, *The King of In Between* will appeal to blues and rock fans alike, Garland Jeffreys' unique, eclectic sound a welcome antidote to music that too often draws from the same deep wellspring instead of painting with the entire bright spectrum of colors you'll hear on *The King of In Between*. (2011)

GOOSE CREEK SYMPHONY
Head For The Hills   (Bo Records)

Decades before the term "Americana" was created so that the cool
kids could listen to country music without seeming, well... uncool...
the good fellows of Goose Creek Symphony were rockin' the early
1970s with their unique and invigorating elixir of hillbilly blues and
country-rock, what Gram Parsons once wisely called "Cosmic
American Music."

Problem is, sitting comfortably somewhere between the Flying Burrito
Brothers and Uncle Tupelo didn't fly too high, commercially, during
the Nixon/Ford years, and after releasing a handful of spectacular
albums that never grabbed the ears of few beyond their rabid, tho'
small fan base, Charlie Gearheart, Paul Spradlin, and crew called it
quits around 1978 or so. Thankfully, sensing that the musical currents
were changing, the Goose got back together in 1990, and they've been
creating new fans ever since with sporadic touring and recording.

The point where the Goose was cooked, if you will, was in 1974 when
Columbia Records made literal pâté out of the band's fourth album,
Do Your Thing But Don't Touch Mine. Saddling them with an
unsympathetic (and evidently first-time) producer rather than let the
band produce themselves as they had been, Goose fans considered this
to be the weakest of the band's works, and when it went nowhere fast,
the label dropped 'em quicker than...well, I don't really need to make
this analogy, do I?

After its "one and done" experience with Columbia, Goose Creek
Symphony retreated to Vancouver B.C. to record their fifth and, for a
while, their final album, *Head For The Hills*. The story here gets
murky, and not too many folks even whisper the truth up in the back
hills of ole Kentucky, but evidently the album would be released and
copies pressed up, but few seemed to have made their way out of the
label's warehouse.

Although not really a "lost album" like the Goose's *The Same Thing
Again*, which was shelved before it got to the pressing plant, *Head For
The Hills* suffered a slow death nonetheless.

The truth is, there's nothing on *Head For The Hills* that departs from the Goose's tried-and-true formula. Reissued by the band itself a decade ago on CD, this new "special edition" reissue of *Head For The Hills* features pristine re-mastered sound, spiffy new cover artwork courtesy of Chris Kro, and it restores a song – "Workin' For The Devil" – that was on the original vinyl but dropped for the earlier CD release.

Since the band's tasty interplay of acoustic and electric guitars, ragin' fiddles, and vocal harmonies wasn't broke in '75 when they recorded *Head For The Hills*, they didn't work too hard to fix it. Although Goose Creek's mix of twang-and-bang was a couple of decades ahead of its time, the ensuing years have proven that their trademark sound has held up remarkably well against the ever-changing face of popular music.

Opening with the traditional "Goin' Down The Road," the band establishes its intent with a laid-back and uber-twangy performance that creates the country equivalent of Phil Spector's "wall of sound" (fence of sound?), with plenty of guitars and fiddles driving the mix.

Gearheart's anti-industry "Number One Gravy Band" lampoons rock star excess with some rather ribald admissions and an outright challenge for the audience to listen to some "down home music." The "Pretty Mama/Hey Good Lookin'" medley successfully welds Gearheart's original romantic-rocker with a cover of fellow traveler Hank Senior's sly hillbilly come-on.

The Goose pulls off a similarly ambitious pairing with "Head For The Hills/Will The Circle Be Unbroken," matching Gearheart's humorous satire of the "back to the country" movement with the Carter Family's original country-gospel anthem. The lost track, "Workin' For The Devil," is a good ole-fashioned, tear-jerking cheatin' song worthy of the Louvin Brothers, while the up-tempo "People Like Me" is the sort of inclusionary "feel good" number that the Goose's closest modern doppelganger, Bonepony, would jam on.

Methinks that Goose Creek Symphony long ago made peace with the fact that they'd never be chart-toppers or world-beaters, and that's OK. All these guys ever wanted to do was make music that people would enjoy, and although it probably wouldn't have made any difference back in the day had *Head For The Hills* received the distribution it deserved, the fact that this timeless music is flying high again is good enough for long-time fans of the Goose. (2009)

GOOSE CREEK SYMPHONY
The Same Thing Again   (Bo Records)

If you've never heard of the Goose Creek Symphony – and most folks haven't – well, here's the truth. While Jeff Tweedy and Jay Farrar were scampering around in Pampers and playing with wooden blocks, Charles Gearheart and the Goose were fusing country and rock sounds like nobody else, plumbing the depths of hillbilly, folk, bluegrass, and rock music almost two decades before any of that "No Depresssion" stuff became trés chic. Goose Creek's unique country-rock hybrid had an earthier, more organic sound than just about anything coming out of Nashville circa 1971-74.

The Same Thing Again is the great lost Goose Creek Symphony album, with songs recorded during sessions in 1973 and '74, the proposed album shelved after the band's break-up, and forgotten until a couple of years ago. Unlike Goose Creek's *Head For The Hills*, which was actually pressed on vinyl and allowed to die a slow death in the label's warehouse back in '76 (since reissued by the band on CD), *The Same Thing Again* never made it past the cassette-tapes-for-friends stage.

Dunno if it would have met with a kinder fate than any of the band's earlier albums, but *The Same Thing Again* is a near-seamless pairing of reckless country soul and good-times hippie-rock vibe. Larry Collins' Okie blues tune "Tulsa Turnaround" – recommended to the band by Waylon Jennings – is reinvented here as a fiddle-fueled rave-up. "Too Much of A Good Thing" is a classic country-funk Goose

Creek story-song with typical down-home morality. "Just Another Rock & Roll Song" mixes exotic Caribbean rhythms with no-frills '70s-era guitar-rock, while the title track is a slow-paced country waltz with smart biographical lyrics and some damn fine pedal-steel.

The Same Thing Again includes a bonus DVD that features music videos for "Tulsa Turnaround" and "The Same Thing Again," both pieced together with still photos and vintage live footage, while the mini-film "On The Bus '73" shows Gearheart and the Goose riding down the back roads of America in their Silver Eagle bus, music intercut with band interviews and home movies of the band at play. Of Goose Creek Symphony, well, as my old granddaddy used to say, "that's some real poop-punting music!" (2008)

GRATEFUL DEAD
Rocking The Cradle: Egypt 1978   (Rhino Records)

Let's be as honest as church mice here, shall we? The corpse that once was the Grateful Dead has long since been flayed, flogged and laid to rest along with the hopes and dreams of so many '60s-era flower children. With better than fifty – count 'em! – fifty live albums on the shelf (many consisting of two or three discs, or more), even the Dead's long-standing reputation as a great performing outfit that typically underperformed in the studio is questionable in light of the growing body of evidence.

In the annals of hardcore Grateful Dead fans (a/k/a "Deadheads," which the Reverend's dictionary defines as "one who has smoked so many flowers as to make their musical judgment suspect), no live performance by the band is more legendary that the Dead's journey to the sands of Egypt during late 1978 to play three nights in front of the Great Pyramid. Outside of the historical significance of the performances, there's little here to recommend, however. A two-CD and one-DVD set in a nifty fold-out pop-up package with images of the pyramids, *Rocking The Cradle: Egypt 1978* is a document of the band's experience, but offers little else.

With audio culled from two of the Egyptian nights for the CDs, and video from one night's concert on the DVD, the band sleepwalks through performances of songs from the upcoming *Shakedown Street* album along with a few older chestnuts. The usual spark of the Dead's free-form live performances seems to be missing here, however, and highlights are few and far between.

The band gets behind a cover of the New Orleans Cajun classic "Iko Iko," slowing down the pace to that of a strutting fly-by with a loping groove and a couple of solos full of rich tones. "I Need A Miracle" offers a few hot licks threaded throughout the long form jam, but an obligatory performance of "Truckin'" suffers from a too-mellow vibe, reducing the song's innate anarchic spirit to a hearty bass line and rushed vocals. Sadly, much of the rest of the album's 18 tracks (and their DVD doppelgangers) are entirely somnambulant.

Don't get me wrong here folks, and please don't deluge *Blurt* editor Fred with barrels of hate mail – the Reverend simply *adores* GD albums like *Workingman's Dead, American Beauty, Blues For Allah*, even *In The Dark* – but methinks that you should spend your lunch money on one of those stellar efforts rather than waste your hard-earned coin on this snoozefest. You'll thank me later... (2008)

GRAVEYARD
Hisingen Blues   (Nuclear Blast Records)

The last few years have witnessed the emergence of a third generation of shaggy-haired youth overtly influenced by the early-to-mid-'70s electric bombast of punters like the almighty Black Sabbath, the riff-happy Deep Purple, the prog-minded Uriah Heep, and the legendary Led Zeppelin.

Said youth have since picked up guitars and sat down to drums and began making a din of their own, leading to bands like the Sword, Wolfmother, Witchcraft, and Rose Hill Drive putting their particular stank on the metallic doom-and-gloom of said musical forebears.

Sweden's Graveyard hail from the nearly-mythical Gothenburg, Sweden's second largest city, an international seaport, and home to possibly more bands per capita than any metropolis outside of Austin, Texas. Influential bands like In Flames, At The Gates, and Dark Tranquility created what is known, in certain circles, as the "Gothenburg sound," a melodic form of heavy metal that hybridized  Scandinavian black metal with hardcore's angst, thrash's fury, punk's attitude, and hard rock's melody and innate audacity. While Graveyard has carved its own path out of the Nordic hinterlands with a sound that is less death and more retro in nature, with their sophomore effort, *Hisingen Blues*, the band has the opportunity to make a bigger critical and commercial splash than any of its regional counterparts.

Following the back cover's admonition to play *Hisingen Blues* at "the highest possible volume in order to fully appreciate the sound of Graveyard," the listener is instantly transported back in time by the opening chords of "Ain't Fit to Live Here." With an urgency that chain-whips both Heep and Zeppelin, the song bursts out of the starting gate with a manic rhythm and clashing guitars that underline Joakim Nilsson's Robert Plant-styled vocal howl. Drummer Axel Sjoberg's backbreaking bursts of sound channel Zep's Bonzo more so than the metronomic blast-beat familiar to Swedish metal fans, Sjoberg pounding the cans like a man possessed by absinthe-guzzling demons.

If "Ain't Fit to Live Here" gets your blood boiling with speed, thrash, and blinding flash, "No Good, Mr. Holden" slows the album down to a near-glacial pace, the band dusting off its old warped vinyl copies of Sabbath's *Vol. 4* and dressing the riffs up nicely for the new millennia. Nilsson's vocals are a little duskier here, no match for Ozzie's banshee wail or Ronnie James Dio's epic grandeur…maybe more like Badlands' Ray Gillen, with a little blues lying barely-concealed beneath the high voltage currents. The guitar solo near the end –

Nilsson's, possibly, or perhaps second stringbender Jonatan Larocca Ramm, is a thing of horrible beauty, kind of like a phoenix rising from the ashes of the song's mesmerizing dinosaur stomp.

Graveyard hits full stride by the time they arrive at the title track, "Hisingen Blues" a full-blown metal-edged monolith with vocals nearly drowned out by broken glass guitar and the massive rhythmic hurricane delivered explosively by Ramm's larger-than-life drumbeats and Rikard Edlund's heavy, fluid, and often-times ethereal bass lines. Balancing carelessly on the fine tightwire between hard rock and heavy metal, Graveyard spices the brew with a little psychedelic-tinged lead guitar and some trippy space-rock sounds. Three songs in, you're hopelessly sucked into the maelstrom that is *Hisingen Blues*.

Whether it's the moody "Uncomfortably Numb," Graveyard's take on mid-70s Pink Floyd and as close as they come to a ballad with nuanced drumbeats, careful guitar strum, and atmospheric vocals, or you fall headfirst into "Longing," the sort of deep-blue tone-poem that Zeppelin created and numerous other bands of the era experimented with, you're going to find something to crow about here. "Ungrateful Are the Dead" is another toxic mind-bender, a musical acid trip with chunks of chainsaw guitar; gruff, nearly-hidden vocals; and a swirling psychedelic heartbeat. *Hisingen Blues* closes with a "bonus track," the blues-rock dirge "Cooking Brew," the song's intro offering shimmering guitar notes spun out of pure molten steel before getting down-and-dirty with a bluesy vibe that is assisted by Nilsson's growling voice and heavy, blackened riffs the band must buy by the ton.

Whether or not Graveyard gets any traction stateside with *Hisingen Blues* remains to be seen; tho' they stand as good a chance as any to break out in these troubled days and times. Both Graveyard and *Hisingen Blues* would have been right at home in 1973 or '74, touring with fellow travelers like Spirit or UFO, building an audience by word of mouth, glomming rave reviews from Rick Johnson and the Mad Peck in *Creem* or *Circus*, and earning heavy rotation on FM radio.

Sadly, AOR has gone the way of the floppy disc as radio stations squeeze in a few songs between commercials. MTV, which fueled the

1980s-era boom in hard rock and metal, pulls in bigger ratings numbers these days by promoting teen pregnancy and drunken anti-intellectualism with its insipid reality programming. Music videos? Fuggitaboutit! As for the music press, present company excluded, few zines/blogs/websites outside of those that genuflect at the altar of Martin Popoff will deign to recognize the greatness of *Hisingen Blues*.

Still, if you enjoy a certain street-smart Cro-Mag edge to your rock 'n' roll, take a welcome trip back in time with Graveyard's *Hisingen Blues*. Inspired rather than tired, Graveyard has built a gleaming city in the sun on top of the ancient musical ruins of its hard rock ancestors. (2011)

HAWKWIND
77 (Secret Records U.K.)

Hawkwind is one of those few rare bands that definitely defy categorization. Formed in 1969 by guitarists David Brock and Mick Slattery and vocalist/saxophonist Nik Turner, the band went through various names and roster changes before settling on Hawkwind. At one point, even Motörhead's Lemmy Kilmister played bass with the band, adding vocals to "Silver Machine," their one hit song, which hit number three on the U.K. charts in 1972. Only Brock has been constant across the band's checkered forty-plus-year history, the guitarist serving as Hawkwind's (meager) tether to reality, the planetary body around which various creative satellites have orbited.

In 1977, punk broke in the United Kingdom, and while conventional wisdom leans toward classifying the stripped-down, raw rock 'n' roll sounds emerging from bands like the Damned and the Sex Pistols as a "musical revolution," people on the street knew better. As documented by the most excellent music journalist Dave Thompson, among others, the impact of punk rock in Britain looks a lot better in the rear view mirror than it did in the "there and now."

One thing is for certain, though – punk, at its heart, *was* revolting against the bloated, over-produced, and commercialized music that was dominating the charts in both the U.S. and England. Even the punks knew better than to mess around with Hawkwind, however, and it can be safely said that any band that counts Johnny Rotten *and* Henry Rollins among its fans had nothing to worry about from the "revolution of '77."

Truth is, in spite of the lip service paid to the concept of "anarchy" by many young punks, Hawkwind epitomized the philosophy like no other band then or since. While the band certainly had its share of interpersonal problems and unhealthy relationships, the revolving door that members were constantly exiting through swung both ways and many musicians have come and gone more than once. Musically, while the band had evolved from 1960s era psychedelic-rock, it was a mutation that quickly grew horns and a tail, venturing off into flights of fancy that nobody could have predicted at the time.

The first bona fide "space rock" band, a Hawkwind song *felt* like you were soaring the cosmos with the band, their sound a unique and original mix of psychedelia, progressive rock, proto heavy metal, and indefinable squalls of electronic squeals, jolting feedback, and raw energy that crackled from their performances like a lightning bolt straight from the hand of Zeus. Throw in acid-drenched lyrics that were obsessed with science fiction and fantasy elements – legendary U.K. fantasy scribe Michael Moorcock (*Elric*) even penned lyrics for the band – along with the sort of deep philosophical meanderings one enjoys with Hunter S. Thompson levels of recreational drug use and you have a recipe for 100% crazy…

Hawkwind's anarchic live performances are the stuff of legend, and the recent two-disc set *77* (issued on England's Secret Records label) collects 17 of 'em from across the entire year 1977, culled from the band's appearances at various outdoor festivals and indoor dives. Hawkwind had already delivered six studio albums and an acclaimed double live set, *Space Ritual*, by the time that punk reared its ugly head in the U.K. and they spent much of the year putting the finishing touches on what would become their seventh LP, *Quark Strangeness and Charm*.

Decried at the time as the band taking a left turn towards a more commercially accessible, pop-oriented sound, you sure couldn't tell it from the performances of the three songs from *Quark* included here.

By this point, with the better part of a decade under their belt, it's clear that anything short of howling at the moon would be deemed "too pop" by the band's rabid fans.

There's no lack of full moon lunacy on display across the 17 songs on *77*, beginning with the band's classic "Masters of the Universe." From their 1971 album *In Search of Space*, "Masters" showcases a band shooting for the stars. Frontman Robert Calvert's hoarse, gravel-throated vocals are used sparingly; instead we get hurricane-strength tsunamis of synthesizer and keyboards creating a rhythmic "woosh" as a backdrop for Brock's wiry, imaginative, and completely out-of-this-world fretwork. By contrast, "High Rise" is comparatively down-to-earth, more prog-rock oriented with flowing instrumentation, classically-styled keyboards, and but a few synth-squeals, relying instead on Calvert's eccentric reading of the lyrics.

The band tries out "Damnation Alley" from *Quark* on the crowd, breaking the song into two pulse-quickening parts stitched together by a short instrumental passage. Calvert's relatively calm vocals are mostly buried...hell, they're overwhelmed...by the Sturm und Drang of the band's claustrophobic wall of sound. I hear the singer saying something about a "strange world" and a "radiation wasteland," making me believe that the song is some sort of ecological warning, but in light of the sheer sonic overkill applied herein, and subsequent references to "Dr. Strangelove" and the "pony express," methinks that the band has been dipping into the sugar cube punchbowl, if you know what I mean (and I think that you do).

"Angels of Life" is equally trippy, Calvert's echoed vocals emerging from a glorious din like the voice of some sort of divine entity while Brock's guitar screams in rage and synthesizers wail like banshees dancing merrily on your grave.

Hawkwind plows straight into "Quark, Strangeness and Charm" to open disc two of *77*, the then-upcoming album's title track belying any hint of commercial considerations save for, maybe, an infectious sense of melody lacking in much of the band's industrial-strength jams. While the vocals are somewhat cleaner than previous, and there's a bit of harmony thrown in for good measure, when the 'passé by 1977' synthesizers kick in like rabid bats flying through a Head East song, any hopes of chart position have been thrown out the window. "Death Trap" is one of the band's most muscular, proto-metal tunes, and while it wouldn't show up on record until 1979's *PXR5* album, it was an exciting live staple in 1977. Calvert's doom-and-gloom take on a dying racecar driver is provided properly chaotic music, swirls of guitar and heavy drumbeats clashing against twisted-metal synths with punkish fury until the song's heartbeat simply fades away.

It's clear from *77* that Brock and company were quite prolific in cranking out the tunes, working a couple of albums ahead of themselves, trying out material on an enthusiastic audience and discarding the bombs. Case in point: "Who's Gonna Win The War," from 1980's *Levitation* album, and "Sonic Attack," a longtime live fave from *Space Ritual* that, nevertheless, wouldn't be waxed in the studio until the 1981 album of the same name. The former is a dirge-like ballad with chanted lyrics and complex, multi-layered instrumentation that takes on a sort of dark beauty with melodic fretwork, washes of synth and keyboards, and rolling drumbeats that create a haunting martial rhythmic backbone. The latter is one of the most powerful songs in the Hawkwind milieu, an odd little anti-war/anti-fascism screed with a uniquely British perspective that pairs eclectic spoken-word lyrics with buzzing, humming synthesizer drone, syncopated drumbeats, and jagged shards of guitar that hit your ears like a rattlesnake strike.

Hawkwind is still plying its trade today, the band recently releasing its 26th album, *Onward*, as bandleader-for-life David Brock celebrates his 70th birthday. The band's musical formula has changed little since the material showcased on *77* and if Brock – Hawkwind's creative heart all these years – has lost a step or two in the interim, or repeats himself occasionally, the fact is that nobody has pursued musical anarchy with the fervor and ferocity of Hawkwind for anywhere near as long. *77* is a delightful find, documenting the band at what is arguably the height of its powers, offering up a classic line-up of talent and an unparalleled selection of songs. A welcome reminder that rock music can, indeed, blow your mind, *77* provides the soundtrack for your own trip to wherever you'd like to go. (2012)

HEAVEN & HELL
The Devil You Know
(Rhino Records)

A couple years back, I believe 'twas, the Ronnie James Dio-era incarnation of Black Sabbath (i.e. 1979-1982) got together to pimp Rhino's freshly-released *The Dio Years* compilation. The two-disc set included some of the best musical finery from the line-up's two early '80s sets, *Heaven & Hell* and *Mob Rules*, as well as a few things from the Dio-fronted obligatory live album (*Live Evil*) and their "reunion" misstep, 1992's *Dehumanizer*.

The Dio Years also included three honkin' new tunes recorded specifically for the set, the foursome of Dio, guitarist Toni Iommi, bassist Geezer Butler, and drummer Vinny Appice using the band name Heaven & Hell (after their first album together, geddit?) because, allegedly, Sharon Osborne refused them the use of the holy, and seemingly priceless Black Sabbath name. The new tunes fell on receptive ears, Heaven & Hell went out on tour in support of *The Dio Years*, and they found a modicum of acceptance from hidebound Sab fans, subsequently squeezing out a well-received live album.

Which, in a roundabout way, brings us to *The Devil You Know*, the first "official" Heaven & Hell studio release, and a fine collection of riff-driven doom-metal, ya know. There's no reason, at this point in the game, to believe that you're going to receive much of anything different from Dio, Iommi, and the gang, and that's just fine by me. The album opens with the plodding, seriously downtuned "Atom and Evil," the intro itself worth the price of admission.

Featuring one of Iommi's best sludge-metal guitar lines and Dio's slow-as-cough-syrup vocals, the song stomps along ungracefully and lets the listener know exactly what to expect from this latest Black...er, Heaven & Hell album. The proggish "Bible Black" opens with a piercing guitar line thrown against an acoustic guitar strum, Dio's slow-boiling vocals evolving from an initial menacing growl into his typical full-blown wail as Appice's drums explode and Iommi's fretwork grinds and howls. "Rock & Roll Angel" is the album's best bet for a radio-ready single, with a sledgehammer riff marching like an angry carnivore behind Dio's over-the-top vocals and a matching suit-and-tie of martial rhythms. The unrelenting doomishness of "The Turn of The Screw" is gussied up with some uncharacteristic Dio vocal gymnastics that evoke memories of the New Wave of British Heavy Metal in their inflection and flexibility.

Dio is known as an arcane lyricist, a fanciful songwriter whose head is filled with dreams of dragons and witches and darkness, and *The Devil You Know* is filled with Dio's typically oblique imagery, words that seem so much more frightening when spit at the listener with Dio's usual power and glory.

The songwriter can have a little fun now and then, however, and "Eating The Cannibals" is Dio's tongue-in-cheek stab at humor. A locomotive rocker with screaming six-string and fast-paced rhythms, Dio's vocals run at a pace similar to Bruce Dickinson's, while Iommi's lightning-quick fretboard runs prove that the man can shred with the best o' them.

The stunning "Follow The Tears" strides the razor's edge between Sabbath's typical doom-and-gloom Sturm und Drang and Euro-styled Goth-metal. The song's strident, unyielding rhythms are paired with crunchy guitar riffs, predatory six-string solos, and Dio's best lyrical cynicism and dark-hued cathedral vox.

The Devil You Know closes out with the same sort of retro-cool, dino-stomp tarpit rock as it opened with, "Breaking Into Heaven" allowing Dio to cut loose with his most frenetic vocals yet, which are themselves layered above Iommi's assaulting guitarplay and the Butler/Appice rhythmic cyclone.

No matter what you want to call it – Heaven & Hell, Black Sabbath, or the Archie & Jughead Good-Times Soda-Pop Quartet, the result is exactly the same – this *is The Devil You Know*. A wolf in sheep's clothing is still gonna eat yer Granny, and Messrs. Dio, Iommi, Butler, and Appice are always going to blow your face off. Sabbath Bloody Sabbath, indeed. Et tu, Sharon? (2009)

HUMBLE PIE
On To Victory / Go For The Throat
(Deadline Music)

Fronted by the dynamic, charismatic Steve Marriott, British blues-rockers Humble Pie enjoyed a brief early 1970s heyday that reached its peak with the band's 1972 album *Smokin'*. Originally formed in 1968 by Marriott and guitarist Peter Frampton, the band would go through various line-ups and musical directions before latching onto Marriott's favored rock 'n' soul hybrid, a boogie-and-blues brew that, combined with an unrelenting tour schedule, would take *Smokin'* to number six on the *Billboard* albums chart.

While subsequent albums would experience diminishing commercial returns, Humble Pie remained a popular live band when Marriott decided to pull the plug after 1975's disappointing *Street Rats* in favor of reforming his 1960s-era outfit the Small Faces. When that reunion went south in a tangle of egos and mediocre music, Marriott put together Steve Marriott's All-Stars and toured briefly before finally forming a new version of Humble Pie in 1979 with original drummer Jerry Shirley, guitarist Bobby Tench (from the Jeff Beck Group), and bassist Anthony "Sooty" Jones.

This Humble Pie line-up recorded a pair of albums – 1980's *On To Victory* and the following year's *Go For The Throat* before health issues prompted Marriott to bust up the band for a second time in 1981.

Reissued as part of a two-disc set, *On To Victory* and *Go For The Throat* were both unfairly maligned at the time of their original release, and both albums deserve another listen by long-time fans and newcomers alike. Rather than rest on past laurels or try to recreate the heavy blues-rock formula that struck gold with *Smokin'*, Marriott's new Humble Pie would sojourn into unexpected musical territories, incorporating Marriott's love of American soul music and R&B with the blues-rock sound with which he had built his reputation. As such, *On To Victory* cleverly mixes these related influences to create a fresh (and funky) sound.

On To Victory scored an unexpected minor hit with "Fool For A Pretty Face," the song's swaggering bravado mixing boogie-blues with raucous soul to good effect. The similar "Infatuation" is built with the same blueprint, Marriott adding backing harmonies behind his growling vocals, blasts of R&B styled horns accenting the mix. A cover of the Holland/Dozier/Holland classic "Baby Don't You Do It" is offered a reckless performance with a lot of charm, Marriott's signature high-flying vox imitating his previous "I Don't Need No Doctor" while the band delivers a stone rhythmic groove in the background. Marriott plays a cover of Otis Redding's "My Lover's Prayer" fairly straight, gospel-styled keyboards chiming reverently behind his anguished vocals, while the high-flying "Further Down The Road" displays Marriott's underrated six-string skills and a killer performance by drummer Shirley.

Experiencing a modicum of sales success with *On To Victory*, the re-formed Humble Pie was hustled into the studio to record a quick follow-up. Released in 1981, *Go For The Throat* could be viewed as a sequel to its predecessor and, in many aspects, its songs are almost interchangeable with *On To Victory*, with a few minor artistic lapses. An overwrought cover of Elvis Presley's "All Shook Up" features some fine guitar and keyboards from Marriott, but an overall embarrassing vocal take. Much better is Marriott's original "Teenage Anxiety," a mid-tempo ballad with emotional vocals, a solid rhythmic construct, and tasteful piano leads.

Marriott revisits an old Small Faces tune he co-wrote with Ronnie Lane, "Tin Soldier" a relic of the psychedelic 1960s but still holding a bluesy, soulful edge with Marriott's inspired vocals and nuanced fretwork, and Shirley's big-beat timekeeping. Another Marriott original, "Driver," sounds like a ZZ Top outtake albeit with more frantic percussion and a chaotic arrangement fueled by ripping guitar, flying harmonica riffs, and explosive drumbeats. The swinging, Rolling Stones-styled "Restless Blood" is pure raunch-n-roll cheap thrills, and "Chip Away (The Stone)" is an unbridled rocker from the early Humble Pie songbook, Marriott's vocals almost lost beneath a storm of stammering guitar, bass, and drums.

This reissue of *On To Victory* and *Go For The Throat* packages both albums on a single CD, accompanied by a second live disc that captures a live 1981 radio broadcast recorded in front of an enthusiastic audience at the Reseda Country Club in Los Angeles, California. The eight-track playlist, although stretching across a full 45-minutes, is curiously short on material from the reformed band's then-current albums. No matter, because starting with a particularly high-octane ten-minute jam on the band's "I Don't Need No Doctor" (originally an R&B chart hit for Ray Charles), this live set strikes like lightning and sounds like thunder, showing why Marriott was always more popular as a live performer than a studio artist.

"Infatuation" takes on a new life on-stage, the band stomping and snorting like a mad bull tearing through a china shop. The band revisits another early Humble Pie gem in "30 Days In The Hole," one of the more popular AOR tracks from *Smokin'*, Jerry Shirley's flying drumbeats and Marriott's out-of-control vocals paired with intertwined guitars and heavy bass lines.

The hit "Fool For A Pretty Face" is well-received, Marriott's vocals edgier and stronger than the studio version, the band's crashing instrumentation building to a cacophonous crescendo. Marriott revisits his childhood with a livewire cover of Gene Vincent's early rock classic "Be-Bop-A-Lula," pulling off an audacious performance, while a cover of Don William's country classic "Tulsa Time" swings as hard as the original with amped-up guitars and sonic drumbeats, although the gravel-throated Marriott's attempt at twangy vocals fall far short of the mark.

Since both *On To Victory* and *Go For The Throat* have long been out-of-print in the U.S. and available only sporadically as a British import, it's good to have both albums available again as part of a single set. While neither album is as engaging or entertaining as early Humble Pie efforts like *Rock On* or *Smokin'*, neither is as bad as critics avowed at the time. Both albums include a handful of truly transcendent musical moments – solid fusions of blues, rock, and soul – and although *On To Victory* is the better and more spontaneous of the two releases, the albums mesh together seamlessly on a single disc. Throw in the red-hot live set, and you have a deluxe edition tailor-made for Humble Pie fans to chew upon for a while. (2012)

IAN HUNTER & MICK RONSON
Live At Rockpalast (MIG Music)

In the absence of legitimate contemporary rock 'n' roll heroes, a sort of "cult of personality" has grown up around a number of admittedly eccentric 1960s-and-70s-era musicians. From Nick Lowe and Robyn Hitchcock to Todd Rundgren and other aging rockers raised in the long shadows of the second World War, the digital era has been kinder to them than most, prompting a rediscovery of their early, acclaimed work by a younger audience, extending their careers long past the ostensible commercial "sell by" date. In many instances, it has enabled these artists to grow old with dignity and grace, allowing them to deliver some of the best music of their lives in the 21st century.

Of all of these fellow travelers, Ian Hunter is the oldest and, perhaps, the most iconoclastic. A late arrival to U.K. glam-rock cult faves Mott the Hoople, Hunter quickly took over the band's creative reins and became its best-known member. (Don't think so? Quick, name another Mott member other than Hunter or guitarist Mick Ralphs…)

Hunter's often-snarky, Dylan-inspired wordplay and the band's guitar-heavy hard-rock sound would earn them a modicum of fame, if little fortune, and by the mid-'70s, realizing that the party was coming to a close, Hunter jumped the Mott ship for a solo career, taking former David Bowie/Lou Reed guitarist, and recent band addition Mick Ronson with him.

Although a direct line can be drawn from Mott the Hoople to the intelligent punk-rock of the Clash and the less-intellectual, but admittedly more commercially successful pseudo-metal of Def Leppard, it is Ian Hunter's sporadic solo career that has influenced a generation of British, as well as a lesser number of American musicians. Beginning with his self-titled 1975 debut, which yielded the classic "Once Bitten Twice Shy," through the end of the decade and a handful of albums that culminated in 1979's *You're Never Alone With A Schizophrenic*, which entered "Just Another Night" and "Cleveland Rocks" to the rock 'n' roll lexicon, Hunter wrote a musical legacy that continues to resonate loudly even in recent works like 2007's *Shrunken Heads* and 2009's *Man Overboard*.

In April 1980, reunited with his friend and longtime musical foil Ronson (management problems having kept the two madmen apart for several years), Hunter performed for the popular German TV show *Rockpalast*. Translating, roughly, as "Rock Palace," the program has been broadcast since 1974, airing performances from, literally, hundreds of rock, blues, jazz, and other artists. Video clips from the TV show have been a staple of YouTube since the dawn of that website, but only within the last couple of years has Germany's MIG Music made a number of full-length performances available on CD and DVD.

Hunter's 1980 *Rockpalast* performance, prominently featuring guitarist Ronson, stands as a true gem among an eclectic and varied catalog offered by MIG Music. Fronting a band that included Ronson, bassist Martin Briley, a pair of keyboard players, and a drummer, Hunter rips through a baker's dozen of songs from both his solo albums as well as his tenure with Mott the Hoople. Performing in front of an enthusiastic German audience at the large Grugahalle arena in Essen, Germany, the first half of *Live At Rockpalast* mimics the tracklist, if not the actual performances, found on Hunter's 1980 live release *Welcome To The Club*.

The album-opening instrumental "F.B.I." is effectively a raucous band intro fueled by Ronson's wiry fretwork and a driving rhythm that leads straightaway into "Once Bitten Twice Shy," the hoary hard-rock chestnut stripped down here, provided a slight boogie-rock framework with Hunter's wry vocals dancing atop a sparse arrangement that explodes into a full-blown rock 'n' roll cyclone.

The beautifully lovestruck "Angeline" (a/k/a "Sweet Angeline," from *Brain Capers*) is the first of several Mott the Hoople treasures recreated here, the song's simple, slightly-twangy construction reminiscent of Nick Lowe's Brinsley Schwartz, Hunter's passionate vocals rising above a cacophony of chiming guitars and cascading drumbeats. A pair of beloved tunes from that band's breakthrough 1973 album *Mott* are provided similar reverence, the wistful "I Wish I Was Your Mother" benefiting from Ronson's elegant guitarplay and Hunter's haunting, weary vocals while the up-tempo "All The Way From Memphis" displays all the reckless abandon and joyful banter of the original.

Of Hunter's modest solo hits, "Cleveland Rocks" may be better known than "Just Another Night" due to its use as the theme of *The Drew Carey Show* for several years, performed there by the Presidents of the United States of America (remember "Lump"?). Hunter's version kicks ass, hands down, the singer declaring the city one of the birthplaces of rock 'n' roll and then kicking out the jams with a high-octane performance that is over-the-top delicious in its unbridled energy.

Hunter's vocals ride a wave of distorted guitars and crashing rhythms, feedback creeping in at the edges as the singer delivers the lyrics with a punkish sneer and a sly grin. "Just Another Night" ain't chopped liver, though…Hunter's swaggering vocals sit comfortably within a blanket of sound, keyboards tinkling above a sweaty, grinding dancefloor rhythm.

Live At Rockpalast includes performances of several of Hunter's lesser-known songs as well as an intriguing cover of the obscure mid-'60s Sonny Bono single "Laugh At Me." A spry pop-rock tune with an undeniable melody, vocal harmonies, edgy guitarwork, and period-perfect alienated teen lyrics, Hunter and crew crank up the pathos and turn up the amps and deliver a riveting performance. "We Gotta Get Out Of Here" debuted on *Welcome To The Club* and, sadly, wouldn't be reprised on any later studio albums. Here the song is a hard-rocking sledgehammer with an infectious chorus, scraps of honky-tonk piano, tense guitar, bashed cymbals, gang vocals, and an overall crescendo of chaotic instrumentation.

The set, somewhat appropriately, closes with the Mott hit "All The Young Dudes" and Ronson's "Slaughter On 10th Avenue." The former, handed to the band by the album's producer David Bowie, is played embarrassingly straight. Ronson's guitar mimics perfectly Mick Ralph's original rakish note-picking, and Hunter's vocals sound every bit as punkish in 1980 as they did in 1972. The upbeat "Dudes" leads right into Ronson's languid instrumental; taken from the guitarist's 1974 solo album by that name, the song starts out slow and jazzy and builds to an enormously satisfying finish.

Ian Hunter and Mick Ronson would more or less carry on their musical collaboration until Ronson's untimely death in 1993, frequently touring throughout the early 1980s as the Hunter Ronson Band of which, sadly, only bootleg recordings seem to exist. When Hunter went on hiatus during the latter half of the 1980s, Ronson continued to record and produce, touring with Dylan and working with artists as diverse as Morrissey, Meatloaf, Roger McGuinn, and John Mellencamp, among others. The two friends would reunite for Hunter's 1990 album *YUI Orta*, and performed together one last time in 1992 during a tribute to Queen's Freddie Mercury that would be documented on Ronson's posthumous solo album *Heaven and Hull*.

For a couple of nights in Germany in 1980, however, both artists were at the top of their game, and *Live At Rockpalast* captures the magic that was Ian Hunter and Mick Ronson together. (2012)

JELLO BIAFRA
In The Grip of Official Treason
(Alternative Tentacles)

Since President Bush's popularity has dropped faster than the Titanic what with this whole "morass" thing going on over in Iraq (and, lest we forget, Afghanistan too), a lot of otherwise spineless twits have raised up on their hind legs and started bashing the administration. Big fat hairy deal! It's easy to kick the man and his friends when they're down and out; it's another thing entirely to challenge the powers that be when, like Cagney, they're "on top o' the world, ma!"

That's where Jello Biafra comes in...for two decades and four Presidential administrations, Biafra has been the proverbial fly in the political buttermilk. The former Dead Kennedys' frontman and punk rock icon has forged an impressive second career as a speaker and social commentator. The Green Party progressive has never been afraid to tackle the big issues, pointing out the hypocrisy and contradictions of public policy regardless of whether it's the Republicans or the Democrats holding the seat of power.

In The Grip Of Official Treason is Biafra's eighth spoken word collection, a massive three-disc set that gathers material from several Biafra performances over the last couple of years. The extended rants on the discs run the gamut of subject matter, from U.S. policy in the Middle East and, of course, the war in Iraq to America's obsession with electronic gadgets and their dehumanizing effect on the social landscape. Biafra's well-researched commentary and insightful observations are delivered with no little amount of humor, a necessary ingredient to keep the bile from rising up at the harsh reality these stories reveal.

Biafra has often been accused of "preaching to the choir," that those listeners most likely to pick up spoken word albums like *In The Grip Of Official Treason* are those who likely already agree with Biafra's anarcho-leftist worldview. However, I don't necessarily agree with this criticism. A look at the album's liner notes shows that pieces like "Punk Voter Rally Cry" and "Die For Oil, Sucker" have been taken from a variety of live performances. From the 2004 "Rock Against Bush" tour stop in Tempe, Arizona to the H.O.P.E. 2006 Hacker Conference in NYC, Biafra is often speaking before audiences that probably don't hold firsthand memories of the Dead Kennedys. Many of his college-age audience members were still in diapers when Biafra released *No More Cocoons*, his first spoken word album, nearly twenty years ago.

For many of Biafra's young listeners, his observations come as a revelation, and the material you'll find on *In The Grip Of Official*

Treason is no different. The wide range of topics covered by Biafra, all obviously thought out in detail and well documented, is stunning and best swallowed in one-disc doses. Even for someone as well-read as the Reverend, Jello still manages to teach me something that I didn't already know, opening my eyes to a new reality, however depressing it may be.

The most amazing thing about *In The Grip Of Official Treason* is that Biafra can still do this gig, that he still holds a glimmer of hope in the face of Democratic betrayal, Republican corruption, and corporate greed. Biafra is the punk rock Diogenes searching for one honest man; or maybe he's the left-wing Paul Revere, warning us of the coming storm. Either way, *In The Grip Of Official Treason* entertains and enlightens, and if it doesn't piss you off, you're just not listening… (2007)

JIM BYRNES
I Hear The Wind In The Wires
(Black Hen Music)

To hardcore fans of the genre, it's no surprise that country music just ain't what it used to be. Sure, the great Willie Nelson has outlived all his old friends to become a beacon of light for the "good old days," but no matter how one slices it, today's focus group-created, franken-protooled country "superstars" like Kenny Chesney, Blake Shelton, the Band Perry and their ilk are no prize pig when compared to the pioneers of the genre like Hank Williams, Johnny Cash, George Jones, Patsy Cline, and other Nashville legends.

Although firmly identified with Canada's thriving blues scene, in truth, singer/songwriter Jim Byrnes has more in common with the Band's Levon Helm than with, say, Muddy Waters. Byrnes – who was born in St. Louis, but moved to Vancouver B.C. better than 30 years ago – and the late Helm both draw heavily from across a wide swath of American musical history, from blues and rock to folk and country. Both artists pursue a distinctive roots 'n' blues musical style and possess warm, deep, and totally unique voices that wrap themselves around the material.

So, when Byrnes decided to record an album of mostly old-school country music tunes with his long-time musical foil, producer, and multi-instrumentalist Steve Dawson, the project doesn't fall as far out of the singer's wheelhouse as one might suppose. With *I Hear The Wind On The Wires*, Byrnes has a firm handle on what made these songs by Ray Price, Hank Snow, the Stanley Brothers, Gordon Lightfoot, and others timeless in nature, so much so that Nashville songwriters are still trying to capture that creative lightning in the bottle today.

Byrnes chose a true honky-tonk classic to kick off *I Hear The Wind In The Wires*, Hank Snow's "I'm Movin' On" a number one hit for the Canadian singer and songwriter, a song recorded by everybody from Snow and Willie Nelson to Ray Charles and Elvis Presley. Byrnes plays it straight down the line, laying his twangy vocals atop a flurry of Scotty Moore-styled guitar licks and squalls of Chris Gestrin's funky roller-rink organ riffs, throwing in a few hollers now and then to lively up the joint. Continuing on in this vein, Byrnes' spin on "City Lights" is a little more jaunty than Ray Price's original, but if Byrnes' vocals sound more melancholy than heartbroken, his anguish is punctuated by Dawson's weeping pedal steel guitar.

When Buck Owens put his Bakersfield sound to Harlan Howard's "Above and Beyond (The Call of Love)" in 1960 he scored a #3 chart hit with the tune. Howard, perhaps Nashville's last great country songwriter, had a way of stripping a lyric down to its emotional core, and Byrnes takes the ball and runs with it, hitting every heartfelt note with his romantic promises, the steel guitar moaning in the background as a lonely piano rides alongside the mid-tempo rhythm. Byrnes' take on the song is closer to Owens' than Rodney Crowell's otherwise solid 1989 cover (which did what Buck's couldn't in hitting #1 on the chart), capturing the original's winsome spirit with a believable passion.

Byrnes' duet with Colleen Rennison on "Pickin' Wild Mountain Berries" is simply precious, the performance skewing closer to the R&B styled, 1960s-era Jo Jo Benson/Peggy Scott hit than to the later Loretta Lynn/Conway Twitty "countrypolitan" version. Rennison's sassy, soulful vocals are a delightful counterpoint to Byrnes' raspy baritone, the two voices playing perfectly off each other on what is admittedly a lighthearted bit of fluff, a real guilty pleasure of a song. On the other end of the spectrum, Byrnes' cover of the 1960 Marty Robbins hit "Big Iron" is pure C&W heaven, Byrnes' voice tailor-made for this rollicking story of an unnamed Arizona ranger with "the big iron on his hip" who faces down outlaw Texas Red in a gunfight only one would walk away from. With Dawson's pleading guitar riding shotgun above a rich instrumental backdrop, Byrnes unfolds the gripping tale and drives it to its tragic conclusion.

Switching gears for a moment, "Sensitive Man" sounds like a vintage Ricky Nelson track, or maybe even modern Threk Michaels, the song's melodic undercurrent and rolling heartbeat matched by its James Burton-styled twang 'n' bang stringplay and Byrnes' conversational vocals leading out at the end. Surprisingly, it's a Nick Lowe composition, which you can hear elements of in the chorus and in Byrnes' delivery, but then again, ol' Nick always did have one foot in the Music City even back with the Brinsley Schwarz band.

I Hear The Wind In The Wires closes out appropriately with Hank's 1952 hit "Honky Tonk Blues," Byrnes retaining the original's bluesy underpinnings even while playing up the song's more playful, raucous side as Mike Sanyshyn's fiddle rages and Gestrin's organ chimes away low in the mix.

Jim Byrnes has always included a fair number of other people's songs on his albums – 2010's Juno Award winning *Everywhere West*, for instance, offers up great covers of R&B (Lowell Fulsom), jump blues (Louis Jordan), and straight blues (Jimmy Reed, a major Byrnes influence) alongside Byrnes' own rootsy originals, and in the past he's covered everybody from Mel Tillis and Irving Berlin to Bob Dylan and Muddy Waters…so it's no secret that the man is a masterful stylist and interpreter of songs.

With *I Hear The Wind In The Wires*, however, Byrnes delivers a true labor of love, challenging himself to try his hand in re-creating an era of country music that, woefully, no longer exists. The results speak for themselves, the performances of Byrnes, Dawson, and band shining brightly from the grooves of *I Hear The Wind In The Wires*, imbuing the material with the same sort of energy and passion that first generation country music pioneers brought to it back in the day. (2012)

JIM JONES REVUE
Here to Save Your Soul
(Punk Rock Blues)

Releasing their self-titled debut album in 2008, the Jim Jones Revue made quite a splash in their native U.K. with a ramshackle sound that fleshed out the trendy stateside punk-blues duo conceit with a full-blown, and full-bore band effort that amped up the noise, threw scraps of honky-tonk madness and psychobilly rant-n-roll into the blender, pushed the button and let those razor-sharp blades fly! For most bands attempting this sort of unlikely hybrid, the sad results would be a foul-tasting musical puree; for the Jim Jones Revue, however, what poured out of the studio was an album of highly-flammable rocket fuel.

The band's debut seemingly caught everybody by surprise, British musical tastemakers only slightly less so than the Jim Jones Revue itself. To prolong their fifteen minutes of fame in a country notorious for whiplash musical trends, and perhaps to stave off a little boredom on the U.K. charts, the band has released *Here To Save Your Soul*, an eight-song singles collection that falls somewhere in betwixt an EP and a full-fledged album. Providing some value in a short-change world, only three of the songs on *Here To Save Your Soul* are from the debut album, a fourth from a late September '09 single, and the others rambunctious B-sides that, honestly, don't sound all that much different than the 'A' sides of the singles.

Bereft of inhibition, the Jim Jones Revue plays every song the same way – balls-out with reckless energy and a complete disregard for polite society. For instance, "Rock N Roll Psychosis," which opens *Here To Save Your Soul*, offers up barrelhouse piano that would make Professor Longhair spin in his grave, Delta-dirty guitar that's heavy on grit and soulful feedback and short on meaningless child's play like technique, and blood-curdling vocals that would put a death-metal glass-gagger to shame. The band's cover of Little Richard's "Good Golly Miss Molly" captures the manic energy and crazed soul of the original with atomic-bomb free-form instrumentation that blurs together into a single sonic wave of ass-stompin' sound-n-fury.

Taking their Little Richard obsession to its logical and tragic end, "Princess And The Frog" jumps completely off the rails, sounding much like what would have happened had Rev. Penniman dropped acid and chugged a fifth of Kentucky bourbon before sliding into the studio (rather than joining the ministry) to record. Elliot Mortimer's piano-pounding hits your greedy little ears like Jerry Lee on 'roids and Robitussin, while the twin guitars of Jim Jones and Rupert Orton follow a strict "scorched earth" policy. The purposely crappy production puts the entire performance behind a thick cloud of sound that recreates the experience of standing in the back of a crowded juke-joint, trying to glom a peep of the band through the smoke and sweat.

Thus goes most of *Here To Save Your Soul*, the band unashamedly refusing to release singles any less devastatingly awesome than their album tracks, and certainly no less recklessly conceived and executed. To be honest, the sound here is so ridiculously lo-fi that it would make a Brooklyn hipster's ears bleed Mississippi River mud, with every nuance and subtlety of the band's performances, if they indeed existed, lost in a thunderous storm of dense echo, feedback, and noise.

Discernible above the din of these eight songs, however, is one of the most encouragingly anarchic outfits to hit rock 'n' roll since the Clash wore short pants and the New York Dolls swapped their dresses for spandex and leather. The Jim Jones Revue puts the "unk" back in punk, and whether they're just a three-chord seasonal joke or rebellious true believers, it just doesn't matter, because for a brief fleeting and glorious moment, rock 'n' roll has been taken off life support for one more slam-dance...and that, children, will indeed "save your soul"! (2009)

JIMI HENDRIX EXPERIENCE
Axis: Bold As Love (Sony Legacy/Experience Hendrix)

Over at *Rolling Stone* magazine, critic David Fricke wrote that Jimi Hendrix's *Axis: Bold As Love* is the "most underloved record ever made by a rock god." I'd have to agree with him – the guitar great's sophomore effort was released less than a year after his groundbreaking debut, capping off a whirlwind period of roughly eighteen months that saw Hendrix introduced to British rock fans, blow away the crowd at Monterey, catapult to stardom, and released two best-selling albums.

Still, bookended by two critically-acclaimed and barrier-punishing works such as *Are You Experienced?* and *Electric Ladyland*, Hendrix's *Axis* is often overlooked by even the hardcore Jimi fanatic. While the young blues-rock guitarist – already a veteran of years playing on the Southern "chitlin' circuit" of R&B clubs – had yet to have time to fully digest the measure of his rising stardom, the wealth of ideas that were spun into *Are You Experienced?* had obviously yet to run out when he began working in the studio with Noel Redding and Mitch Mitchell on *Axis*. While not entirely as heart-stopping groundbreaking as his debut, *Axis* rocks hard nonetheless.

Opening with an odd, disconnected voice, the sci-fi jest "Exp" devolves into an instrumental assault on the senses with screaming psychedelic guitars, feedback, oscillating metal thunder, and repetitive riff patterns – all in under two minutes – before leading into the soulful blues song "Up From The Skies." With Jimi's best zoot suit vocals up front, and the band delivering a spiraling funky groove, Hendrix layers on his tense psych-blues guitar notes. The semi-metallic hard rockin' "Spanish Castle Magic" is more in line with the material on *Are You Experienced?*, Hendrix's strident and imaginative fretwork providing a strong crosswind to the blustery rhythms laid down by Redding and Mitchell.

"Wait Until Tomorrow" is one of those overlooked entries in the Hendrix canon, a mid-tempo folk-rock ballad, of sorts, with almost spoken vocals, delicate guitarplay, and Mitchell's potent drumbeaten backdrop. The locomotive rhythms driving "Ain't No Telling" are marred by a mix that places Hendrix's spry vocals too deep in the mix, his guitar barely rising out of the quicksand to make his point, the result an engaging rocker that nevertheless could have been much better.

Songs six through nine represent the heart and soul of *Axis: Bold As Love*, beginning with the ephemeral "Little Wing." Covered by everybody and their brother – from alt-rockers like Concrete Blonde to blues guitarists like Eric Clapton and Stevie Ray Vaughan – the song's familiar refrain and easily-recognizable melody masks one of Hendrix's more emotional instrumental performances. The song's brevity is somewhat deceptive, as well, hiding one of Hendrix's most poetic, if somewhat oblique, songwriting triumphs.

It's a classic song, no doubt, a mesmerizing moment that leads into the monster protest song "If 6 Was 9." With a guitar riff that is equal parts blues and rock, Hendrix shouts out his powerful vocals above Mitchell's explosive drums and cymbals, Redding's bass throbbing with immediacy. By the time that Hendrix kicks it into overdrive, his out-of-this-world soloing is weirdly transcendent.

"You Got Me Floatin'" is a died-in-the-wool rocker that pointed to musical directions that Hendrix would later take with Electric Ladyland. Above an insistent rhythm, Jimi's guitar darts in and out of the mix with fierce imagination, his vocals almost lost in the mix – a good thing, this time, adding to the song's overall chaotic vibe – while the vocal harmonies provide another dimension to the performance. The important middle of the album finishes with "Castles Made of Sand," a psychedelic-tinged blues-rock poem that mixes reality with fantasy, tragedy with whimsy as Hendrix's swirling leads and fluid rhythm guitar prop up his inspired vocal turn.

Although the middle four songs are the heart of the album, *Axis* doesn't peter out afterwards…Redding's "She's So Fine," featuring the bassist on vocals, is a more conventional rocker with psychedelic flourishes, a British pop undercurrent (I'm thinking of the Who and the Kinks), galloping drumbeats, and sublime fretwork from Hendrix. The chameleonlike "One Rainy Wish" begins as a lovely ballad before changing its colors, becoming a raging rocker before calming down into a head-spinning pastiche of lofty vocals and layered guitars.

The title track, of sorts, "Bold As Love" brings Hendrix's blues pedigree in contrast to his status as rock 'n' roll godhead, the song offering bluesy vocals with folkish lyrics, jazzlike guitar flourishes, and a subtle rhythmic foundation courtesy of Redding and Mitchell.

As part of Sony Legacy's reissue series of the Hendrix catalog, the original albums are accompanied by a DVD that includes interviews with engineer Eddie Kramer, producer/Hendrix manager Chas Chandler, and Experience band mates Noel Redding and Mitch Mitchell, as well as scraps of rare live performance footage. Here they speak about the making of several songs from *Axis: Bold As Love*, including "Little Wing" and "If 6 was 9." The deluxe packaging includes a beautiful CD booklet that includes song lyrics, never before seen photos and concert graphics, and insightful liner notes from writer Jym Fahey.

Honestly, the blues take a backseat to psychedelic rock and experimental sounds on *Axis: Bold As Love*. Hendrix's blues and soul background is woven throughout the album, its presence strongly felt as the guitarist's musical influences come to the fore in a strong set of songs that stretched the boundaries of rock music at the time while taking full advantage of studio technology.

Unlike the songs on Hendrix's debut album, which had been field-tested during months of heavy touring, the material on *Axis* represented the guitarist's conquering of a different challenge: the recording studio. Working with engineer Kramer, Hendrix pushed the confines of the studio to their extremes, creating a wealth of songs that would seldom be performed live by the band. The material stands with the best of Hendrix's milieu, however, representing a major step forward in the guitarist's creation of his legacy. (2010)

JIMI HENDRIX EXPERIENCE
Live At Berkeley
(Legacy Recordings)

It's no secret among the cognoscenti that blues-rock guitar great Jimi Hendrix was an inconsistent onstage performer. When he was hot, he burned as bright as a supernova, but when he was not, he could be dull and lackluster. It was part of the blessing and the curse of Hendrix's talents, that he often seemed to view live shows as an inconvenience thrust upon him by his manager when instead the guitarist would rather be sequestered in the studio experimenting with sound.

In an effort to scour the tape vaults of anything remotely of commercial value, Experience Hendrix – the corporation formed by the late guitarist's relatives to preserve Jimi's legacy and exploit the hell out of his musical catalog – has for years released live recordings for a rabid fan base to devour. *Live At Berkeley*, featuring a Jimi Hendrix Experience comprised of Hendrix, long-time friend and bassist Billy Cox, and drummer Mitch Mitchell, captures the band's second set at the Berkeley Community Theatre from Saturday night, May 30, 1970. The album documents a solid eleven-song performance with good, although not great sound (well, it *was* recorded over 40 years ago), definitely showcasing Hendrix at his best onstage.

The performance found on *Live At Berkeley* has long been a fan favorite, and as both sets were originally filmed and recorded that Saturday night, both have been frequently bootlegged on LP and CD in the four decades since. For fans that live their lives aboveground, however, with no previous (bootlegged) exposure to this particular band performance, the Berkeley shows are a revelation. The second set documented by *Live At Berkeley* cranks up slowly, like the first glowing embers of an out-of-control wildfire. "Pass It On," which fuses Hendrix's "Straight Ahead" with improvised lyrics and lots of flamethrower solos, is loose and funky, with Cox and Mitchell delivering a ramshackle rhythm behind Jimi's chaotic leads.

By the time the band hits three songs in and "Lover Man," this rock 'n' roll locomotive is beginning to fire on all cylinders. Hendrix's hurried vocals are propelled forward by Cox's wickedly twisted and fast-paced bass line, Mitchell's explosive percussion allowing the guitarist to embroider the song with what sound like experimental, stream-of-consciousness styled solos that further Hendrix's redefining of electric guitar. "Stone Free" is a rampaging rocker with Hendrix's half-buried vocals overshadowed by his wiry fretwork, Cox's throbbing bass, and Mitchell's crashing cymbals. By the time that Jimi cuts loose with his solo two and a half minutes in, he's clearly entered the stratosphere and running on pure adrenalin and imagination.

Of course, Hendrix doesn't ignore the fan favorites on *Live At Berkeley*, trotting out both the reliable "Hey Joe" and the legendary "Foxey Lady" for an enthusiastic audience. The former is provided its usual malevolence with Hendrix's darkly-elegant guitar lines and mournful vocals while the latter is pumped-up larger than life with an extended and amplified performance of the familiar intro as Hendrix's axe howls and squeals with feedback. The arrangement of "Foxey Lady" lends itself to improvisation, and Cox coaxes a heavy bass sound as the foundation beneath Jimi's screaming guitarplay. Another of the band's early hits, "Purple Haze," is provided a similar treatment, scorched-earth guitar layered above the driving drumbeats and sledge-hammer bass. Hendrix stretches out the song's well-worn riff with short, but sharp solos and heaps of echo and buzz.

It wouldn't be Jimi Hendrix if he didn't trot out a couple of songs from the bluesier side of his milieu, and in Berkeley that night he delivered a powerful reading of his "I Don't Live Today." Mitchell's fluid, tribal rhythms intro the song with a short drum solo before Hendrix kicks in with an electrifying barrage of guitar licks. Call it "blues on steroids" if you will, but the song is one of the finest, albeit misunderstood of the Hendrix catalog, his blustery solos channeling more emotion and empathy in a few seconds than a lot of guitarists can muster across an entire album.

This album's "Voodoo Chile (Slight Return)" represents one of the guitarist's blockbuster performances, ten-minutes-plus of fiery blues and rock fused into an incredible display of talent and audacity with otherworldly lyrics and an incredible Mitch Mitchell drum clinic that keeps up with the guitarist nearly step for step.

You'd be hard-pressed to find a live Hendrix performance with more electricity than that documented by *Live At Berkeley*. The refashioned Jimi Hendrix Experience begins the second set with a slow rolling boil and builds to a livewire crescendo, closing out the performance with a lengthy jam that (figuratively) blows the roof off the Berkeley Community Theatre. However – and this is a big "if" here, folks – considering that this performance was released a mere nine years ago when Experience Hendrix had its deal with MCA Records, is buying it again a real necessity?

There are no additional tracks on this new reissue, only a mild upgrade in sound and, well, honestly, if you have this CD already, there's no reason to upgrade. Spend your money on the DVD/Blu-ray release of *Live At Berkeley* with the new footage instead. On the other hand, if you're a Hendrix newbie and haven't heard this stuff before, run to your local music retailer and grab up a copy of both the *Live At Berkeley* CD and the DVD. Now, if we could only get a CD release of the Experience's first Berkeley set, the hardcore faithful would shut up and be happy! (2012)

JIMI HENDRIX EXPERIENCE
Winterland   (Experience Hendrix/Sony Legacy)

By October 1968, the Jimi Hendrix Experience was on top of the rock 'n' roll world. The band's December 1967 album *Axis: Bold As Love* would rise to number three on the *Billboard* magazine Top 200 albums chart, on its way to eventual multi-Platinum™ sales. Hendrix and the original Experience line-up of bassist Noel Redding and drummer Mitch Mitchell would sell out six shows over three nights at San Francisco's famed Winterland arena in advance of the impending release of their ground-breaking *Electric Ladyland* album.

A handful of performances from the three October 1968 Winterland concerts were previously released in 1987 by Rykodisc as *Live At Winterland*. In September 2011, however, Sony Legacy Recordings, working with Experience Hendrix, provided these legendary shows the respect they deserve with the release of both a single-CD compilation of the performances as well as a deluxe four-disc boxed set with performances from all three nights. The single-disc *Winterland* set stands well on its own, representing an amazing document of the band's incredible three-night stand in San Francisco.

From the first note of *Winterland*, the band blazes right into the slippery groove of "Fire," a red-hot rocker with a rattletrap riff, some of Jimi's most sexually suggestive lyrics, and an undeniable grouping of short, shocking solos that dance feverishly alongside Mitchell's crashing cymbals and drumbeats. Running a rapid-paced three-anna-half minutes, this performance would make for raucous radio airplay. After a short spoken intro, the band spins headfirst into the familiar "Foxey Lady," a brief psychedelic passage leading into the bold, larger-than-life riff that serves as the song's foundation. This live version is stretched slightly from the original, but remains raw, muscular, and stunning with Hendrix's guitar squealing like an animal in heat as Mitchell bangs the crap out of the cans.

Hendrix's trademark freefalling extended jam on Bob Dylan's "Like A Rolling Stone" is simply stunning on *Winterland*. Running eleven minutes, Jimi's performance runs the gamut from electric folk-rock to soulful blues, the entire song peppered with brilliant fretboard magic that is at once both subtle and dazzlingly audacious. Redding's bass play rides low in the arrangement, and Mitchell's chaotic percussion creeps in from the edges, but this is Jimi's showcase moment. The garage-rock staple and Hendrix hit "Hey Joe" is no less remarkable, Hendrix's dark-hued performance drenched in malevolent emotion.

One of the highlights of this *Winterland* compilation is the band's raging cover of Eric Clapton and Cream's "Sunshine of Your Love." While the original was a murky mix of psychedelic rock and British blues, Hendrix's live take on the song doesn't mimic Cream's as much as deconstructs it, changing the tempo and re-making it into an inspired instrumental performance that showcases the skills of all three players, with Jimi embellishing Clapton's guitar parts with his own impressive flights of fancy. One of Hendrix's most beloved songs, "Little Wing" is a mid-tempo ballad, with poetic lyrics and a hypnotizing melody, Jimi's familiar haunting riff running through the song. Hendrix's solos here are wonderfully dreamlike, often echoing the melody but sometimes flying off into the ether with reckless abandon.

The angst-laden lyrics of "Manic Depression" foreshadow punk rock a decade early, but the song's soundtrack is a cacophonic symphony of tortured guitar, thundering drumbeats, and blustery, deep bass lines. The powerful "Voodoo Child (Slight Return)" is the perfect fusion of blues and rock, taking the blueprint written by Clapton, Jimmy Page, and those other Brits that fancied themselves bluesmen and setting it on fire. This performance hits your ears like a nuclear bomb, Hendrix's soulful vocals all but lost beneath a hurricane-strength squall of feedback-drenched guitar and galloping drumbeats. The classic "Purple Haze" continues this instrumental slaughter, the opening riffs pumped up on adrenaline and steroids as the Experience rattles the rafters with an explosive, unforgettable take on one of their signature songs.

The long out-of-print *Live At Winterland* doesn't hold a candle to this 2011 version. While I don't have the original Rykodisc version for comparison, I can tell that only six songs from that CD are reprised here, and from the running time it appears that these are different performances anyway. No matter, really, because even if you have that album, you're going to want this one, which is as fiery a collection of Hendrix live jams as will ever batter your ears into blissed-out submission.

Hardcore fans, of course, are going to want to invest the $50 or so for the deluxe four-CD *Winterland* box set, which includes a rare Hendrix interview. The *Winterland* box includes some solid obscurities as well, like a cover of Howlin' Wolf's "Killing Floor" with Jefferson Airplane bassist Jack Casady, and the band's rowdy take on the Troggs' "Wild Thing." Either way you roll, you can't go wrong, and the single-disc "highlights" CD of *Winterland* stands well on its own as an incredible live document of the Jimi Hendrix Experience. (2011)

JOE COCKER

Joe Cocker!   (Hip-O Select)

Years before he became the tragic burn-out parodied by John Belushi on *Saturday Night Live*, Joe Cocker was just another young soul rebel trying to grab the brass ring. The British singer came up through the ranks of various skiffle and jazz-blues bands like many of his contemporaries, but he distinguished himself from the rest of the pack through his gritty, rough-hewn R&B vocals and a car wreck performing style that had him staggering around on stage, flailing his arms in the approximation of a disoriented sand piper, and belting out songs in his best Ray Charles croak.

Cocker's debut album, 1969's *With A Little Help From My Friends*, represented more than just another rocker finding gold with Lennon and McCartney's songwriting skills. His soulful take on the Beatles tune scored his first Top 40 hit and put Joe Cocker on the pop music map. He followed it up quickly with a similar, sorta self-titled collection, *Joe Cocker!*, that featured a mix of covers of folks like Dylan, Leonard Cohen, and John Sebastian along with originals penned for the album by Leon Russell.

Because Cocker was a superb stylist, there was very little drop-off in his performances during the months separating his first and second albums. Backed by the Grease Band, a solid group of punters led by keyboardist Chris Stainton and including the six-string skills of guitarist Henry McCulloch, as well as melodious backing vocals by Merry Clayton, Rita Coolidge, and Bonnie Bramlett, Cocker blows through the songs here like a runaway freight train.

Several of the tunes featured on *Joe Cocker!* would become live standards for the singer in the years to follow. Russell's "Delta Lady" is probably the best-known here, a fine gossamer bit of British soul better known, perhaps, for its soaring chorus and backing harmonies than for Cocker's stellar vocal performance.

Cocker's take on John Sebastian's Lovin' Spoonful gem "Darling Be Home Soon" is pure magic, Cocker perfectly capturing the song's desire and emotion. A cover of New Orleans R&B legend Lloyd

Price's "Lawdy Miss Clawdy" is a real raver, even if Stainton does end up nicking pieces-and-parts of Alex Chilton's "The Letter" for his keyboard melody.

Beatles Paul McCartney and George Harrison, impressed with Cocker's previous take of "With A Little Help From My Friends," gave permission for the singer to use "She Came In Through The Bathroom Window" and "Something" for *Joe Cocker!* The former is an unabashed soul-rocker with McCulloch's imaginative, slightly-twangy fretwork, while the latter is a showcase for Cocker's interpretive skills, his high-flying vocals matched by delicious backing harmonies and Stainton's half-gospel/half-psychedelic keyboard flourishes; McCulloch also throws in a few choice notes just to lively things up.

Cocker would go on to find a greater measure of fame and notoriety in the wake of his 1970 Mad Dogs & Englishmen tour, which would yield both an acclaimed film and an album, and which would also help launch Leon Russell's solo career. By mid-decade, though, due to alcohol, Cocker had become a mere shadow of his former self. He would recover from this stumble and forge a satisfying and moderately successful career, but never again would he reach the Icarus-like heights that he did with *Joe Cocker!* (2009)

JOE GRUSHECKY
East Carson Street (Schoolhouse Records)

The 1970s gave rise to a sub-sub-genre of rock 'n' roll known as "Rust Belt" or "Heartland rock." Street-smart and lyrically savvy, the style welded the garage-rock and soul music of the previous decade with a harder edge to create a sort of "working class blues." Bruce Springsteen is, perhaps, the most critically-acclaimed and commercially successful troubadour of this poor boy's symphony, with Bob Seger, John Mellencamp, and others bringing up the rear guard.

Rust Belt rock has long since become passé…Bruce, bless his soul, is a multi-gajillionaire who, no matter how hard he tries, has lost his affinity with us po' folk. Seger has retired to a ranch somewhere on the outer fringes of the apocalyptic urban wasteland once known as Detroit, Johnny boy has sold his soul to the man, and other practitioners of this antique brand of rock have long since disappeared due to commercial indifference, or they discovered house music, or something…except for Pittsburgh's Joe Grushecky.

As far as Rust Belt rock goes, Grushecky is the last man standing, and as shown by his latest, *East Carson Street*, Joey G. ain't giving up an inch to history, either. His first album with long-time band the Houserockers since 2004, *East Carson Street* features Grushecky's typical lyrical acumen, his whip-smart story-songs accompanied by unbridled, guitar-driven music that isn't afraid to rawk when the situation calls for it.

Also as usual, the material on *East Carson Street* is semi-biographical and partially observational, and easily recognizable to anybody that has actually worked for a living. The homespun homilies of the album-opening "Chasing Shadows" ("slow down and enjoy it, life ain't a race," "don't waste your time chasing shadows") take on gargantuan importance when mixed with piercing guitars, crashing drumbeats, and Grushecky's wonderfully gravel-throated vocals.

The scorching fretwork opening "It's Too Late (Can't Turn Back Now)" lays the groundwork for the song's insightful, introspective lyrics, keyboards chiming urgently as guitars pile up notes like cars on the freeway.

The mid-tempo folk-rock of the title track does Johnny Mellencamp and his "Small Town" one better, Grushecky musing on the importance of friends and family, the price of fame too high a toll if it means giving up life on "East Carson Street." It's a lovely song, a great sentiment, and a quietly defiant statement against the myth that one has to discard the past if they want to find the future. Grushecky's old pal and songwriting partner Bruce Springsteen drops by for the anthemic rocker "Another Thin Line," the song featuring three? four? guitars ringing clearly between the shared vocals, the song itself another positivist plea for faith in an often cold world.

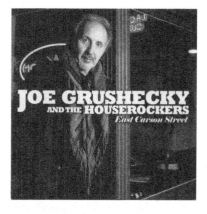

It's another collaboration on *East Carson Street*, however, that stands out, Grushecky and fellow Steel City songwriter Bill Deasy penning the excellent folk-rock dirge "Broken Wheel." With alternating vocals and menacing guitar strum, the song tells of a man at odds with himself, possibly on the run from the law, a man with no apparent way of surviving the ordeal. It's a haunting song with an old west feel and a rock 'n' roll vibe that puts all of those wussy indie-rock scribes to shame.

Grushecky's "The Sun Is Going To Shine Again" is a classic Rust Belt rocker in the vein of his earlier Iron City Houserockers band, a bright tale of love conquering the brutalities that life often brings…the job, the bills, all the petty little injustices that fade away when you have somebody to share them with you, beat 'em down, and render them meaningless. Joined by fellow rocker Willie Nile on vocals, the song is an encouraging reminder of the good things in life. "Down River" is an honest look at mortality by the veteran rocker, who has probably lost more friends by now than he cares to remember. The song's beautiful lyrics are sung with reverence by Grushecky against a gentle rolling soundtrack that creates an elegant emotional atmosphere.

Better than 30 years since the Iron City Houserockers hit the scene with their excellent debut album *Love's So Tough*, and nearly 40 since Grushecky first played with the Brick Alley Band, the man still rocks with an energy and commitment that boys half his age can't muster. While the addition of his 20-something-year-old son Johnny has certainly brought a youthful vigor to the Houserockers band, the truth is that Joe Grushecky has been following the siren's call of rock 'n' roll for most of his life, and he isn't about to give up now. *East*

Carson Street shows that, while Grushecky may not have found the fountain of youth, unlike almost all of his contemporaries, neither has he forgotten the sheer joy of making music. (2010)

JOHN CIPOLLINA/NICK GRAVENITES BAND
West Coast Legends Vol. 1   (SPV Recordings)

Guitarist John Cipollina is best known as a founding member of, and lead guitarist for Quicksilver Messenger Service, one of the leading bands of the late '60s San Francisco psychedelic-rock explosion that included the Jefferson Airplane and the Grateful Dead. Cipollina brought his imaginative guitar playing and flawless technique to a handful of QMS albums before leaving the band in 1970, foremost among them the 1969 psychedelic classic *Happy Trails*.

After splitting from Quicksilver, Cipollina would spend nearly 20 years trying to duplicate the modest success enjoyed by QMS, forming bands like John Cipollina's Raven and Copperhead, or hooking up with established outfits like Terry & the Pirates or British prog-rockers Man. Part of the reason for the talented Cipollina's relative obscurity is that while he could play guitar like nobody's business, he wasn't a singer or songwriter, and his onstage presence was entirely based around his instrument.

By contrast, singer, songwriter, and guitarist Nick Gravenites was a natural bandleader, a charismatic singer of some skill, an excellent songwriter (his "Born In Chicago," a hit for the Paul Butterfield Blues Band, would become a blues standard), and a fair-to-middlin' rhythm guitarist. The two men met when Gravenites produced Quicksilver's debut album, and they continued to collaborate musically almost until Cipollina's death in 1989. The chemistry that developed between Cipollina and Gravenites was magical, not unlike that of Ian Hunter and Mick Ronson, the sort of artistic collaboration that comes along only once in a blue moon.

Credited to the John Cipollina/Nick Gravenites Band, *West Coast Legends Vol. 1* is part of a series of CD and DVD releases on the German SPV label that document notable performances from the legendary German television program *Rockpalast* (translated as "Rock

Palace"). First aired in 1974 and continuing to this day, *Rockpalast* has broadcast performances from, literally, hundreds of rock, blues, jazz and other artists – from reggae legends like Bob Marley and Black Uhuru to prog-rockers like Camel and Spock's Beard, from jazz-fusion bands like Weather Report to rockers like Tom Petty and Them Crooked Vultures.

West Coast Legends Vol. 1 captures a lively November 1980 performance from the two guitarists, the Cipollina/Gravenites Band rounded out by bassist Al Staehely from Spirit, and drummer Marcus David of Clover. The four men knock out an inspired mix of psychedelic-tinged hard rock and Chicago blues-inspired blues-rock; the songs are mostly penned by Gravenites, but the six-string pyrotechnics are definitely provided by Cipollina.

West Coast Legends Vol. 1 kicks off with Gravenites' fond reminiscence of the Windy City, "Southside" a rollicking blues-infused number that exhibits a funky groove, a sassy attitude, and Gravenites' throaty vocals. While the band delivers a fluid rhythm, Cipollina carves out a little space for himself with a sharp-edged and bluesy solo. The outfit really finds its footing with the slick, slippery "Junkyard In Malibu" from Gravenites' 1980 album *Bluestar*. Gravenites' vocals are gruff and fairly fast-paced, but Cipollina's scorching leads couldn't have lit up the stage brighter if he'd been shooting tracer bullets from the barrel of an M-16 rifle.

"Signs of Life" is a Staehely original, a boogie-rocker sounding not unlike another Spirit alum's band, Jo Jo Gunne. With rollicking fretwork and a locomotive drumbeat, Staehely's vocals are unremarkable but the lyrics are OK, and Gravenites' spry rhythm guitar and Cipollina's serpentine lead breathes fire into the performance. Gravenites' "Small Walk-In Box," which would end up on his 1982 album *Monkey Medicine*, was already designed as a lengthy instrumental jam; here the song is extended a few minutes further with shards of clashing guitars, soaring solos, David's machinegun drum-and-cymbal work, and Staehely's jazzy bass riffs.

Cipollina revisits his Quicksilver Messenger Service past with his signature tune, a cover of folk singer Hamilton Camp's "Pride of Man." With Staehely providing fiery vocals and the rest of the band adding harmonies, the song's melody is constructed on Cipollina's taut guitar riffs. An explosive solo mimics the melody, and David's consistent drumbeats furnish a solid rhythmic foundation. Another Staehely original, "Hot Rods And Cool Women," is a greasy lil' slice o' Texas boogie, a mid-'70s throwback with sizzling fretwork, a nasty backbeat, and a bar-b-q grin.

Gravenites' "Buried Alive In The Blues" was scheduled to be recorded by Janis Joplin for her landmark *Pearl* album, her tragic death resulting in that album's instrumental rendition. Here the song is delivered at full-throttle by Gravenites, the band delivering a massive groove that is equal parts Southern twang and Southside Chicago blues. Cipollina's nimble guitarplay displays a different dimension to his talent, while Gravenites' soulful vocals are propelled by a hearty bass line and galloping drumbeats.

Bo Diddley's classic "Who Do You Love," which had received the full Quicksilver treatment back in '69, is revisited on *West Coast Legends Vol. 1* with a vengeance, the band kicking out the jams with an eleven-minute instrumental work-out. With Staehely and David re-creating the infamous Diddley beat, and Gravenites pounding out a heavy rhythm above hoarse vocals, Cipollina embroiders the song with his white-hot lead guitarwork. The unusual arrangement throws in plenty of light and dark, with guitars jabbing out of the silence, drumbeats working against the bass line, scraps of noisy feedback, and the odd sound recreating the uncertainty of an Avalon Ballroom acid trip circa '68.

John Cipollina never recorded a proper solo album throughout his lengthy, albeit tragically-shortened career, and it's unlikely that he could have created something as special as *West Coast Legends Vol. 1* if he *had* eventually ventured into the studio. The guitarist always felt more at home on stage anyway, and provided the canvas primed for him by Gravenites' excellent and open-ended songs, Cipollina delivers a stunning tour de force of sound and sonics. While Cipollina and Gravenites would collaborate together on a handful of wonderful and overlooked albums of psychedelic blues-rock, this live document is a near-perfect representation of both underrated artists' talents. (2011)

JOHNNY WINTER
Still Alive and Well   (Columbia Records)

When blues-rock guitarist Johnny Winter released his fifth studio album, *Still Alive and Well*, in early 1973 he'd been away from the decade's thriving and ever-changing music scene for nearly three years. During this time, Winter had been hospitalized for heroin addiction and had already run through two bands – his original blues-rock trio and the hard rock-oriented Johnny Winter And, with Rick Derringer and members of the McCoys. While the former band had experienced some chart success with Winter's self-titled debut album and its follow-up, *Second Winter*, the first Johnny Winter And album in 1970 barely charted, a relative failure partially redeemed by the band's moderately-successful 1971 live album.

Winter put together a kind of new band for *Still Alive and Well*, with guitarist Derringer and bassist Randy Jo Hobbs from Johnny Winter And, and drummer Richard Hughes, who would be part of Winter's bands for three or four years. With Derringer producing, and including guest musicians like Todd Rundgren and Mark "Moogie" Klingman (later of Rundgren's band Utopia), *Still Alive and Well* was a welcome comeback album from the talented guitarist, hitting #22 on the *Billboard* albums chart and featuring a number of songs that Winter would perform well into his lengthy career.

Still Alive and Well blows into town with a flurry of notes, Winter's scorching intro to the well-known B.B. King hit "Rock Me Baby" leaving nothing but flames and ash behind as the singer's roaring vocals are met by a percussive avalanche. Winter has always claimed that he wasn't much of a singer, and while his vox here won't be mistaken for King's smooth-as-silk croon, there's plenty of soul and fire riding atop the ripping guitar licks and fatback rhythms. Dan Hartman's "Can't You Feel It" is a similar barn-burner – dialed back a notch, perhaps, but evincing a Southern rock groove with a heart of pure blues. Songwriter and multi-instrumentalist Hartman was a member of Johnny's brother Edgar's band at the time, keeping it all in the family.

The first of two Rick Derringer-penned songs on *Still Alive and Well*, "Cheap Tequila" is a delightfully greasy ballad in a Rolling Stones vein, with imaginative lyrics and a country-blues vibe. The song benefits from Winter's appropriately heartsick vocals, a big joyful chorus, and light-fingered mandolin pickin' courtesy of Mr. Johnny which, intertwined with Derringer's electric guitar, makes for some truly mesmerizing instrumentation.

The first of Winter's two original songs here, "Rock & Roll," is a Texas-styled boogie-blues romp in the finest Z.Z. Top style, which means that it has plenty of electrifying slide-guitar work, stomp 'n' stammer percussion, and gruff vocals that barely rise above the livewire six-string rattle.

Mick Jagger and Keith Richards of the Stones wrote "Silver Train" specifically for Winter, and he did a heck of a lot more with the song than the Glimmer Twins ever would. Opening with a choogling locomotive rhythm, Derringer's slide-guitar, and "Moogie" Klingman's honky-tonk piano-pounding, Winter's vocals provide a curious cross between Jagger and Howlin' Wolf, at once both growling and twangy, driven to rise above the strident, busy instrumentation.

It's a raucous performance by the entire band, and not the last to infect these grooves. By contrast, "Ain't Nothing To Me" is a sleazy barroom ballad, a sordid tale of booze and violence that offers up Derringer's weepy pedal steel and Winter's wry country-western styled vocals. Why one of those bright-eyed MBAs with one of Nashville's Music Row labels hasn't had one of their white-bread artists cover this old-school honky-tonk treasure is a mystery to me.

The Derringer-penned cover song was tailor-made for the Texas blues-rock guitarist, its tale of triumph and defiance sung with all the heat and energy of a revved-up jet engine. Winter's playful, razor-sharp vocals are matched by Hughes' relentless drumbeats and crashing cymbals, his high-flying guitar solos swooping and soaring like an F-15 Eagle in battle. "Too Much Seconal" sits at the opposite end of the musical spectrum, the jazz-blues dirge not lacking in fervor but delivered in a much more laid-back manner. Winter's elegant slide-guitar and mandolin are met by Jeremy Steig's fluid flutework, the woodwind's notes dancing around the steel-stringed instrumentation and creating a fever dream-like effect.

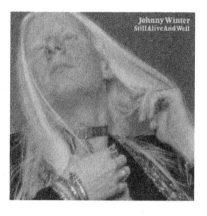

The original vinyl version of *Still Alive and Well* closed out with a cover of the Stones' "Let It Bleed," faithfully delivered by Winter and crew with a little less twang and a little heavier rock 'n' roll sound than the original. The 1994 CD reissue includes two bonus tracks – rowdy covers of Little Richard's "Lucille," which is pure juke-joint vamp with a funky, walking rhythm and scraped, trembling fretwork, and Dylan's "From A Buick Six," which amps up the Scribe's oblique lyrics with rattletrap instrumentation, a boogieing backbeat, and shards of rhythmic guitar. Both songs could have easily been included on the original LP, fitting in both stylistically and in the reckless energy of their performances.

Some 40+ years after its release, Johnny Winter's *Still Alive and Well* remains the guitarist's highest-charting, best-selling, and most critically-acclaimed work. Musically, the album runs the gamut of rock, blues, and what we'd today call alt-country, providing the listener with plenty of twangbangin' good fun while still managing to pacify the purists with a handful of traditionally-styled blues tunes. While Winter would go on to make albums equally as great (*Guitar Slinger, Third Degree*, and *I'm A Bluesman* all come to mind), he'd never again achieve the perfect blend of roots 'n' blues that he did with *Still Alive and Well*, an essential entry in the Johnny Winter canon. (2014)

KANSAS
Two For The Show   (Legacy Recordings)

At the time of its initial 1978 release, *Two For The Show* provided a
welcome breather for a band that had cranked out an amazing five
albums in the space of slightly more than three years. This
unparalleled burst of creative energy was matched by ascending
commercial fortunes, Kansas having achieved multi-Platinum™ sales
status with albums like 1976's *Leftoverture* and the following year's
enormously popular *Point of Know Return*. As the band rolled across
America in support of the latter album, they knew that it was time for
the obligatory live set, thus shows in Michigan, Maryland, and New
York City were recorded for posterity.

Released as a gatefold double-album with mock Norman Rockwell
cover, *Two For The Show* is, in many aspects, *the* quintessential '70s
decade live rock album. In a move that would be unheard of in this
ProTools era, all the songs here are presented entirely live, without
overdubs or enhancements of any sort.

While this means that some of the original album's thirteen extended
songs fall prey to lackluster performances, more often than not, the
recording captures the unique prog-rock flavor and instrumental
virtuosity that was (and is) Kansas. This 30th anniversary reissue of
Two For The Show has been expanded into a massive, two-disc, 24-
song woolly mammoth with ten additional, previously unreleased
songs, packaged in a deluxe gatefold cardboard digipak.

For a generation raised on video games, whose familiarity with
Kansas may be primarily through the "Rock Band" or "Guitar Hero"
game soundtracks, *Two For The Show* may be a real eye-opener. The
band's penchant for instrumental solos and lengthy jams pre-dates
'90s-era bands like Phish and their ilk, every song here sounding
curiously out-of-time in today's digital, three-minute, celebrity
soundtrack world.

Well-known Kansas tracks like "Point of Know Return," "Carry On
Wayward Son," and "Dust In The Wind" are accompanied by obscure-
yet-entertaining fare like the bluesy, hard rocking "Lonely Street," the

Keith-Emerson-meets-the-Phantom-of-the-Opera "Miracles Out of Nowhere," or the funky proto-metal booger-rock of "Sparks of The Tempest."

Live rock 'n' roll albums are considered hopelessly obsolete by the musical digerati these days, so it figures that double-gatefold-live relics like *Two For The Show* would smell a lot like a Naugahyde leisure suit to the eternally-cooler-than-thou crowd. Then again, with the next generation of teen-aged whizz kidz rediscovering the joys of vintage vinyl, searching for artists that actually know how to play their instruments, perhaps the unique Kansas blend of pop, prog, and hard rock isn't really as ancient as the hipsters would have you believe, eh?! (2008)

KING CRIMSON
In The Court of The Crimson King   (Discipline Global Mobile)

Whether you choose to blame King Crimson for creating progressive rock, or rejoice in the genre's pervasive instrumental virtuosity, there can be no argument that the band's landmark 1969 album *In the Court of the Crimson King* was the shot across the bow that began this whole "prog-rock" thing. Bandleader and guitarist Robert Fripp, aided and abetted by skilled musicians like bassist Greg Lake, multi-instrumentalist Ian McDonald, and drummer/percussionist Michael Giles – with lyrical assist from wordsmith Peter Sinfield – together took post-psychedelic rock to the brink of madness and back again with a trailblazing mix of avant-garde rock, free-form jazz, and heavy Baroque classicism.

As one of the cornerstones of '70s rock, and a major influence on everybody from lesser-known bands like Camel and Gentle Giant to world-beaters like Yes and Pink Floyd, *In the Court of the Crimson King* has been reissued ad nauseum, in various guises and quality, in the years since its fortunate inception. Since Crimson headmaster

Fripp oversaw the 30th anniversary re-release of the album ten years ago, why should you pony up a double-sawbuck for this shiny, *brand new* 40th anniversary re-re-release? Good question, grasshopper…cough up the cash 'cause the Reverend sez so!

First of all, for the first time in four decades, this is truly Fripp's baby to do with as he wishes, released through the artist's own Disciple Global Mobile (DGM) label. The mercurial guitarist could have chosen anybody to assist him in the re-mastering process, and he hand-picked Porcupine Tree/Blackfield mastermind Steven Wilson to work his own unique brand of magic on these songs.

Thus you have an ambitious two-disc set, one CD and one DVD, the first disc featuring a brand-spankin'-new 2009 stereo mix of the album's five songs, taken from the original multi-track master tapes. Throw in a couple of alternate tracks, and the full version of "Moonchild" (the original album featured an edited version), and Bob's yer uncle!

At the risk of sounding like a late-night commercial for slap-chop or some other such gadgetry, that's not all you get! Disc two, the DVD, is where Fripp and Wilson get their geek freak on, packing the disc with various audiophile versions of the album, from a larger-than-life-sounding MLP lossless 5.1 Surround version for those of you who really want to prog out on your home theatre sound-system to a pristine-sounding lossless PCM stereo version of the 2009 mix from the first disc, as well as an entirely alternate take of the album from the original masters.

If that wasn't enough, they slip in a video clip of the band performing "21st Century Schizoid Man" from their legendary July 5, 1969 debut concert in London's Hyde Park. The accompanying booklet includes a lot of photos, new liner notes from Fripp and writer Sid Smith, song lyrics, and enough info on the re-mastering process to engage even the most serious audiohound.

"Yeah, old timer, but what does the music sound like?" Like nothing you've ever heard before, kiddies! Benefitting from Fripp and Wilson's OCD-like attention to detail, the previously only-mildly-scary "21st Century Schizoid Man" leaps out of your speakers like a saber-yielding golem, going for your ears with a truly oppressive menace. The instruments sizzle and spark like a downed electric line, at times rattling around your skullplace like a nasty bit of shock therapy. The ethereal "Moonchild" features some of the most gorgeous and inventive instrumentation that you'll ever experience, with Lake's  wan vocals matched by the song's pastoral ambiance.

The Rev's personal fave, the title track, takes on a heretofore unknown majesty and grace, with the instrumental swells and exotic lyricism riding on a lush magic carpet of imagination. The bonus tracks are equally impressive, with the extended version of "Moonchild" taking a great song and stretching out the best parts of it while the "duo version" of "I Talk To The Wind" takes the song even deeper into the sort of folk-rock fairytale land that would be plumbed so successfully by Fairport Convention. "Wind Session," extracted from the session that created the fantastic intro for "21st Century Schizoid Man," is a cut-and-paste exercise mostly interesting to the hardcore faithful.

Overall, this 40th anniversary edition of *In The Court Of The Crimson King* trumps all other versions in the history of mankind, save for the original 1969 gatefold vinyl release that kick-started the entire prog-rock mess to begin with. Forty years later, the album stands alone in the rarified stratosphere reserved for true classics of rock music, and it still sounds as unique, daring, and challenging today as it did in 1969. (2009)

KING CRIMSON
Red　　　　　(Discipline Global Mobile)

In the five years between the release of *In The Court Of The Crimson King* and the band's seventh album, 1975's *Red*, King Crimson had easily undergone a half-dozen line-up changes, the only constant being frontman and founder Robert Fripp. At odds with Fripp's unique musical vision and perspective, band members would jump ship at the slightest provocation, leaving King Crimson as basically the power-trio of Fripp, bassist/vocalist John Wetton, and drummer Bill Bruford when it came time to record *Red*.

To his credit, Fripp managed to coax original band member Ian McDonald into the studio to lay down some red-hot alto sax alongside another former Crimsoner, soprano saxophonist Mel Collins. Fripp also recruited former members Robin Miller and Marc Charig to contribute oboe and cornet, respectively, and violinist David Cross, who had already bolted from the band, was represented by a previously-taped performance. It was this ramshackle King Crimson line-up that would haunt London's Olympic Sound Studios during the summer of 1974 to create *Red*, an album that would become the band's short-lived swansong.

By mid-1974, King Crimson's breakneck recording schedule and growing popularity as a live band had them perched in an odd position, just inches away from the commercial breakthrough that might have made them players in the same league as Pink Floyd and Yes.

However, physically beaten-down by a half-decade of touring, and brow-beaten by music business hijinx, Fripp found himself standing at an artistic and spiritual crossroads, and he unceremoniously announced to Wetton and Bruford that he would be withholding his opinion during the sessions for *Red*, a curious position for, perhaps, the band's guiding force to take.

Wetton and Bruford accepted the challenge, Fripp reduced to a lesser status in a band that he clearly saw on the ropes. The resulting album, fractured as it was by the sound of the band falling apart, is nothing short of a masterpiece and one of the most important and enduring works in the extensive King Crimson catalog.

Red kicks off with the barbed-wire tension of the instrumental title track. A tour de force of clashing instrumentation working at odd angles off one another, the semi-metallic "Red" was more intense and aggressive than anything Crimson had attempted previously, as if all the wounds of years in the rock 'n' roll trenches were all exposed at once.

From here, *Red* takes a decidedly different tact with a pair of shorter vocal tracks. The filigree instrumentation and wan vocals of "Fallen Angel" harkens back to the band's earlier folk-rock compositions, albeit with heavier ambience courtesy of an impressive Wetton/Bruford bass/drums dynamic and the injection of flailing, chaotic hornplay. In some ways, the dark-hued "One More Red Nightmare" foreshadows the band's later 1980s-era work with syncopated rhythms, wiry angular guitarplay, and more shadowy instrumental textures.

The fantasia-colored landscape of the live, improvised "Providence" is supported by David Cross's nightmarish violin and Fripp's monstrous fretwork, while the twelve-minute-plus "Starless," part of the band's live set for months, is codified here as an amalgam of the early and the future Crimson sound. Wetton's melancholy vocals are matched by the mournful horns of Collins and McDonald, while Fripp's guitar fills in the corners with subtle anguish.

The two-disc 40th Anniversary Series reissue of *Red* provides the definitive version of this influential album, with a handful of bonus tracks including a heavier-than-metal "trio version" of the title track that, stripped down to its guitar/bass/drums foundation, sounds even more menacing than the original leviathan. The DVD bonus disc includes a lossless 5.1 surround mix of *Red* produced by Porcupine Tree's Steven Wilson, as well as a lossless PCM stereo mix with an additional bonus track thrown in for good measure. The best part of the DVD, however, for those of us with pedestrian ears unable to pick up on Wilson's majestic remixes, is the inclusion of four video performances taken from a 1974 French TV appearance, including a spirited take on "Starless."

Although Fripp would announce shortly after the album's completion that King Crimson had "ceased to exist," *Red* would become an influential and important part of the band's canon nonetheless. A prog-rock album for people that didn't like progressive rock, the unyielding heaviness of *Red* is said to have inspired rockers as diverse as Black Flag's Henry Rollins, Nirvana's Kurt Cobain, and Tool's Maynard James Keenan, among others. After a brief solo career, and a pair of classic collaborations with Brian Eno, Fripp would later re-form King Crimson in 1980 with Bruford and guitarist Adrian Belew…but that's a story for another time. (2009)

LIVING COLOUR
The Chair In The Doorway   (Megaforce Records)

They say that you can't tell a book from its cover, but that's just a hoary old homily our grandparent's grandparents came up with to try and teach us something about rushing to judgment…or else it's an indictment of contemporary education, I'm not really sure which. But in our modern society, marketing has taught us that the cover *is* the book, or at least a reasonable facsimile of such, and we all know since childhood that the cookie portrayed on the front of the package has little to do with the vaguely chocolate-flavored crumbs that we'll pick out of the box and shove into our greedy little maws while sitting mindlessly in front of the TV set.

But I digress…honestly, you shouldn't judge the first album in five years from the reunited Living Colour from its amazingly ugly CD cover. Chosen from among thousands of entries by the band's fans across the globe, there's nothing about the cover artwork here that would lead one to believe that this is a slammin' new batch o' tunes from one of the most innovative and influential bands of the early 1990s.

Heck, there's nothing here that wouldn't be mistaken for some bad video game software, much less scream "rock 'n' roll!" at the top of its leather-plated lungs. 'Tis more the shame, too, 'cause *The Chair In The Doorway* is an album that deserves to be discovered by the hard rock/heavy metal hungry masses that have embraced the likes of Nickelback to get their cheap thrills.

Whether it was a change in musical trends, or the waning of their creative juices, Living Colour's brilliant late 1980s shooting stardom flamed out after the release of 1993's *Stain*, which was seen as somewhat of a letdown after the blinding white light/white heat of the band's 1988 debut, *Vivid* and its 1990 follow-up, *Time's Up*. The band went on hiatus for the better part of the decade, reuniting in 2000 and hitting the music biz treadmill again in '03 with the critically-acclaimed, commercially-ignored *CollideØscope*, and they have subsided mostly on live gigs and live albums in the years since.

Although *The Chair In The Doorway* may not reverse Living Colour's unfortunate commercial fortunes, the guys certainly have nothing to hang their collective heads in shame over, either. Carefully-crafted over the past half-decade, the album provides a nice balance of sly funk-metal and lyrical bombast, the band filling the grooves with plenty of creative rhythms and exciting fretwork.

Corey Glover's voice is a bit more ragged than it was 20 years ago, but he's still capable of both a soulful metallic croon and a roughneck howl. Bassist Muzz Skillings and drummer Will Calhoun comprise one of the best rhythm sections in contemporary music, period, with Skillings' basswork vibrating out of the mix while Calhoun's tub-thumping ranges from subtle, seductive brushwork to devastating blasts of furious energy. As for guitarist Vernon Reid, I've loved every note the guy has cranked out since I first saw him perform back in '87, and in my mind he's one of the most underrated, and madly imaginative guitarists of the past 20 years.

What can the longtime, never-say-die Living Colour fan expect from *The Chair In The Doorway*? Well, the more things change, the more they stay the same. The band continues to grow in subtle and sometimes strange ways – heck, the engaging "That's What You Taught Me" could easily pass for a mainstream hard rock tune with Reid's conventional soloing, Glover's passionate vox, and a radio-ready rhythmic backdrop.

But the adventurous "Burned Bridges" throws a few more studio tricks into the mix, with oscillating fretwork and subdued-but-powerful vocals underpinned by a driving backbeat.

"The Chair" is the album's monster track, with a dangerous slamdance groove met headfirst with spacey, reckless, anarchic guitarwork and fierce vocals. The obligatory throwback tune here may be "DecaDance," the song invoking memories of *Time's Up* era jams with its Godzilla-sized rhythm and barbed wire solos, but "Heads Up" could be a *Vivid* outtake, with plodding dino-stomp rhythms and plenty of socially-conscious moxie mucking up the grooves.

Time and trends may have passed Living Colour by, but that doesn't mean that the band can't still create vital, exciting, balls-to-the-wall hard rock 'n' roll as they have with *The Chair In The Doorway*. Although they don't sound nearly as innovative as they did in 1988, they're certainly more musically subversive. Forget about the cover, it's what's inside that counts…and in this case, there's plenty for everybody to enjoy. (2009)

LOVE
Forever Changes   (Rhino Records)

One of the most beloved and enduring albums in the canon of rock music, Love's *Forever Changes* was initially released in 1967 to yawns and commercial indifference. The third and final album released by the Los Angeles band's original line-up, *Forever Changes* barely slipped into the *Billboard* Top 200 albums before sinking back out of sight…until it was rediscovered by eager rock fans during the alt-rock daze of the '90s.

Love was formed by the brilliant singer/songwriter Arthur Lee in 1965, Lee's artistic vision often supported and complimented by underrated guitarist Bryan MacLean. In any other band, MacLean would have been the primary talent, but in Love he often toiled beneath the long shadow of Lee's genius. After leaving the band in 1968 in the wake of *Forever Changes'* release, MacLean would tinker away at songs and solo material before leaving the music biz altogether. The rest of the band provided an incredible cohesion and chemistry to Lee and MacLean's original material.

Love's first couple of albums – 1966's self-titled debut, and the following year's *Da Capo* – featured a guitar-driven, folk-rock sound with waves of psychedelic candy-coloring and washes of electric-blues and jazzy flourishes. Neither album particularly lit the world on fire, but both were strong artistic statements.

Originally, the label wanted session players to back Lee and MacLean, respectively, on their songs, due to the band's growing personal problems and drug use; indeed, two tracks on *Forever Changes* were recorded with studio pros. When all the members of Love finally got together to make the album, nobody could have imagined what would come out of the sessions.

A grand collection of baroque-pop with elements of psychedelic-rock, folk, and R&B with uncharacteristic horns and strings, *Forever Changes* is a masterpiece of musical composition and lyrical brilliance. The songs crafted by Lee and MacLean were years ahead of their time, deep tapestries of sound with lush threading of various colors.

The Spanish flamenco flavor of MacLean's enchanting "Alone Again Or" stands in direct contrast to the trebly guitarwork of the psych-rock naildriver "A House Is Not A Hotel." The gentle hippie soundscape of "Andmoreagain" is supported by a lilting melody and gossamer orchestral flourishes while the overtly cynical "Bummer In The Summer" is an old-fashioned garage-rock freak-out.

Lyrically, *Forever Changes* provides a signpost of storm clouds on the horizon. Largely written and recorded during the "Summer of Love," the album's poetry frequently portrays a society undergoing change. Portending a long, dark night ahead, songs like "The Red Telephone" and the surrealistic, anti-war "Live And Let Live" deliver a forceful, sometimes frenzied message despite their lush backing soundtrack. Lee had stated in interviews that he literally felt that his life was coming to an end at this time, and his sub-conscious reflections on race and society have taken on a timeless quality.

So, what's the difference between this *Forever Changes* "Collector's Edition" and the last time around, when Rhino reissued the album in 2001? Well, to begin with, this one is a whopping two-disc set, the first presenting the original album in all of its pristine glory. The second disc offers an "alternative mix" of the album, eleven songs, only one of which was included on the 2001 CD. To these ears, the "alternative mix" of the album sounds inferior, lacking the same texture and depth of the originally released recordings.

Another ten "bonus tracks" replicate those on the last reissue, adding previously unreleased versions of "Andmoreagain" (instrumental backing track) and "The Red Telephone" (tracking sessions highlights), neither of which are essential, or even add much to the experience save for the hardcore believer.

The lively, rocking obscure B-side "Laughing Stock" is a welcome addition, while a boisterous, unreleased cover of "Wooly Bully" is a bona-fide album outtake, and a heck of a lot of fun. A mono single remix of "Alone Again Or," with dynamic sound and warmth, makes a strong case for taking rock back to its (mono) roots. Informative new liner notes from Andrew Sandoval are complimented by a handful of photos.

Should you spring for the "Collector's Edition" of *Forever Changes*? If you're a fan of the band, you probably already have. If you're unfamiliar with Love, mildly curious, or haven't heard this landmark work, you should give it a listen. After all, hundreds of rock critics couldn't be wrong when they voted *Forever Changes* as one of the best albums of all time, could they? (2008)

MERL SAUNDERS & JERRY GARCIA
Well-Matched – The Best of Merl Saunders & Jerry Garcia
(Fantasy Records)

Lost amidst the mythos that continues to build around the Grateful Dead is a simple, undeniable fact – Jerry Garcia was a hell of a guitarist. Prone towards leading the Dead into extended onstage instrumental free-for-alls that would often redefine the sound of the song being played, Garcia is best remembered as the grandfather of the mid-'90s "jam band" movement. However, Garcia was also a curious and intelligent guitarist, with an insatiable thirst for knowledge and the ability to assimilate and master any musical style thrown his way, from rock and blues to bluegrass and jazz.

Nowhere are Garcia's talents as a musician and his drive to play on greater display than with *Well-Matched – The Best Of Merl Saunders & Jerry Garcia*. When not on the road with his day job – pushing the Grateful Dead towards rock mythology with constant touring and live performances so damn enchanting that fans still talk about them today – for several years, Garcia would climb onstage with a smoking club band led by jazz pianist Merl Saunders. Saunders was a veteran of the West Coast jazz and blues circuit, playing with cats like Lionel Hampton, Miles Davis, and Taj Mahal. Now you would think that after playing for months at a time on the road with the Dead that Jerry would want to kick back at home and forget the guitar for a while. But Garcia seemed to cherish working in a live environment with challenging musicians, and thus a friendship was forged with the equally talented Saunders.

Well-Matched draws its performances from the lone live album that the unnamed Saunders/Garcia band released along with a number of Saunders' studio albums, where he and Garcia and a hand-picked coterie of musicians would recreate the chemistry of those live jams. Constant throughout these sessions were little-known but talented bassist John Kahn and drummer Bill Vitt, along with folks like David Grisman, Vassar Clements, Tom Fogerty, and even the Tower of Power horns. Make no mistake, though, 'cause this is definitely the Merl and Jerry show, the two powerful musicians riffing off one another, creating an exciting fusion of jazz, blues, rock, and R&B that is breath-taking in its ambition and amazing in its execution.

Saunders, Garcia and pals were playing for the fun of it, and it shows in the loose, energetic performances provided tunes like the Doc Pomus chestnut "Lonely Avenue" or on their imaginative reading of Dylan's "Positively 4th Street." The Saunders' original, "Merl's Tune," is an impressive instrumental work-out that showcases the player's abilities while the Motown classic "I Second That Emotion" enjoys a loping groove and Garcia's lofty vocals.

A fine rendition of J.J. Cale's "After Midnight" with guitarist Tom Fogerty of CCR is matched by an inspired, soulful cover of Jimmy Cliff's reggae classic "The Harder They Come." *Well-Matched – The Best Of Merl Saunders & Jerry Garcia* shows the skills of both of these wonderful musicians in a different light, and should be a "must have" disc for any Grateful Dead fan, if only so they can fully appreciate Jerry Garcia's range and incredible diversity. (2007)

MITCH RYDER
Detroit Ain't Dead Yet (The Promise)   (Freeworld)

Back in the fall of 1980, when Detroit rocker Bob Seger was riding high on the charts and packin' 'em into the stadiums with his *Against The Wind* album, he sold out every show during an unheard-of nine-night stand in the Motor City. For these triumphant homecoming shows, Seger hand-picked Detroit rock 'n' soul legend Mitch Ryder as his opener, a gracious act that jump-started Ryder's second shot at the brass ring.

Born William Levise, Jr. in Hamtramck, a city within the city limits of Detroit, Ryder got his start singing as a teen with a local soul band named the Peps before forming his own Billy Lee and the Rivieras. Discovered in 1965 by producer Bob Crewe, the band was re-named Mitch Ryder and the Detroit Wheels, and they would go on to score a string of early hits like "Jenny Take A Ride," "C.C. Rider," and "Devil with a Blue Dress On." When the hits dried up, Ryder made the sojourn to Memphis to record the amazing *The Detroit/Memphis Experiment* with Booker T and the MG's in 1969.

Returning home, Ryder put together the ground-breaking rock outfit Detroit, which released a single 1971 album that yielded a hit with an energetic cover of Lou Reed's "Rock and Roll." By 1973, though, Ryder was experiencing problems with his voice, and he retired from music.

He still had the itch, however, and his self-produced 1978 comeback album *How I Spent My Vacation* led to the aforementioned gigs opening for Seger; more indie releases; a major label deal and a John Mellencamp-produced, critically-acclaimed album that went nowhere fast. Although Ryder's overshadowing influence could be heard in '80s-era hits from folks like Seger, Mellencamp, and Springsteen, the man couldn't get arrested with his own work.

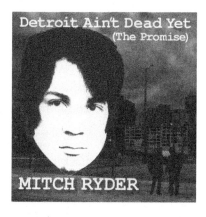

Flash forward almost 30 years and, much like the gardens that are starting to crop up in the abandoned lots around the urban wasteland formerly known as Detroit, Mitch Ryder is still punching away at success. He never really went anywhere you know…Ryder remained somewhat of a star in Europe, and he has continued to record and release albums to the present day. In the closing days of 2009, he teamed with producer Don Was – another Motor City talent – to record *Detroit Ain't Dead Yet (The Promise)* in L.A. with a top notch batch of musicians. Working with a set of largely original songs, Ryder has delivered a spirited performance that equals his mid-'80s creative peak.

Ryder's calling card has always been his uncanny ability to blend blues, soul, and rock 'n' roll into a single artistic entity, and it's no different on *Detroit Ain't Dead Yet (The Promise)*. Ryder's whiskey-soaked vocals still ooze with blue-eyed soul better than anybody ever has; nowhere is this more evident than on the album-opening track, the semi-autobiographical "Back Then." Ryder's vox slip-n-slide across a funky soundtrack with characteristic swagger, growling when necessary and hitting the high notes when appropriate as the band lays down a vicious groove.

And so it goes…the Southern-fried soul of "My Heart Belongs To Me" benefits from some Steve Cropper-styled geetar pickin', a lively rhythmic backdrop, and Ryder's passionate vocals. The intelligent, sometimes shocking "Junkie Love" is a frank discussion of addiction that benefits from 1970s-styled rolling funk-n-soul instrumentation, lively vocals, and Randy Jacobs' squealing fretwork. A beautiful cover of the great Jimmy Ruffin soul gem "What Becomes Of The Broken Hearted" was recorded live and showcases Ryder's emotion-tugging vocal abilities while "The Way We Were" is a haunting, topical tale of society's decline that rocks as hard as it rolls.

Detroit Ain't Dead Yet (The Promise) isn't an exploitative cash-grab taking advantage of some over-the-hill, broken-and-broke-ass rocker. No, this is the one-and-only Mitch Ryder, still kicking ass and taking names at age 65, delivering a monster set of songs that combine the artist's 1960s rock 'n' soul roots with his edgy 1980s solo work. With a sympathetic producer in Don Was, who worked with Ryder in the 1990s with his own Motor City band Was (Not Was), Ryder is able to make a late-career statement that stands tall alongside anything he's ever done. Detroit ain't dead yet, and neither is Mitch Ryder... (2010)

NEAL MORSE
? Live   (Radiant Records/Metal Blade)

When Neal Morse left Spock's Beard, the band he had formed 20 years earlier with his brother Alan, after the 2002 release of the album *Snow*, prog-rock fans wondered what the popular musician was going to do next. Morse had become a born again Christian and, in a 2003 interview with this writer, he was clearly conflicted not only as to what his next move would be, but he also showed doubt about where his faith would take him.

It's an old adage, to be sure, but the Lord *does* help those that help themselves, and Morse and Spock's Beard have both done well since parting company. For Morse, he found refuge in his music, bringing the same enormous talent, creativity, and intellect to his newfound musical direction as he did when writing and performing with Spock's Beard. Since the split, Morse has continued his participation in the prog-rock supergroup Transatlantic with Dream Theatre's Mike Portnoy, Pete Trewavas of Marillion, and the Flower Kings' Roine Stolt, releasing two live albums culled from American and European performances.

More importantly, however, Morse has recorded four solo albums in as many years, developing his voice as a Christian rock artist, expanding his musical palette beyond traditional prog-rock to incorporate elements of folk, jazz, and classical music in a soundtrack to his lyrically intricate compositions. *Testimony*, from 2003, was Morse's first album after leaving the band, and it deals with his pre-and-post-Christian life from a unique perspective. The following year's *One* was a self-assured concept album, while the provocatively-named *?* ("question mark") matches Morse's journey of self-discovery with his most fascinating music to date. The

controversial *Sola Scriptura*, from early in 2007, tackles difficult lyrical material (Martin Luther and the reformation), featuring an ambitious musical signature.

Fans have long clamored for a live album from Morse that features his solo material, and the artist has responded with the electric, invigorating *? Live*. Recorded in Berlin in July 2006, the first disc of this two-CD set recreates the *?* album in its entirety. Backed by a talented group of European musicians (instead of the prog superstars that typically populate his albums), Morse puts them all through their paces with a spirited and spiritual performance.

"The Temple of the Living God" opens with swelling piano and haunting guitar before spiraling into a multi-layered, cacophonic blend of manic keyboard fills, urgent guitar lines and grand themes. "The Outsider" is a succinct interlude with sparse instrumentation and elegant beauty while "Into The Fire" displays the fervor of a tent revival with scorching guitar and keyboards. "Solid As The Sun" has a jazzy, almost New Orleans-styled Professor Longhair feel to its undercurrent, with metallic guitar riffs scraping across the vocals.

The second disc of *? Live* features tracks from Morse's album *One* – nearly three-quarters of the album, actually – and includes the first tentative onstage performance of Morse's son Wil on the moody "The Man's Gone." The lengthy "The Creation" is a veritable symphony, Morse's passionate vocals backed by lush instrumentation and interesting melodic flights of fancy. Though some may beg to differ, the song is symbolic of what is good and entertaining about progressive rock, crossing stylistic borders with rapidly-changing timing, contagious rhythms, keyboard wizardry, tastefully fluid guitar leads, and powerful performances all around.

? Live closes with an eighteen-minute encore medley of material, including Transatlantic's wonderful, folkish "We All Need Some Light" along with "Open Wide The Flood Gates," "Solitary Soul" and "Wind At My Back" from the underrated Spock's Beard album *Snow*. In many ways, the clues were there on *Snow*, signaling Morse's fascination with messianic themes and subsequent approach to his solo work. Taken as a whole, *? Live* provides an entertaining and eye-opening 77-minutes of quality listening, where the strength of the music may well be overshadowed by the power of the message.

Prog-rock fans who have shied away from Neal Morse's solo work in fear of his Christian leanings should reconsider. Much as he did with Spock's Beard, Morse is creating vital, imaginative and important music, using his talents to stretch the conservative barriers of both progressive rock and Contemporary Christian music.

Morse may not have found the CCM success and acceptance that he desires – yet – but there's no doubt in this humble scribe's mind that, at some point in the future, as long as Morse continues to create challenging, magnificent music as he has on *? Live* and his post-conversion solo albums, his influence on Christian music and thought will be profound. And, his stuff rocks! (2008)

NEAL MORSE
Lifeline   (Radiant Records)

As the founder of neo-prog legends Spock's Beard, Neal Morse carried the torch of '70s-styled progressive rock throughout the '80s and '90s. In the face of the ever-changing currents of punk, hair metal, grunge, alt-rock and, finally…ugh…boy bands and pop divas…Morse led his merry pranksters through a series of albums, both conceptual and otherwise, that championed songwriting, instrumental virtuosity, and erudite literary sense over the loutishness of power chords and the glitter of pop-cult celebrity.

When he left Spock's Beard to sojourn out on his own after becoming a born again Christian, Morse had a personal crisis of faith that resulted in brilliant recordings like *Testimony* and *One*, the artist lyrically exploring his newfound faith in a decidedly prog-oriented musical landscape.

With *Lifeline*, Morse's ninth solo effort and his fifth original studio album since breaking with his former band, Morse has attempted to craft a collection of songs that matches the extended instrumental compositions of Spock's Beard with his personal fondness for Beatlesque pop and his life-affirming, contemporary Christian lyricism.

It's a shaky tightrope that Morse is attempting to balance on here, but *Lifeline* manages to deliver without the need for a safety net. With the help of his long-time pals, bassist Randy George and Dream Theatre drummer Mike Portnoy, Morse mixes his still-fervent faith with brilliant songcraft and skilled instrumentation. *Lifeline* is, perhaps, the most overtly autobiographical of Morse's work, quite a feat considering his penchant for confessional lyrics, but it's also a document of his lifelong journey from the dark to the light.

Throughout it all, Morse never comes across as "holier than thou," instead sounding joyous and thankful to be making music on his own terms. Words aside, *Lifeline* is Morse's most animated collection, musically ranging from the almost-metallic "Leviathan," a humorous sea-serpent tale with screaming guitar and funky blasts of horn, to the lushly-orchestrated "Fly High." The folk-rock of "The Way Home" mixes soaring harmonies with decidedly late 1960s Brit-folk acoustic guitarplay to create a modern version of Genesis or the Strawbs.

The cornerstone of *Lifeline*, however, is the twenty-eight-minute-plus masterpiece "So Many Roads." An epic song-suite that displays many shades of fanciful coloration, the backing soundtrack zig-zags from classically-styled keyboard romps and swelling choruses of grandeur towards folkish lyrics and full-bore rock jams, Morse masterfully taking the best elements of Yes, the Beatles, Pink Floyd and, yes, Spock's Beard, and imbuing them all with his own unique musical vision.

As prog-rock continues to grow in popularity with audiences searching for something other than label-manufactured rock bands and cookie-cutter singer/songwriters, Neal Morse stands at the forefront of the movement as a true believer and a trailblazer. When he first brought Christian themes to progressive rock, there was no little uncertainty as to how prog fans in the U.S., Europe and Asia would accept Morse's good intentions. Better than half-a-decade later, Morse is flying higher than ever, creating music that incorporates the best of both prog-rock and CCR, reaching fans in both camps in the process. (2008)

NILS LOFGREN
Old School   (Vision Music)

At this point in a career that has now spanned five decades, singer, songwriter, and guitarist Nils Lofgren is better known as the trampoline-jumping, comically-large-hat-wearing, guitar-wielding member of Bruce Springsteen's band than he is for the string of critically-acclaimed solo albums that he released, pre-E Street, between 1975 and '85.

His status as a buddy of the Boss notwithstanding, the fact is that Lofgren has the sort of rockin' credentials that younger musicians would sell their souls to Old Scratch to put on a resume. A musical prodigy who studied jazz and classical music as a child, Lofgren picked up a guitar at age 15 and dedicated his life to rock 'n' roll, forming the acclaimed D.C. area band Grin at age 18. Grin's popular live shows brought the guitarist to the attention of Neil Young, who brought Lofgren in to play on his classic *After The Gold Rush* album.

Grin recorded three acclaimed albums circa 1971/72 but scored only a single minor hit with the Lofgren song "White Lies." In the wake of that band's break-up, Lofgren toured with Young and contributed to the singer's *Tonight's The Night* album. Lofgren launched his solo career with the 1975 release of his self-titled debut, an album notable for original songs like "Be Good Tonight," "Back It Up," and "Keith Don't Go," a musical plea to Rolling Stones guitarist Keith Richards. The following year's *Cry Tough* won equal critical acclaim as the debut and experienced similar modest sales, but subsequent releases like 1977's *I Came To Dance*, 1979's *Nils*, and 1983's *Wonderland* would result in declining commercial fortunes, and in 1985 Lofgren accepted Springsteen's offer to join the E Street Band.

In between Springsteen tours, Lofgren toured with Mrs. Springsteen, Patti Scialfa; as part of Ringo Starr's All-Star Band; and again with Neil Young. During his lengthy tenure playing behind the Boss, Lofgren largely put his solo career on the back burner, but he still managed to release a handful of albums during the 1990s and 2000s, studio efforts complimented by various compilations and live material from the archives. Lofgren's last album was 2006's *Sacred Weapon*, and now five years later the rock 'n' roll lifer returns with his 15th studio album, *Old School*.

Much like fellow Bruce-buddy Joe Grushecky, Lofgren is a grizzled veteran of life in the rock 'n' roll trenches, an elder statesman with a snowball's chance in hell of scoring that ever-elusive, career-making hit. Also like Joey G., however, Lofgren's role as cult favorite frees the artist from undue commercial expectations, resulting in as honest and sincere a work as one can expect in these jaded early years of the new millennium. *Old School* is exactly that, a collection of largely original material that doesn't stray far from Lofgren's signature sound and breaks little new ground, but rather wraps the listener in a familiar blanket of classic, guitar-driven rock.

The title track opens *Old School*, the song's funky groove and hot git licks barely concealing the singer's lyrical laments about these darned kids today, Congressional critters, reality TV, and dysfunctional families. While Lofgren sounds like an old man screaming "get off my lawn" at anybody walking down the street, the performance sizzles with a fat rhythmic groove, timely blasts of horns, and a slight vocal contribution from Foreigner's Lou Gramm. The following "60 Is The New 18" fares slightly better. A mid-tempo rocker with a tempered perspective, Lofgren is self-effacing at times, concerned at others, as he faces coming out the other side of middle age with an edgy, rocking, jumpy new wavish sound that hits the ears like it's 1981 all over again.

Lofgren finds his usual introspective groove by the time the lovely, acoustic "Miss You Ray" rolls around. A heartfelt tribute to R&B legend Ray Charles, the song is really much more: a fond reminiscence of life and family, delivered in a gentle, quivering voice and accompanied by Lofgren's elegant fretwork. The charming "Love Stumbles On" veers the closest to Lofgren's beloved mid-'70s solo work, evoking a sort of musical and lyrical cross between Grin, Grushecky's Iron City Houserockers, and Springsteen's early albums. While the lyrics are Dylan oblique, there's no mistaking Lofgren's beautiful, plaintive vocals and bittersweet guitarplay.

One of the highlights of *Old School* is Lofgren's take on musician and songwriter Bruce McCabe's hauntingly beautiful "Irish Angel." A romantic ballad of heartbreak delivered with a slight Celtic lilt, Lofgren's gruff, forlorn vocals are matched by his delicate piano and Spanish-tinged fretwork. Another master stroke is provided by the muscled, hard-edged soul-rock romp "Ain't Too Many Of Us Left," Lofgren joined on vocals by Stax Records great Sam Moore. An autobiographical tale that tries to make some sort of sense of aging in a rapidly-changing world, Moore's soulful backing vox add a wonderful gravitas behind Lofgren's fierce guitar riffs.

Old School closes with the mid-tempo "Why Me," another nod to Lofgren's 1970s work, with maybe a dash of 1980s-era Springsteen thrown in on the lyrical phrasing for good measure. The song asks more questions, perhaps, than it answers, the protagonist staring down his mortality with an almost fatalistic acceptance, humble yet defiant. Lofgren's guitar screams and howls angrily in the background, lending a sort of Dylan Thomas, "do not go gentle into that good night" spirit to the song, the artist delivering one of the strongest, emotionally-charged performances of his lengthy career.

While Lofgren's *Old School* won't set the charts on fire, it offers plenty to chew on for the guitarist's long-time fans while providing enough contemporary style and grace to attract some new followers. Lofgren's voice has dropped somewhat from his high-pitched teens and 20s, weathered into a more soulful instrument, and his guitar playing has never been better, displaying great elegance and grace. An artist definitely ripe for rediscovery, *Old School* is a vital, engaging work by a rock 'n' roll veteran. (2012)

NIRVANA '69
Cult   (Global Recording Artists)

Way back, in the pre-grunge mists of Merry Ole England, there was a band called Nirvana. No, not *that* Nirvana – years before Kurt Cobain was born, and while he was still in diapers, this British outfit was wowing critics with a unique musical vision that mixed folk-influenced rock 'n' roll with elements of psychedelic pop, jazz, classical, and even baroque chamber music. Comprised of Irish musician Patrick Campbell-Lyons and Greek composer Alex Spyropoulos, Nirvana turned quite a few heads, wowed a handful of British music critics, and sold a bucketload of records – literally, however many records could fit into a large-sized bucket. Yeah, that few…

The buzz around Campbell-Lyons and Spyropoulos caused Island Records founder Chris Blackwell to sign the pair, and with a bevy of professional studio musicians and a small orchestra, Nirvana recorded 1967's *The Story of Simon Simopath*, which is widely considered to be the first bona fide "concept album," the odd couple beating such world-renown acts as the Who, the Kinks, and the Pretty Things to the punch. Although the band's music was exceptionally difficult to perform live, Campbell-Lyons and Spyropoulos pieced together a touring band nonetheless, opening for bands like Traffic and Spooky Tooth, resulting in a subsequent minor U.K. hit single in "Rainbow Chaser."

Campbell-Lyons and Spyropoulos would record two more albums together, 1968's *All of Us*, which was similar in sound and scope to their debut, and *Black Flower*, an allegedly difficult recording which Blackwell refused to release. That problematic third Nirvana album finally saw limited release in 1970, but by 1971 the pairing had run its course, with Campbell-Lyons and Spyropoulos splitting amicably. Campbell-Lyons would release two more albums under the Nirvana name before launching a solo career that fizzled out in the mid-'80s, when he reunited with Spyropoulos and re-launched Nirvana, the pair making new music well into the 1990s.

Imagine young Master Cobain's surprise when Campbell-Lyons and Spyropoulos filed a lawsuit against him and Geffen Records in 1992 for the appropriation of their band's name. A rumored large cash pay-off allowed Cobain's crew to continue using the Nirvana name, while Campbell-Lyons and Spyropoulos kept on trucking, virtually unknown in the United States, but evidently keeping a sense of humor about the whole affair, even recording a version of Cobain's "Lithium" at one point.

By the time of the Seattle Nirvana's commercial ascent to the peaks of stardom, the British Nirvana's first two original albums had become a sort of Holy Grail of 1960s psych-rock collectors, fetching handsome prices on eBay and elsewhere, leading to a rash of CD reissues, some legitimate and some questionable, that only spread the band's myth even further.

Since many of these CD reissues of Nirvana's *The Story of Simon Simopath* and *All of Us* were import discs, the band still remains a bit of an obscurity here in the U.S., notable mostly to the sort of hardcore collector type that will spend hours digging through crates to find that one album by Gandalf, the Millennium, the Left Banke, or Kaleidoscope to add to their teetering stacks o' wax. Credited to Nirvana '69, the newly-released *Cult* (Global Recording Artists) is a long-overdue CD compilation of early material from the British Nirvana, offered on these shores for what may be the first time.

Enquiring minds want to know, does this 1960s-era Nirvana live up to the hype spread around by the collectors' community for the past three decades? Well, the short answer is, yes and no. Only the simple-minded and/or clueless would really believe that Nirvana '69 sounds *anything* like Cobain's world-beating trio, so those of you expecting some sort of earth-shaking, proto-grunge cheap thrills can dash off to Pitchfork and see what new band you're supposed to download this week. As for the rest of you, throw out any preconceived ideas you may have about psych-pop, British folk-rock, or any of that because, the truth is, Nirvana sounds both like nothing you've ever heard before and, curiously, like a lot of what you already love. If you're a fan of such 1960s-era fellow travelers as the Zombies, Love, or the Left Banke, you'll probably dig *Cult* nearly as much as any album by those folks.

To say that Campbell-Lyons and Spyropoulos had a grandiose musical vision is to put it mildly, and as shown by the nearly two-dozen tracks collected on *Cult*, the only limitations on the pair's immense musical ambition seemed to be the restrictions of the studio itself. *Cult* includes seven of the ten tracks from *The Story of Simon Simopath* and nine of twelve from *All of Us* (the album's actual title is too long for even me to recount here), as well as a handful of single B-sides, and even a new song in "Our Love Is The Sea." While the bulk of *Cult* is pleasant enough psychedelic pop – a mind-bending musical garden that the Reverend only walks through a couple times a year – there are rare flashes of brilliance here that certainly justify the band's legend.

Island Records definitely missed the boat by only issuing a pair of singles from the first Nirvana album, as I count four red-hot slabs from *The Story of Simon Simopath* that had a puncher's chance to hit the U.K. charts hard circa 1967. In an era where singles were the currency of commercial pop music, it was almost malpractice to throw only one single into the marketplace.

The band's album-opening "Wings of Love" is a wistful little romantic number chock-full of poetic imagery, sweeping orchestration, a lovely melody, and odd little instrumental rumblings here and there which raise it about your normal "Summer of Love" fare. "Lonely Boy" would have made another rad single, the melancholy vocals clad in baroque-pop trappings with a dash of background harmonies, and an overall whimsical vibe.

"Satellite Jockey" is simply brilliant, reminding of both the Kinks and the Move, but pre-dating the Electric Light Orchestra with a complex pop melody welded to a classical construct. The album's actual single, "Pentacost Hotel," is a charming, elfish song with the sort of soft/loud dynamic that Cobain would later use to sell millions of records. *This Nirvana* slaps cascading instrumentation and orchestral finery onto a psych-pop framework with great results. The band's only charting single, 1968's "Rainbow Chaser," would later be included on their sophomore album, and while it shows slight artistic growth over the aforementioned material from their debut, it doesn't stray far from the classical-pop hybrid blueprint they used on that album. With swirls of orchestral instrumentation, the melody here is somewhat more syncopated, with wan vocals lost amidst the washes of violin and cacophonic percussion.

Curiously enough, "Tiny Goddess" was actually the band's first single, but wasn't included on the first album. I'm not sure why, because the song's ethereal arrangement, thundering percussion, flowery lyrics and vocals, and dazzling instrumentation fit like a glove with that album. Perhaps with a stronger melody "Tiny Goddess" might have delivered the band's first hit.

There are a couple of other high points from *All of Us* included on *Cult*, including the up-tempo "Girl In The Park," a spry pastiche of late 1960s pop/rock and sunshine pop that hides its symphonic foundation beneath lively vocals and a strong melodic hook. "The St. Johns Wood Affair" is a catchy little number that blends jazzy flourishes with an unusual arrangement, sparse instrumentation, and a few surprising musical twists and turns before it's all over.

Of the B-sides, etc to be found on *Cult*, they don't detour much from the material from the main albums, although both "Life Ain't Easy" and "Darling Darlane" both stand out, the former a hauntingly beautiful ballad with a lush orchestral background and melancholy vocals, the latter a mid-tempo romantic pop song that melds scraps of 1950s-era rock (think Gene Pitney) with a 1960s psychedelic sensibility (more like the Bee Gees than the Beatles).

As for the "bonus tracks" included on *Cult*, "Requiem for John Coltrane" is an unexpected outlier, mixing lonesome jazzy hornplay with odd noises and overall sonic chaos unlike anything the band had previously recorded. "Our Love Is The Sea" presents the 2012 version of Nirvana; benefiting from modern production and improved studio tools, the song builds upon the band's 1960s legacy to deliver a fantastic bit of musical whimsy.

The British Nirvana never found the fame and fortune that their later stateside namesakes did, but they were nonetheless influential far beyond their meager commercial returns would suggest. The making of the band's first two albums involved a number of talents that would benefit from the experience of working with Campbell-Lyons and Spyropoulos to go on to bigger and better things. This list includes producers Tony Visconti (David Bowie, Marc Bolan); Jimmy Miller (The Rolling Stones); and Guy Stevens (Mott the Hoople, The Clash) as well as studio engineer Brian Humphries (Traffic, Pink Floyd), plus musicians like Billy Bremner (Rockpile).

All in all, if you're a fan of 1960s-era psychedelic pop, you're going to love Nirvana, and *Cult* is a fine introduction to, if not a substitute for, the band's near-mythical original albums. (2012)

ORPHANED LAND
The Never Ending Way Of ORwarriOR   (Century Media Records)

Orphaned Land is an anomaly in the world of rock 'n' roll – a popular, border-hopping Israeli heavy metal band that also enjoys a large Arab and Palestinian audience. Formed in the early 1990s as Resurrection, the band changed its name to Orphaned Land to avoid confusion with a Florida-based death metal band. Although the band has been, shall we say, less than "prolific" throughout its on-again, off-again career – *The Never Ending Way Of ORwarriOR* is only the fourth Orphaned Land album in almost two decades, and its first in six years – every new album from Orphaned Land both shocks and surprises with a mix of traditional Middle Eastern folk music and boundary-busting progressive metal that underlines and supports the band's intelligent, conceptual lyrics.

While Orphaned Land's last album, 2004's *Mabool*, drew its inspiration, literally, from the Biblical tale of Noah's Ark, the story and concept behind *The Never Ending Way Of ORwarriOR* is a little less specific. Loosely translated, the "ORwarriOR" is a champion of light and order facing down the forces of evil and chaos on battlefield

Earth. While the story may be somewhat difficult to follow for European and American audiences – lyrics are sung in English, Hebrew, and Arabic – the energetic music is so invigorating and exciting, the band's instrumental virtuosity so impressive, that it doesn't really matter.

This ain't your daddy's heavy metal, that's for sure, and listeners tuning in to hear Iron Maiden or Motley Crue will be sorely disappointed. For prog-metal fans with tastes more attuned to, say, Porcupine Tree or Dream Theater, however, *The Never Ending Way Of ORwarriOR* will prove to be a real treat. While some traditional metal tropes remain, such as skull-busting rhythms and shredded-lightning fretboard runs, Orphaned Land brings a much more refined and subversive vision to its music. The album-opening "Sapori," for instance, features exotic vocal harmonies, martial rhythms, and the haunting leads of female vocalist Shlomit Levi soaring above a sea of clashing instrumentation and symphonic-metal riffing.

The explosive "From Broken Vessels" offers up grating black-metal howls from vocalist Kobi Farhi, whose broken-glass gargle is accompanied by a muscular soundtrack that includes clean vocal harmonies and time-signature changes that only superhuman math-metal monsters like Meshuggah could duplicate. And so it goes throughout *The Never Ending Way Of ORwarriOR*, the album mixing the sublime with bludgeoning sonic overkill, often during the course of a single song.

The too-brief-by-half "Bereft In The Abyss" is, by turns, almost pastoral in its grace, with an elegant acoustic-guitar threaded beneath Moroccan rhythms and gorgeous harmony vocals. "Olat Ha'tamid" sounds like a Middle Eastern bazaar caught on tape: the bustling crowds, the heat, and the haggling captured against an esoteric instrumental backdrop, strains of traditional folk crashing against riff-driven hard rock.

The grand, epic "The Warrior" is the album's centerpiece, a swelling cinematic soundtrack and spoken (Hebrew?) lyrics leading into a moody, atmospheric, metallic Sturm und Drang that sits uncomfortably beneath the vocals like a fiery hot ember. The guitar playing of Yossi Sassi Sa'aron and Matt Svatizky here is simply amazing, their instruments entwined in some sort of battle to the death that results in biting tones that leave scorched earth in their wake.

Taken altogether, *The Never Ending Way Of ORwarriOR* provides an exhilarating ride across a musical landscape that, upon first blush, will seem to be exceedingly hostile to foreign ears (i.e. those of us not of Middle Eastern descent). The challenge is worth the sojourn, however, for even if you can't quite suss out the story behind the lyrics, the band's intent is clear, and the complex, multi-layered and textured music created by Orphaned Land takes the concept of progressive metal to an entirely higher level. Mixed with love by Porcupine Tree's resident genius Steven Wilson, who also contributes keyboards to several songs, *The Never Ending Way Of ORwarriOR* represents a form of "thinking man's (and woman's) metal" that expands the genre's sound like no other work previous. (2010)

PAT TRAVERS
Boom Boom (Out Go The Lights)   (MVD Audio)

Blooze-rock guitarslinger Pat Travers is fondly remembered for his incredible string of late 1970s/early 1980s albums that began with his self-titled 1976 debut and ran through such blistering six-string showcases as *Makin' Magic* and *Putting It Straight* (both 1977); *Heat In The Street* (1979), *Crash And Burn* (1980) and, of course, the signature *Live! Go For What You Know* (1979), which yielded Travers' best-known tune, his red-hot and scorching cover of the Stan Lewis blues classic "Boom Boom (Out Go The Lights)." When the Reverend lived in Detroit circa 1979-81, you couldn't turn on WRIF-FM radio without hearing Travers' trademark guitar licks and distinctive vocals.

Unlike many so-called "classic rock" artists, Travers survived the onslaught of, first, punk rock and, later, "new wave" to carry stadium-approved guitar rock into the new decade. By the mid-'80s, however, Travers' trademark one-two punch of blues and rock had fallen out of favor with the MTV generation and he sat the rest of the decade on the bench, coming back into the game with *School of Hard Knocks* in 1990. Since that time, Travers has continued to plow the fertile earth of electric blues and rock 'n' roll cheap thrills, releasing a handful of decent studio albums – some with an abundance of original material – as well as a slew of remarkably consistent live discs, working through the years with other such respected rock journeymen as Aynsley Dunbar, Carmine Appice, Jeff Watson, and T.M. Stevens.

The secret to Travers' ongoing longevity is that, through the years, neither his original songs, nor his inspired choices in cover material, have been all that complicated. My old buddy Grimey once said of ZZ Top's early albums, "anybody could play that stuff," and that's also true of Pat Travers. What separates the bearded wonders from Texas – *and* the six-string wunderkind from Canada – from the great unwashed masses is that although *anybody* can play this stuff, few are as capable of doing it with such energy, passion, and originality.

Which brings us, in a roundabout way, to *Boom Boom (Out Go The Lights)*, a rather worthwhile collection of Travers' guitar rave-ups from the good folks at MVD Audio. While it might be easy to dismiss the disc as *justanotherPatTraversalbum*, in spite of the ultra-groovy high-contrast Brian Perry cover art, with its reassuring deep maroon framework, you would have to be the worst sort of imbecile to pass this gem by in the "classic rock" bin of one of the few remaining record stores. Turn said disc to its reverse and take a gander at the glorious baker's dozen of songs awaiting your purchase and tell me, honestly, closeted blooze-rock fan, that this collection of original Travers' scorchers and rare cover tunes wouldn't just ROCK YOUR F'KN WORLD!!!

Ostensibly this is an album of live performances, and since MVD licensed the content from Cleopatra Records, my best guess is that this elixir is of late 1990s vintage, perchance from the same shows that populated the 1997 *Whiskey Blues* live album. Regardless, *Boom Boom (Out Go The Lights)* showcases Travers' skills just as strongly as any of his late 1970s releases, the middle-aged axeman finding new ways to breathe life into aging chestnuts like "Snortin' Whiskey," "Crash And Burn," and the ubiquitous title track. It's with Travers' performance of songs by fellow travelers like Z.Z. Top, Lynyrd Skynyrd, Cream, and Aerosmith that a full measure of the artist is provided, however.

Given the man's undeniable blooze-rock credentials (and I use the British slang term "blooze" since London is where the Canadian guitar prodigy cut his eye teeth), it should be expected that Travers would kick serious ass with tunes like the Texas mudstomp of Z.Z. Top's "Waitin' For The Bus" (a bull's-eye right down to the Gibbonesque vox) and "Jesus Just Left Chicago" (ditto).

Travers even acquits himself honorably on the redneck swamp sludge of Skynyrd's "Gimme Back My Bullets," while he should be able to play molten electric Chicago slag like Willie Dixon's "Evil" in his sleep. But two of the covers here simply scream aloud from the smackdown laid down upon their pointy heads by Travers and his unnamed crew.

Travers' energetic, soulful reading of Stevie Wonder's wonderful "Superstitious" puts that of his former idol Jeff Beck to shame, the stellar fretwork displayed here is torn from somewhere deep down in the man's rock 'n' roll soul. While the band struggles to keep up with Travers' madman performance, the guitarist is walking on clouds with an extended solo so damn hot that it will leave blisters on the listener's fingers.

The other notable cover that DEMANDS your attention is the unlikely choice of "Lights Out" by British rockers U.F.O. With lightning bolt leads building upon galloping rhythms, Travers strays from his usual bluesy milieu to cut loose with reckless abandon on the strident hard rock classic, his vocals chasing some ghosts we can't see, his trusty six-string coaxed and coerced into spitting out alien sounds that more respected "guitar gods" like Satriani or Vai can't even muster up in their dreams.

Before you dismiss *Boom Boom (Out Go The Lights)* as *justanotherPatTraversalbum*, you should rustle up a copy and hear it for yourself. These thirteen songs are the perfect forum for Travers' free-wheeling, swashbuckling six-string style, the album capturing the sound of a man whose time has clearly passed but he doesn't GIVE A DAMN! Freed from commercial expectations, label demands, creative concerns or any of the constraints of the modern music biz, Pat Travers is able to simply do what he does best – rock! (2007)

PAUL COLLINS
King of Power Pop!   (Alive Naturalsound Records)

Given his impressive pedigree – a founding member, with Peter Case, of original L.A. power pop pioneers the Nerves during the 1970s, and of the Beat (later Paul Collins' Beat) during the '80s – Paul Collins has certainly earned his status as power pop nobility. In his quest to claim the power pop crown, which has lain dormant since the late 1980s when Nick Lowe abdicated the throne, Collins sojourned to the holy land, the Motor City, home of the Knack, the Romantics, and Nikki Corvette, to record in Detroit's notorious Ghetto Recorders studio.

Working with producer Jim Diamond, who has helped shape the sound of such garage-dwelling fellow travelers as Outrageous Cherry, the New Bomb Turks, and the White Stripes, Collins bangs-and-crashes his way through thirteen high-octane slabs of outright power pop majesty, a baker's dozen, if you will, of sugar-coated sonic delights.

King of Power Pop! kicks off the party with the declarative "C'mon Let's Go!," a call-to-arms for Collins' would-be subjects that features ecstatic slabs of cascading Duane Eddy-styled six-string, a bouncy rhythm, and the soothing harmonies of Ms. Corvette behind Collins' gruff-but-lovable tenor.

King of Power Pop! only amps up the wattage from here…"Do You Wanna Love Me?" evokes the British invasion, with a driving rhythm and sloppy garage-dawg harpwork courtesy of the Romantics' Wally Palmar. "Doin' It For The Ladies" wears its '60s-era influences proudly on its sleeve, with delicious harmonies beating out a sort of beach blanket bingo on your eardrums.

The stellar opening guitar on "Don't Blame Your Troubles On Me," provided by longtime Collins' foil Eric Blakely, does little to conceal the song's Yardbirds-romping stomp-and-stammer roots, while the hoarse vocals and muscular soundtrack of "Off The Hook" only add to the song's anguished heartache, a necessary lyrical theme in the power pop kingdom.Collins solidifies his bona-fides with a pair of wired, inspired covers, beginning with the Box Tops' classic "The Letter."

Rather than attempting to mimic Alex Chilton's blue-eyed Memphis soul original, Collins instead strips the song down to the essentials – emotional teardrop vocals, menacing guitar, and crashing drumbeats. The result evokes the grandeur of the original while adding an invaluable contemporary rock 'n' roll sheen to the affair. A cover of the Flamin' Groovies' "You Tore Me Down" is provided a

loving reading with crooned vocals and a thick, beautiful tapestry of instrumentation. It's with "Kings of Power Pop," a semi-autobiographic history, that Collins makes his final claim to the title, with self-effacing lyrics, great vocal harmonies, and gorgeous guitars that will spin your head in circles.

Leave it to the commoners of the blogosphere to endlessly debate Paul Collins' status in the power pop firmament; as for this humble rockcrit, given the uniquely high quality of tuneage on *King of Power Pop!*, with nary a duff track among the thirteen, I say give him the crown. He's earned it with better than three decades of uncompromising loyalty to the power pop aesthetic. Paul Collins may never become the rock star he dreamed of, but 13 albums in, he deserves our fealty, dammit! After all, as his royal highness himself sings, "the kids just want to have fun!" (2010)

PENDRAGON
The History: 1984-2000   (Metal Mind/MVD Audio)

For over twenty years, British neo-prog stalwarts Pendragon have bucked commercial trends in favor of exploring the classically-minded, folk-influenced style originally forged by bands like Genesis, Strawbs, and Renaissance. Unlike contemporaries Marillion, Pendragon has never achieved a great amount of chart success in the U.K., but rather are revered by loyal audiences in countries like France and Poland. Neither band ever made much of a splash with American prog-rock aficionados, but in Pendragon's defense, there hasn't been a lot of their music made available to audiences on this side of the pond. Originally released exclusively in Poland and enjoying a brief US release back in '01, *The History: 1984-2000* has been compiled from a half-dozen Pendragon albums and should whet the appetite of stateside proggers to seek out the band's other excellent work as import discs.

The History: 1984-2000 is a fine showcase of Pendragon's chosen milieu. Although guitarist/frontman Nick Barrett and keyboard wizard Clive Nolan, along with bassist Peter Gee and drummer Fudge Smith, are all superb musicians, it is the band's enormous musical chemistry that drives these songs. Although some jaded U.S. prog fans may find Pendragon's unique sound to be less aggressive than they like, with less emphasis on technical virtuosity and more importance placed on the song, these four gifted artists are incredible musicians nonetheless.

Pendragon reminds me a lot of early 1970s Pink Floyd, with each song's lyrics, structure and underlying soundtrack considered above mere instrumental interplay. As such, mesmerizing tunes like "Total Recall" or the eerie medieval "The Black Knight" represent a finely crafted combination of intelligent, imaginative lyrics and unpredictable musical composition.

Pendragon's *The History: 1984-2000* includes two haunting acoustic performances of songs from early albums, "The King Of The Castle" and "Paintbox," that were recorded exclusively for this volume. Stripped of electricity, the songs are redefined as soaring folk ballads with a pastoral edge. The album also includes an ultra-cool performance video of "The Last Waltz" culled from the band's 1997 album and DVD *Live At Last!* that you can watch on the old computer.

The History: 1984-2000 is an excellent introduction to the many charms of Pendragon, and hopefully the band will receive its overdue welcome from American audiences so that we can see more of their work reissued stateside. (2007)

PETER TOWNSHEND
The Definitive Collection   (Hip-O Records)

As the guiding force behind rock legends the Who, guitarist/
songwriter Peter Townshend's induction to the Rock & Roll Hall Of
Fame was all but guaranteed. One of the original, first wave "British
Invasion" bands that assaulted the colonies in the aftermath of the
Beatles, the Who were blessed with a wealth of talent. All four
members of the Who would have stood out in nearly any other band
and, indeed, three of these four musicians would eventually succeed in
their own solo endeavors.

Frontman Roger Daltry was a strutting, larger-than-life figure with a
big voice and rock star charisma. Bassist John Entwistle played rock
'n' roll with an improvisational jazz sensibility, and was a better
songwriter than most of his contemporaries. Drummer Keith Moon
was an anarchic wildman, bashing and crashing the skins with reckless
abandon. Then there was Townshend…an immensely gifted
songwriter, a powerful guitarist and a whirling dervish onstage,
leaping and spinning and seemingly flying on the wings of the music;
he was also intellectual, introspective and often spiritually troubled.

Townshend was a prolific songwriter, one of the greatest in the history
of the rock genre. His creative accomplishments with the Who are
second only, perhaps, to those of John Lennon of the Beatles. What a
lot of people seem to forget, however, is that Townshend also enjoyed
a significant solo career, receiving overwhelming critical acclaim and
some degree of commercial success. Townshend recorded demos of
just about every song he ever wrote for the Who, and discarded more
songs than the band ever recorded. A lot of this material has shown up
in various "odds 'n' sods" collections through the years, and
Townshend's own demo versions of songs have made his *Scoop*
albums a series much sought-after by collectors.

The Definitive Collection is a brand-new collection of Peter
Townshend solo material. Now I'm a little wary of record label hype,
and calling any compilation album "definitive" is, perhaps, stretching
the definition of the word. In the case of Peter Townshend's *The
Definitive Collection*, however, I'm going to set my reservations aside

and instead revel in the music. Featuring material culled from Townshend's 35-year "solo" career, *The Definitive Collection* does a worthy job of presenting the many faces of this rock legend.

Townshend's first solo effort, *Who Came First*, was a low-key affair released in 1972 as an outlet for the songwriter's growing catalog of material. Collecting songs unsuitable for the Who as well as more personal, spiritually-oriented material, the album offered an insightful glimpse into the depth of Townshend's songwriting talents. "Sheraton Gibson," an underrated cut from *Who Came First*, is a wonderful, lively song about life on the road and the accompanying loneliness, Townshend's vocals darting in and out of the mix, complimented by his fluid, mesmerizing guitarwork.

From *Rough Mix*, Townshend's acclaimed 1977 collaboration with ex-Faces' bassist Ronnie Lane, "Street In The City" is a melodic, observational song that relies on Townshend's winsome vocals to rise above the rich string-orchestral arrangement. Also from *Rough Mix*, "My Baby Gives It Away" is a twangy rocker with a loping groove and rapid-fire lyrics. *Rough Mix* is the jewel of Townshend's solo career, a rambling collection of roots rock, British folk and country overtones and well worth checking out on its own.

The Definitive Collection also includes three songs from *Empty Glass*, Townshend's 1980 solo breakthrough and his best-selling album to date. The album was written as Townshend struggled with the death of Who drummer Keith Moon. The personal nature of the lyrics and their combination of pop melodies and gutter-punk rockers took *Empty Glass* to the number five position on the charts.

The album's radio-ready singles were easy choices, but "A Little Is Enough," an engaging love song with new wavy synth overtones and a driving beat is a fine addition to the collection, sounding amusingly retro albeit featuring, perhaps, some uncharacteristically inane lyrics. He redeems himself with "Let My Love Open The Door," the hit single combining the most attractive elements of '80s synth-pop with old-fashioned harmonies and a killer hook. Befitting its title, "Rough Boys" shows a little more muscle, with forceful Townshend vocals performance, imaginative keyboards and some tasty six-string riffing.

Townshend followed *Empty Glass* with the obtusely-named *All The Best Cowboys Have Chinese Eyes* in 1982. Overall Townshend's most maddening album, both loved and hated by his fans, its arty, pretentious songs have withstood the test of time. The album's "Slit Skirts" is a dynamic song, with interesting lyrics, an infectious chorus, and various musical twists and turns with signature changes and intriguing instrumental interludes.

"The Sea Refuses No River" could just as easily have been one of Townshend's compositions for the Who, a grand, majestic song that showcases some of Townshend's most subtle vocals and his skills as an arranger. The song is, perhaps, one of the most overlooked of the artist's canon.

By the mid-'80s Townshend seemed to be going in a thousand directions at once, and seemingly lost sight of his creative strengths. "Face The Face," from 1985's *White City: A Novel*, is an intriguing choice for this collection, an almost experimental piece that starts off small, with an atmospheric intro, dissonant piano, and clanging sounds building to a steady rhythm, kind of like a train coming down the track, straight at your stalled-out car.

Townshend's multi-layered vocals are one part electronic wizardry and one part gospel fervor. "A Friend Is A Friend," from *The Iron Man: A Musical*, is a slight slip of a song – perhaps that misbegotten album's best, but a pale choice nonetheless. The two tracks included from 1993's *Psychoderelict* fare somewhat better; a concept album ridden with spoken word interludes and weak material, "English Boy" is nevertheless a knock-down rocker with one of Townshend's best vocal performances in a decade and some truly unusual musical undercurrents.

The Definitive Collection is a fairly decent overview of the ups and downs of Peter Townshend's solo career, replacing the decade-old *The Best Of* collection with a better song selection. I personally would have liked to have seen one of the Who's classic tunes from Townshend's *Deep End Live!* album included here. Also, all of the best stuff from this compilation – and then some – was included two years ago on the double-disc *Gold* collection, part of the industry's efforts to cannibalize itself through countless variations on the same compilations. However, if you remain among the uninitiated that just wants a taste of Townshend, *The Definitive Collection* is the way to go; go for the *Gold* if you want a deeper drink of the artist's talents. If you like what you hear, grab copies of *Empty Glass* and *Rough Mix* to get a full measure of Townshend's greatest work. (2007)

ROBERT GORDON
Robert Gordon with Link Wray / Fresh Fish Special
(American Beat Records)

One of the very cool things about the punk revolution of '77 was the major label's begrudging willingness to listen to new sounds. With many of the arena-rock giants of the era either dying off or rapidly becoming irrelevant, record labels were forced to cast an eye about for something new and exciting to exploit. They didn't really understand this punk rock stuff and, truthfully, most of it scared them half to death. This is what the kids were listening to, tho', and they had to put out *something* to bolster flagging album sales, so…

The labels subsequently began a feeding frenzy that extended well into the "new wave" daze of the early 1980s, throwing out albums by new artists with alarming regularity, tossing them up against the wall to see what stuck. This haphazard approach resulted in a wealth of truly crappy music, but it also gave voice to many creative and influential artists of enduring stature. It was an exciting time to be a fan of music, because one really never knew what the next new band would bring to the table.

Even by the relatively relaxed standards of the late 1970s, it's still a wonder that rockabilly Robert Gordon ever landed a label deal in the first place. Not that his music was terrible; on the contrary, his unique take on the rockabilly sound was firmly rooted in a heartfelt love and appreciation for the music. Rather than attempt to mimic the style, as the Stray Cats would do with varied success half-a-decade or so later, Gordon's musical homage was authentic and natural. In every way that counted, Robert Gordon *was* a rockabilly singer, standing in as stark a contrast to the punk rockers of the day as they did to the "dinosaurs" they had allegedly replaced.

It probably didn't hurt that Gordon was signed to producer Richard Gottehrer's Private Stock label, which was distributed by RCA Records, the label home of rockabilly icon Elvis Presley. Gordon found a kindred spirit in Gottehrer, and recruiting, perhaps, the greatest rock guitarist of the '50s – Link Wray – the singer, the producer and the six-string marvel ventured into the studio during two different months in 1977 to record what would later become two legendary albums – *Robert Gordon with Link Wray* and *Fresh Fish Special*, both released in 1979.

The first of the two albums, *Robert Gordon with Link Wray*, finds the singer taking tentative steps towards recreating the rockabilly sounds that inspired him as a teen. The results are encouraging: tunes like the raucous "Red Hot" or the slinky "Summertime Blues" really tear up the asphalt while slow dances like "Sweet Surrender" place an emphasis on Gordon's fine vocals, his infectious baritone swooping and soaring across the lyrics.

Wray's guitar swings pretty freely, subtly spicing up the material, but my one complaint would be that the band never really cuts loose and sets the studio on fire. Save for a couple of Wray originals, most of the tunes here are vintage nuggets, well chosen, and some of them, like "Flyin' Saucers Rock & Roll," threaten to leap right off the turntable. The album is a fitting tribute to Gordon's influences, nearly-forgotten original rockers like Gene Vincent, Eddie Cochran, and Johnny Burnette.

Gordon and Wray hit their stride with their second collaboration, *Fresh Fish Special*. Recorded shortly after the tragic death of Elvis Presley, the King's spirit is channeled throughout these performances. The album's musical format is loosened up a bit – think Elvis circa '65 rather than the rockabilly 'E' of '55 – to include tunes like the classic New Orleans swinger "Sea Cruise" or the crooning ballad "Blue Eyes (Don't Run Away)."

There's plenty here to satisfy the listener's inner-rockabilly, however, from the shuffling "Five Days, Five Days," with Wray's tasty guitar licks complemented by the Jordanaires' vocal harmonies, or the grand, Presley-esque "If This Is Wrong."

Gordon knocks an obscure Elvis cover, "I Want To Be Free" from the movie *Jailhouse Rock*, right out of the park with a soaring performance, while the rollicking "Twenty Flight Rock" swings like an out-of-control wrecking ball. One of Gordon's biggest fans, Bruce Springsteen, hand-delivered the eloquent "Fire," which the singer makes his own with an inspired performance, and "Red Cadillac And A Black Mustache" is your typical sordid '50s-era tale of love gone wrong, the song's shuffling beat paired with one of Gordon's best vocal interpretations.

These two classic late 1970s albums helped kickstart a rockabilly revival that resulted in '80s-era bands like the Stray Cats and Matchbox, and continues to inspire roots-rockers like the Reverend Horton Heat and the Legendary Shack Shakers. The new reissue label American Beat Records recently released *Robert Gordon with Link Wray* and *Fresh Fish Special* on a single CD, re-mastered for an invigorating sound and with short liner notes.

Although neither of these fine albums made much of a commercial splash at the time of their release, they've gone in-and-out-of-print several times through the years and have displayed greater longevity than many better-known and better-selling artists. More than a relic of a time long passed-by, these albums are a treasured document of an almost-anything-goes era where an entertaining performer like Robert Gordon could make his voice heard. (2007)

ROY BUCHANAN
Live At Rockpalast   (MIG Music)

Roy Buchanan is probably the best guitarist that you've never heard. Although he found a modicum of success with the twelve albums he released during his lifetime, two of them achieving Gold™ sales status (a heady accomplishment in the 1970s), his influence reaches far beyond the meager commercial returns of his work. The "Master of the Telecaster" provided inspiration for fellow guitarists like Jeff Beck, Gary Moore, Danny Gatton, and ZZ Top's Billy Gibbons, among others with his heady brew of blues, roots-rock, R&B, and country music.

After an amazing string of eight studio and a single live album recorded and released during the brief space of nine years, by 1981 Buchanan was burned out. The vagaries of the recording industry, and his labels' attempts to conform his talents to a saleable commodity had left him disgruntled and disillusioned. The guitarist would virtually disappear, taking a four-year hiatus to re-think and re-

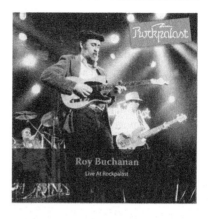

charge his batteries. Lucky for us, Alligator Records' Bruce Iglauer convinced Buchanan to return from his self-imposed exile, giving the guitarist artistic control in the studio that would result in some of the best recordings of Buchanan's career.

Live At Rockpalast is taken from a February 1985 performance by the guitarist and his band for the popular German TV show *Rockpalast*, and would mark Buchanan's return to music…and what a return it would prove to be! Buchanan's performance here, prior to the recording of his Alligator debut *When A Guitar Plays The Blues*, shows an artist and musician back in fighting form and shaking off the ring rust. Leading a band that included (seldom used) singer Martin Stephenson, keyboardist John Steel, and bassist Anthony Dumm – all members of U.K. pop/rock band the Daintees – as well as drummer Martin Yula, Buchanan cranks through a baker's dozen of original blues-flavored roots-rockers and favorite covers, much to the delight of the enthusiastic German audience.

The set kicks off with the spry "Thing In G (Short Fuse)," a funky instrumental romp that sounds not unlike some of the material Stevie Ray Vaughan would be vamping on a couple of short years later. While the band provides a supple rhythm, Buchanan embroiders the song with his red-hot fretwork, the guitarist firing on all cylinders as he throws in sly blues, jazz, and rockabilly references throughout the four-minute firecracker. Buchanan's subsequent take on Booker T & the MGs' classic "Green Onion" is unlike any you've ever heard…while the band offers up a standard take on the song's keyboard riffing and swaggering drumbeats, the guitarist stomps all over tradition with his wild-ass flamethrower solos, which bounce off the arrangement like a madman careening off the walls of his rubber room. It makes for an energetic and unpredictable performance, and a heck of a lot of fun.

Buchanan was well-known and revered for his ability to fuse blues, rock, and country music into an earthy, organic sound, and nowhere did he ever do it better than with "Roy's Blues (Roy's Bluz)." An intricate instrumental backdrop frames the almost whispered, briefly spoken lyrics as Buchanan's fretwork ranges from low-key blues and roots-rock to jagged shards of angular jazz licks and twangy, barbed-wire country tones. It's not blues as we know it, but it's breathtaking nevertheless, the song stretched out to ten minutes by Buchanan and band so that by the time he hits the crescendo almost six minutes in, when the raucous vocals fly out of nowhere, you're left exhausted.

By contrast, Buchanan's instrumental "Blues In D" is a more traditional blues shuffle, with the guitarist showing his mojo hand through a number of passages throughout the song. Above a standard Chicago blues bass/drums rhythm, Buchanan tacks on an incendiary display of six-string pyrotechnics, emotion pouring from his fingertips in a performance that is pure instinct and adrenalin. He takes much the same tack with songwriter Don Gibson's "Sweet Dreams," Buchanan's mournful, tear-jerking solos echoing the song's heartbreak lyrics, adding a bit of blues hue to this instrumental take on a beloved country classic.

Like just about every other guitarist that came of age during the 1960s, Buchanan was touched by the incredible sounds that issued from the instrument of the late Jimi Hendrix. Buchanan's take on Hendrix's "Hey Joe" – the song a garage-rock standard first hit big by the Leaves in 1965 and later adapted by Hendrix as the Experience's first single – skews more towards Hendrix's vision in this performance. Although Stevenson's vocals are unremarkable, it's Buchanan's mangling of his instrument that draws your attention, his solos incorporating scraps of blues, rock, and some otherworldly sounds that even Jimi couldn't reach. The following version of Hendrix's "Foxey Lady" soars even further into the stratosphere, the vocals overshadowed and hidden beneath Buchanan's unbelievable, high-flying guitar and the muscular rhythmic soundtrack provided by Dumm and Yula.

Buchanan's "Messiah (Messiah Will Come Again)" is provided a truly ethereal performance here, the song's unlikely fusion of blues and rock with classical music overtones unique to Buchanan's particular experience and perspective. His haunting guitarplay here is elegantly beautiful and tragically dark, the guitarist wringing every bit of energy and emotion from his fretboard.

The mood is heightened greatly, however, by the upbeat "Night Train," a rockabilly-tinged instrumental with a ramshackle framework that rocks and rolls like the wheels on a freight train. Buchanan closes *Live At Rockpalast* with "Wayfaring Pilgrim," another haunting instrumental that showcases his immense abilities, great tone, and masterful blending of musical styles.

The 1985 release of the acclaimed *When A Guitar Plays The Blues* represented the beginning of a fertile period of Roy Buchanan's career, the guitarist quickly recording 1986's *Dancing On The Edge* and the following year's *Hot Wires* before his tragic death in 1988. Returning to the trenches in 1985 after a four-year break, Buchanan sounds recharged, revved-up, and ready-to-roll on *Live At Rockpalast*. There are few live documents of this unique and influential guitarist available, and this one is well worth your hard-earned coin. (2012)

SANDY BULL & THE RHYTHM ACE
Live 1976   (Drag City Records)

One of a legion of young soul rebels who emerged during the early 1960s with guitar in hand, Sandy Bull was in the same league as fellow travelers like John Fahey, Leo Kottke, and Britain's Bert Jansch. Unlike those aforementioned contemporaries, however, who pulled the majority of their inspiration from blues and folk music, often with a smattering of jazz, Bull's restless musical spirit would lead him to incorporate elements of classical, Indian, and droning Arabic raga style into his playing.

Also unlike his fellow string-benders, Bull largely eschewed the traditional three-to-four-minute pop song format in favor of extended instrumental jams that would allow him to stretch out like an improvisational jazzman and get to the heart of the performance, providing his breathtakingly intricate compositions with greater texture and tone. Bull would also pick up a bass guitar, banjo, and oud once in a while, his proficiency in these various instruments lending a dangerously-exotic vibe to his compositions.

Signing with the noted folk label Vanguard Records, Bull released a handful of albums circa 1963-72, the most acclaimed of these, his 1963 debut *Fantasias for Guitar and Banjo*, recorded with jazz percussionist Billy Higgins (who had played with Ornette Coleman, John Coltrane, and Herbie Hancock, among others). Featuring the twenty-minute, side-long "Blend," the album featured Bull's myriad of influences and introduced him as a serious, talented musician. But by the time of the release of 1972's *Demolition Derby*, Bull had sunk deeply into drug addiction, and he seemingly disappeared from music altogether until resurfacing in 1988 with the acclaimed *Jukebox School of Music* album.

The truth is, Sandy Bull hadn't turned his back on music during the 1970s, and after going through rehab, he relocated to San Francisco and began performing again, including the May 1976 appearance opening for Leo Kottke at the Berkeley Community Center that is captured by *Live 1976*. Re-mastered from a long-lost tape made by friend and engineer Hillel Resner, Drag City's vinyl-only release of *Live 1976* shines a light on Bull's enormous talents with a set of performances and soft-spoken intros that paint a fuller portrait of this unfairly obscure instrumentalist.

Accompanied by "The Rhythm Ace," his electronic drum machine, and a four-track TASCAM recorder on which he would often place backing bass and drums to accompany his live lead instrument, Bull displayed the technological acumen of a prog-rock virtuoso while unfolding his largely acoustic-based, dream-like compositions. *Live 1976* opens with "Oud," a seven-minute-plus instrumental performed with the pear-shaped Middle Eastern stringed instrument that Bull had come to favor. The performance is simply magical, mesmerizing in its depth and tone as Bull explores several varying musical landscapes within the confines of the song.

A brief interlude follows where he jokingly introduces "the band" and demonstrates the abilities of "The Rhythm Ace," a still-unfamiliar bit of technology in the mid-'70s. With "Love Is Forever," Bull tries his hand at a more-traditional, albeit elongated pop song, his imperfect but aching vocals accompanied by elegant acoustic fretwork, the drum machine, and syncopated riffing on an electric oud. Inspired by the Drifters, Bull introduces "Driftin'" as a "beach tune," a pre-recorded bass line providing support beneath Bull's spry, soulful guitarplay that weds an odd folk-rock sound to a lofty R&B framework, with a little weepy country steel twang laid in on top as an exciting counterpoint.

Bull's humorous introduction to "Alligator Wrestler" explains the childhood interlude with the song's protagonist and veers off course into a story from his rehab before tying it all together with a nice bit of metaphor. The song itself is an energetic, upbeat instrumental that evinces a swamp-rock vibe, adding a loping, funky rhythmic track with heavy bass and some of the oddest, Southern-styled chicken-pickin' that you'll ever hear. Running nearly nine-minutes, the performance is exhausting and awe-inspiring, and is the beating creative heart of *Live 1976*.

The album ends with "New York City," the performance falling just shy of eight minutes and displaying a more urbane, sophisticated edge to Bull's playing than previous tracks. The guitarist's nimble licks are paired with a jazzy, syncopated rhythm resulting in an inspired piece that easily places Bull alongside such vaunted contemporaries as Larry Coryell and Al Di Meola as a skilled jazz-fusion stylist.

While continuing to perform, often outside of the public's eye, throughout the 1980s, Bull would eventually land in the rural countryside near Nashville, building a home and studio and raising a family. He would return to the recording world with the aforementioned *Jukebox School of Music*, followed by 1991's *Vehicle* and 1996's *Steel Tears*, both albums released on his own independent Timeless Recording Society label, all three treated with deference by critics.

Although passing away in 2001 at the too-young age of 60 from cancer, Sandy Bull left behind a body of work that, while not large by contemporary recording standards, nevertheless represents the best qualities of his playing – creative, efficient, meticulous, imaginative, and adventuresome. *Live 1976* is a welcome addition to this catalog that serves to bolster Bull's growing reputation, the album a warm and entertaining collection that reveals another dimension of this underrated instrumentalist's enormous talents. (2012)

SIR DOUGLAS QUINTET
The Mono Singles '68-'72   (Sundazed Records)

Although long respected by critics, hipsters, and historians for their important place in rock 'n' roll history, only belatedly has the Sir Douglas Quintet begun to receive its props for expanding the 1960s-era garage-rock vocabulary beyond retro-Elvis crooning and faux Fab Four harmonies. While the band was originally put together by Houston producer Huey P. Meaux as a Cajun facsimile of an amalgam of British Invasion bands, left in the hands of the capable Doug Sahm and friends, the Sir Douglas Quintet became something else entirely.

The original Sir Douglas Quintet recorded a handful of songs with Meaux, scoring a Top Twenty hit in 1965 with the Tex-Mex flavored classic "She's About A Mover." Fleeting fame would follow, met by a string of good, but not particularly successful singles released by various Meaux-owned labels, culminating in *The Best of the Sir Douglas Quintet* album, a collection of the aforementioned flotsam and jetsam. When the band was arrested for marijuana possession after returning home to Texas from a 1966 European tour, Sahm got out of jail, broke up the band, and took off to San Francisco, followed shortly by the Quintet's saxophonist Frank Morin.

In California, Sahm saw the light and formed a new version of the Sir Douglas Quintet with friend Morin and a bunch of guys who subsequently came and went. Playing regularly around Frisco, the band signed with a Mercury Records subsidiary, and recorded a true debut album in 1968's *Sir Douglas Quintet + 2 = Honkey Blues*. It's at this point that our tale takes off and the era documented by Sundazed's *The Mono Singles '68-'72* begins, the album collecting all

22 songs – 11 singles total, with B-sides – released by Mercury and its subsidiary labels during the stated period.

While these songs have been compiled before – most notably as part of the 2006 box set *The Complete Mercury Recordings*, this single-disc set places them firmly in the spotlight all by their lonesome selves. Whether you prefer the mono or the stereo versions of these songs is a matter of personal taste, really – I find myself on the fence, liking the mono versions of some songs better, the fleshier stereo mixes of others – the groundbreaking nature and entertainment value of the songs is beyond argument. As a rabid Doug Sahm and Sir Douglas Quintet fan, I'm happier than an armadillo in the sun to have multiple versions of all of these classic tunes.

The Mono Singles '68-'72 begins with an atypical pair of 1968 singles, "Are Inlaws Really Outlaws" and "Sell A Song." The former is a muted, Stax Records/Southern soul jam with bleating horns and conversational vocals, while the latter is similar to what Delaney & Bonnie would be doing later in the 1960s, Sahm's R&B torch vocals supported by Wayne Talbert's gospel-tinged piano and scraps of guitar until the song devolves into an improvised instrumental work-out with jazzy horns. Both songs are interesting in a curious, prurient, historical context but neither is indicative of the sound that the Sir Douglas Quintet would later innovate.

By late '68, Sahm would have a reconstituted Quintet in place with his old friend Augie Meyers on keyboards, where he belonged, and then the band really started cooking. "Mendocino" was the result of the new band line-up, the song's Tex-Mex flavor enhanced by Meyers' buoyant keys, Sahm's understated vocals, and a melodic hook large enough to hang your hat on. The song cracked the U.S. Top 30, blew up even bigger in Europe, and put the Quintet back on the international stage. The B-side was the wistful "I Wanna Be Your Mama Again," a mid-tempo slice of Texas soul with Sahm's lonesome vocals, some inspired piano-play by Meyers, and just a touch of psychedelic swirl creeping in around the bluesy edges of the song.

"Mendocino," the hit single, would subsequently spawn *Mendocino* the album, which in turn would yield a couple more minor hits. The first was the yearning "It Didn't Even Bring Me Down," a great example of the emotionalism Sahm could bring to a song with both words and vocals, the music a mix of horn-driven R&B led by Morin's tasteful tenor saxophone and Texas-flavored blues-rock. The flip side was the jaunty "Lawd, I'm Just A Country Boy In This Great Big Freaky City," another homesick ode about life in bad old San Francisco that is as alt-country in sound and texture as anything to follow by the Byrds and/or Gram Parsons.

Sahm missed Texas something awful during his stay in the Bay area, and it made for some great songs. The other single from *Mendocino* was the wonderfully wry blues-gospel-rock hybrid "At The Crossroads," a slow-paced ballad with chiming organ and as mournful a vocal performance as you'll ever hear. Sahm's verse "you can teach me life's lesson, you can bring a lot of gold, but you just can't live in Texas, if you don't have a lot of soul," is pitch-perfect in its yearning, the sentiment punctuated by an elegant score of descending piano notes. Turn the single over and you have the equally delightful "Texas Me," a fiddle-driven country tale of Sahm's move to Frisco, a mid-tempo rocker with plenty of twang and an undeniable yen for life back in Austin.

Somewhere during all of this, Mercury released the non-album single "Dynamite Woman," a swinging little number with gobs of Cajun fiddle, Meyers' steady Farfisa work, Sahm's vocals almost lost in the mix beneath the spry instrumentation. "Too Many Docile Minds" picks up, musically, where "Dynamite Woman" left off, adding a bit more melody to the arrangement but otherwise sounding very similar. Why they were left off the album is anybody's guess, 'cause both are fine performances.

Reunited with producer Meaux, the Sir Douglas Quintet would release *Together After Five* in 1970. The album's lead-off single was the mid-tempo Tex-Mex rave-up "Nuevo Laredo," an ode to the Texas border town that features a recurring keyboard riff, joyous blasts of Mexican-influenced horns, and more than a little mariachi flavor. "I Don't Want To Go Home" is a contemporary 1960s-styled country ballad that would have been at home in either Texas or Tennessee. It's right about here that Sahm veers off course, *The Mono Singles '68-'72* offering a pair of Nashville-born singles that Mercury released under the "Wayne Douglas" name in an attempt to crack the country charts.

Although both "Be Real" and the Music City remake of "I Don't Want To Go Home" are fine examples of old-school country featuring some of the city's best session players – folks like pedal-steel maestro Pete Drake and honky-tonk pianist Hargus "Pig" Robbins – both were a little too raw and, well, dated to appeal to then-contemporary country radio's sophisticated "countrypolitan" audience that placed a premium on slick production and slicker appearance. Sahm returned to the Sir Douglas Quintet for 1970's *1+1+1=4* album, from which were released a couple of singles, "What About Tomorrow" a relatively-unremarkable country-rocker and "(I Found Love) A Nice Song" a bluesy ballad with jangly piano-pounding and a dynamic vocal performance by Sahm, with just a little nuanced guitar thrown in for good measure.

To be honest, Sahm's return from Nashville to San Francisco seemed to only prolong the inevitable homeward journey, and the subsequent handful of single releases seemed to be a catch-as-catch-can mixed bag of styles. "Catch The Man On The Rise" is a bluesy rocker that walks a path that Joe Cocker would sprint down a couple of years hence, while the psychedelic tropes of "Pretty Flower" seems an unnatural fit for the Lone Star State transplant. Sahm finally gave in and went back home to Texas in time for 1971's *The Return of Doug Saldana*, a welcome return to form after the middlin' country-rock of *1+1+1=4*. Tex-Mex ruled the soundtrack to the autobiographical "Me And My Destiny," a great folk-rock song with deep roots in the multi-cultural Texas music tradition that Sahm cherished and, indeed, helped popularize.

The B-side of "Me And My Destiny" was a heartfelt cover of Freddy Fender's 1959 regional hit "Wasted Days, Wasted Nights" which, perchance, would launch Fender's country music stardom during the ensuing decade. Delivered straight, as a 1950s-styled soul burner, Sahm's version is very cool with emotional vocals, a swinging horn line, and piano flourishes all around. With *The Return of Doug Saldana* achieving mixed commercial results, the Sir Douglas Quintet would call it a day.

Sahm appeared as a drug dealer in the 1972 film *Cisco Pike* starring Kris Kristofferson, offering up the pro-drug song "Michoacan" for the movie's soundtrack. Released by Mercury as the last Quintet single, the jaunty Mexican-flavored number is a mid-tempo polka featuring Meyers' familiar Farfisa and Sahm's playful vocals. The B-side, "Westside Blues Again," is a bluesy, smouldering R&B tune that features a great, growling Sahm vocal and scorching fretwork complimented by Rocky Morales' 1950s-styled tenor sax riffs.

Doug Sahm would launch his solo career with 1973's acclaimed *Doug Sahm and Band*, recorded with what remained of the Sir Douglas Quintet, including Meyers and future Texas Tornados bandmate Flaco Jimenez. It was a testament to the esteem that his fellow artists held Sahm that he was able to enlist talents like Bob Dylan, Dr. John, and David Bromberg to appear on his solo debut.

Sahm would continue to create and record essential and creative music throughout the 1980s and 1990s, both as a solo artist and with the more commercially-successful Texas Tornados. Although Sahm would later resurrect the Sir Douglas Quintet name on occasion, he'd never break as much ground as he did with these 22 songs recorded over four years. (2011)

SPIRIT
West Coast Legends Vol. 3   (WDR Media/SPV)

I'll tarry not a moment to consider this, nor brook any argument otherwise, but Spirit *was* the great lost band of the 1960s. The band was formed in 1967 by five talented musicians that had healthy mixed backgrounds in folk, jazz, blues, and rock and their unique musical chemistry brought all of these elements to the table. The original Spirit line-up cranked out four critically-acclaimed albums in the space of three short years, culminating in 1970's landmark *Twelve Dreams of Dr. Sardonicus*. Along the way, Spirit scored a #25 hit with the song "I Got A Line On You" from the band's 1968 album *The Family That Plays Together*, which itself would inch into the Top 30 of the charts.

By 1978, though, Spirit had all but dropped off the edge of the major label radar, the band's tumultuous history leaving just guitarist Randy

California and his stepfather, drummer Ed Cassidy, holding the reins of this once-proud rock 'n' roll innovator. These two talents carried the Spirit torch through the 1980s and into the late '90s with numerous cobbled-together rosters, this impressive marathon sprint resulting in roughly a dozen live and studio releases on numerous independent labels. They would fall short of the finish line, though, with California's tragic death in 1997 while trying to save his young son from a vicious undertow while vacationing in Hawaii, the guitarist believed drowned.

In March 1978, however, California and Cassidy, along with bass player Larry "Fuzzy" Knight, took Spirit to Germany for a live performance to be broadcast by the legendary *Rockpalast* television show. First aired in 1974 and continuing to this day, *Rockpalast* has broadcast performances from, literally, hundreds of rock, blues, jazz and other artists – from reggae legends like Bob Marley and Black Uhuru to prog-rockers like Camel and Spock's Beard, from jazz-fusion bands like Weather Report to rockers like Tom Petty and Them Crooked Vultures. On this night, in Essen, Germany, Spirit held court for nearly two hours in front of an enthusiastic audience.

The show opens with the mighty Ed Cassidy banging away on the cans in his trademark fluid, rhythmic manner, pounding out a hybrid rock, blues, and jazz solo that exhibits the best qualities of all three genres. Gradually, the rest of the trio glides in on a steely wind, the band freestyling the "Rockpalast Jam" with a monster bass line courtesy of Knight, and frontman Randy California's incendiary fretwork. The jam shows all that was good about California's guitar style, technique picked up at the knee of the one and only Jimi Hendrix when Randy was a mere teen. Since those first lessons with the master, the student had expanded his sonic palette into an impressive musical weapon.

Fully engaged with the *Rockpalast* crowd, Spirit cranks-n-spanks a set of well-chosen covers and golden oldies…and these songs really *are* pure rock 'n' roll gold, mined from the vastly underrated Spirit catalog circa 1968-1970. The fan favorite "Mr. Skin," referring to drummer Cassidy's bald dome, suffers from the lack of the original version's lush, moody instrumentation and full band harmonies behind then-frontman Jay Ferguson (split to Jo Jo Gunne around 1971 and riding a crest of solo success by '79). The three-piece Spirit makes up for these shortcomings with amplification and audacity, California kicking up dust with the song's now-familiar solo, his use of sustain and feedback creating a glorious din.

The timeless "Nature's Way," another gem from the band's wonderful *Twelve Dreams of Dr. Sardonicus* LP, floats in with a mesmerizing blend of lofty vocals and ethereal instrumentation, the song's complex construction revealing itself in due time as California lets loose with a multi-colored solo full of reckless energy and shimmering beauty. The previously-unreleased (in 1978) "Hollywood Dream" was a new addition to the Spirit canon at the time, and the song rocks like a scalded dog, California's lyrics inspired by life lived by these journeyman rockers. Knight's bass throbs mechanically like a jackhammer, Cassidy's Godzilla-sized drumbeats echo like the voice of god, and California's raffish fretwork rattles and buzzes like a jackknife comet.

Originally released on 1969's *Clear* album, California's prescient "1984" – inspired by George Orwell's dystopian novel – would ironically run into censorship by U.S. radio programmers worked into a lather about the song's anti-authoritarian lyrics. This live performance is even better than the LP original, imbued with menace by a bass line on a bombing run and California's somber vocals and molten string-pulling. The guitarist channels his mentor Jimi with a lively cover of the garage-rock classic "Hey Joe." The trio adds to Hendrix's considerable cover of the song with dirtier sound, fatter bass, and a barrage of drumbeats. California doesn't so much as mimic Jimi's electrifying original solo as exaggerates it times ten, throwing in jazzy licks and metallic riffs alongside the prerequisite blood, sweat, and tears. The performance is riotous, chaotic, and entirely rocking…

Another *Twelve Dreams* cut, "Animal Zoo," is necessarily sparser than the original, but California's vocals flow effortlessly through the song's difficult lyrical meter. Knight's bass covers the rhythm originally provided by a second guitarist, and the song devolves at some point to an improvised reprise of the "Rockpalast Jam" before ending in an abrupt blurt. The obligatory 1970s-era drum solo is accommodated by "It's All The Same," Cassidy's blistering speed and innate rhythmic sense put to the test by two of the largest drums that I've ever seen, the legendary cult drummer performing a portion of the impressive solo sans sticks or mallet.

Spirit's biggest hit, "I Got A Line On You," is revved-up and rocked-out with all the trappings you need for a great performance: blastbeat drums, a humming bass line, and the song's own integral riff – familiar to any listener whose sense of rock 'n' roll history extends back further into the mists of time than Creed or Limp Bizkit. California spits out the lyrics at a breakneck speed, hands clawing at his instrument, frantically trying to keep up with the pace as the song seemingly takes on a life of its own like some sort of evil golem. After a dozen fine performances, the band leaves the stage, only to return for an encore nearly half as long…and every bit as energetic…as the main show.

Another nod to Hendrix is made with Spirit's inspired cover of Dylan-by-way-of-Jimi on "All Along The Watchtower," which California first put on wax a year earlier on the *Future Games* album. This classic rock treasure has been recorded by everybody from Dave Mason and Neil Young to the Dream Syndicate and Eddie Vedder. While Jimi's version remains the gold standard above all others, this rendition by Spirit kicks ass like a steel-toed boot. While California's vocals sound a bit tired by now, and the rhythmic backdrop is, unfortunately, more subdued than I would prefer, when California breaks into his inevitable solo, the whole thing explodes like a shotgun shell fired at a rotten pumpkin. While Randy attempts to take the song, note-by-note, soaring into some otherworldly stratosphere, Cassidy's tribal drumbeats keep the performance grounded on Mother Earth.

A second encore brings "Downer (Tampa Jam)," a short, shock rocker that bleeds into a good ol' fashioned hippie jam. The broadcast closes with "If I Miss This Train," a bluesy guitar-driven number on which California is assisted by Allman Brothers Band guitarist Dickey Betts, whose band Great Southern had performed earlier that night before Spirit. At the time, *Rockpalast* was an open-ended broadcast, i.e. the show was over when the amps stopped buzzing, which allowed the producers to capture magical moments like this on tape. California and Betts duel like a couple of grizzled gunfighters, the Spirit guitarist pursuing a tough-as-nails, caked-in-mud sound while Betts' sweet Southern tones display plenty of down-home twang and honey-covered soul.

Spirit's *West Coast Legends Vol. 3* is a fine addition to the *Rockpalast* series, the DVD preserving the band's historical performance on video, a rare recording of this particular Spirit line-up. Some of these performances have been previously-released on albums of dubious provenance – like 1997's *Made In Germany* – and *West Coast Legends Vol. 3* is also available on CD in truncated form. Skip the shorter CD and go for the full-blown DVD to get the entire, mind-blowing Spirit musical experience. (2011)

STEVE HILLAGE
Live In England 1979   (Gonzo Multimedia)

An important member of progressive rock's royal family, guitarist Steve Hillage had his fingers in a number of groundbreaking and influential prog-rock outfits of the late 1960s and early '70s. With keyboardist/guitarist Dave Stewart (no, not the Eurythmics guy), Hillage formed the group Uriel, which evolved into prog cult faves Egg after Hillage's departure for school.

The guitarist popped up a couple years later to form the short-lived prog outfit Khan with Stewart, the band releasing one acclaimed album, 1972's *Space Shanty*, after which Hillage hooked up with former Soft Machine guitarist Daevid Allen in the influential psychedelic experimental prog band Gong. Hillage contributed fretwork and songwriting to three of Gong's most important albums: 1973's *Flying Teapot* and *Angel Egg*, and 1974's *You*.

After reuniting with Stewart and Egg to record that band's third and final album, 1974's *The Civil Surface*, Hillage hung out his shingle and begun flying solo with the 1975 release of his excellent debut album, *Fish Rising*. A number of acclaimed albums would follow, including 1976's *L* and the following year's *Motivation Radio*. By the mid-'80s, however, Hillage had turned to production, working on albums by Simple Minds and Robyn Hitchcock before virtually disappearing from music altogether. He would resurface in the 1990s, working with electronic dance band the Orb before launching his own electronic outfit System 7, with which he has explored the far reaches of popular music well into the 2000s.

In 1979, however, Hillage and band were touring in support of that year's *Live Herald* album, itself a collection of fine performances of material from across the previous half-decade of Hillage's career. *Live In England 1979*, a two-disc CD/DVD set, takes the *Live Herald* tracklist one step further… capturing a February 1979 performance by Hillage at The University of Kent, this Gonzo Multimedia release offers up over an hour of mind-bending prog-rock audio but also a video version of the performance.

Live In England 1979 opens with the psychedelic-tinged six-minute rocker "The Salmon Song," taken from Hillage's debut disc, that offers up plenty of screaming guitars courtesy Hillage and his old friend Dave Stewart, and some amazing percussion work by drummer Andy Anderson.

"Unzipping the Zype" is a freeform band jam that includes synthesizer wizard (and longtime Hillage partner) Miquette Giraudy and bassist John McKenzie along with Hillage, Stewart, and Anderson, every band member getting an instrumental moment in the spotlight while Hillage and Giraudy share vocals. The song is a spacey amalgam of prog-rock, jazzy licks, electronic riffing, and heady percussion.

Hillage's take on Donovan's "Hurdy Gurdy Man" is taken from the guitarist's album *L* and twisted into a hallucinogenic musical landscape that the composer wouldn't recognize. With Giraudy's synth swirls providing a multi-hued backdrop, the band's gorgeous vocal harmonies, and Hillage's imaginative guitar licks take the hippie anthem to an entirely higher plane of consciousness. Ditto for the band's take on George Harrison's classic "It's All Too Much" (taken from the Beatles' *Yellow Submarine* album), the performance graced by dancing synths, melodic vocals, and gorgeous guitar lines.

Two bonus tracks on *Live In England 1979* are actually live performances from an uncredited 1977 show, perhaps the Rainbow Theatre show in London that was partially documented by *Live Herald*. Both "Hurdy Gurdy Glissando" and "Electrick Gypsies" are culled from Hillage's *L* album, the former ostensibly inspired by the Donovan tune, Hillage and crew taking their vision to deliciously mind-altering extremes, the performance a third eye-opening psychedelic brew of soaring guitars; buzzing, throbbing synthesizers; breakneck percussion; and fluid bass lines that mix jazzy and classical elements into the prog-rock stew. The latter is a more straight-forward 1970s-era hard rock number but with plenty of proggy flourishes like phased fretwork, jazzy percussion, odd time changes, and oscillating synth riffs livening up the performance.

The DVD portion of *Live In England 1979* offers up pretty much the entire audio portion of the set, minus the 1977 live bonus tracks but including the ethereal dueling acoustic and electric guitars of "Radio," a simply stunning performance that emerges from billowing clouds of smoke-machine generated fog, as well as the scorching "Light in the Sky," another period rocker with plenty of spacey visuals, Giraudy's oddball vocals, and Hillage's lively fretwork. The DVD also includes a 2006 interview with Hillage and Giraudy talking about the *Live Herald* album and the tour documented by *Live In England 1979*.

Overall, *Live In England 1979* offers up a fine representation of the Steve Hillage Band on stage as well as the guitarist's creative state of mind during the latter part of the 1970s as Hillage explored the outer reaches of the psych, prog, and hard rock universes. The CD and DVD are a lot of fun, and a welcome reminder of Hillage's immense and often underrated talents and his hallowed status as one of progressive rock's great guitarists and composers. (2013)

THE BLACK KEYS
El Camino   (Nonesuch Records)

The Black Keys found unexpected success with their 2010 breakthrough album *Brothers*, which earned the duo of Dan Auerbach and Patrick Carney three Grammy® Awards. While *Brothers'* mix of psychedelic-tinged blues, rock, and soul music struck a chord with listeners, the album's hit single, the groove-fattened "Tighten Up," became ubiquitous, blasting from TV sets and radios across the fruited plains.

The Black Keys have delivered a fast follow-up to *Brothers* in the form of *El Camino*, a solid collection that draws upon its predecessor's timeless mix of styles with a pure-at-heart blast of retro-soul and rock 'n' roll. Unlike the band's previous collaboration with producer Danger Mouse, 2008's *Attack & Release*, which experimented in lofty sonic atmospherics, there are no loose musical threads here. Instead, *El Camino* hits fast-and-hard with inspiration that spans the decades, the Black Keys turbo-charging their trademark garage-blues sound with elements of soul, electric funk, and punch-drunk throwback rock 'n' roll.

El Camino cranks from the jump with lead single "Lonely Boy," which sports a riff-happy melodic hook every bit as large and in charge as that on "Tighten Up." Auerbach's slightly-echoed vocals are overwhelmed by the song's dangerously infectious sing-along chorus and Carney's propulsive drumbeats. Infusing a bedrock of rock 'n' soul with a maddeningly effective recurring riff and plenty of engaging "whoa whoa whoa," the song will stick in your brain long after you've heard it, like some funky brain chigger.

You'll find no creative drop-off from the radio-friendly peaks of "Lonely Boy," *El Camino* rolling through its eleven songs in a shockingly efficient 38 minutes, leaving the listener gasping for breath and wanting another taste. The martial rhythms of "Dead and Gone" belie the song's melodic R&B heartbeat, while "Little Black Submarines" is a Zeppelin-styled folk-rock ballad with melancholy vocals and elegant, atmospheric fretwork. "Money Maker" is a raucous blues-rock stomp with muscular rhythms while "Nova Baby" revisits the retro-soul vibe of the opening track with a gorgeous melody and sticky chorus.

The Black Keys have come a long way from their three-chord garage-blues origins as an ersatz Rust Belt White Stripes doppelganger, finding their own voice in a high-octane blend of styles that is as classic as it is contemporary. (2012)

THE BLUEFIELDS
Pure   (Underground Treehouse Records)

Probably the closest that the Nashville rock scene has ever come to the birth of a bona fide "supergroup," the Bluefields are comprised of former Georgia Satellites' frontman Dan Baird (who, more recently, fronts his own Dan Baird and Homemade Sin band); Jason & the Scorchers' charismatic guitarslinger Warner E. Hodges (also a Homemade Sin band member); and singer/songwriter Joe Blanton, formerly of such beloved Music City rock 'n' roll institutions as the Enemy and Royal Court of China. All three men have a lot of miles under their belts, all three have experienced the fragile joys of a major label record deal, and all three have pursued solo careers with varying degrees of success. Nevertheless, their individual pedigrees are impeccable…

That these three musicians came together is an act of provenance, perhaps, or maybe just the Holy Trinity (Chuck, Elvis & Bob) looking down from the Mount Olympus of Rock 'n' Roll. Blanton had returned to Nashville after a decade-long hiatus spent in the hinterlands pursuing the brass ring with an acclaimed, albeit impoverishing solo career.

Blanton reconnected with his teenage pal Hodges (the two cutting their musical teeth together on the roughneck late '70s Nashville punk scene), the guitarist in turn introducing Joe to Dan, the three subsequently finding acres of common ground. As these things happen, they decided to write and play together 'cause, well, that's what rock 'n' roll lifers do, and the trio convened to Blanton's secret, subterranean recording studio, dubbed by the newly-formed Bluefields as the "underground tree house."

I'm not sure whether it was the trio's rapidly-formed musical chemistry, or if jars of pure-D white lightning corn liquor were passed around the basement studio, but *Pure*, the Bluefields' debut album, serves up a righteous helping of shit-kickin', guitar-driven, Southern-fried twang-rock that fans of both the Satellites and the Scorchers will nod their collective heads in approval of, although the Bluefields really sound nothing like either of those bands. Blanton takes the lead vocals on most of the

tracks, the man really one of the best singers in the Music City, criminally overlooked among the glut of clones marching in lockstep through the halls of the record label offices that line Nashville's notorious "Music Row."

Hodges does what he's always done best, and that is to bash and mangle that plank of wood and steel, tearing sounds out of his instrument previously unheard of by man or beast while Baird, the M.V.P. of any session he's involved with, plays the fat-string, adds a little of his trademark Keith Richards-styled rhythm guitar where needed, pitches in on backing vocals, and even adds keyboards if necessary. Friend of the band Steve Gorman, from the currently-on-hiatus Black Crowes, adds his thunderous drumbeats to the majority of the songs. The bottom line, though, is that regardless of the talent assembled, it's the music that matters…and *Pure* offers up more than a few surprises.

The album kicks off with "What You Won't Do," the song's brief instrumental intro displaying more than a few strains of Led Zeppelin's Eastern-fueled musical mysticism. When the band kicks in, Gorman's blast-beats ring loudly and the intertwined guitars are simply smothering. The instrumentation is thick, like an intoxicating smoke, the arrangement more than a little Zeppelinesque but with more twang and bang for your buck, mixing roots-and-hard-rock with a bluesy undercurrent to great effect.

The jaunty "Bad Old Days" is both a gripping morality tale and a humorous page straight out of the Dan Baird songbook. With a rolling,

Southern boogie-flavored soundtrack, the lyrics recall a tale of woe that all three band members have lived in one manner or another. Sobriety doesn't come easy, those crazy old days are in the rear view mirror, and with guitars that swing with anarchic glee, "Bad Old Days" is an unbridled rocker tailor-made for radio…if radio still played rock 'n' roll, that is…

"Don't Let Me Fall" is an old-school romantic ballad, the sort of song that, with enough hairspray and metallic hooks, would have had the spandex-clad bottle-blondes pulling out their lighters twenty-five years ago. In these days and times, though, Blanton's vocals are timelessly heartworn, Hodges' Duane Eddy-styled background riffs a perfect accompaniment. The band doesn't stay morose for long, though, launching directly into "Nobody Loves You," a pop-tinged rollicking boogie-rocker with an '80s new wave vibe built on a spry rhythm, ambitious rolling drumbeats, and shards of wiry guitar.

By this time in the album's sequencing, the Bluefields sound like they're having way too much fun, a hypothesis easily proven by the Zep-styled reprise of "Repair My Soul," a larger than life, foot-stomping hard-rocker. Built on a foundation of dirty Delta blues, the song is raised to the heavens on the strength of intricate (and inordinately heavy) guitars that sound like a clash of the titans, and Gorman's unbelievable drum tones, which sound eerily like the angry ghost of John Bonham banging on the cans. With lyrics dealing with sin and salvation, if this one doesn't scorch the hair from your head and get your feet a moving, then you're probably deaf (or a Justin Bieber fan…shudder).

As good a song and performance as "Repair My Soul" may be…and make no mistake true believers, it's one of the best rock songs you'll hear in your lifetime…the Bluefields trio scale the heights of the aforementioned Mount Olympus with the incredible "Flat Out Gone." A runaway locomotive of choogling guitars, racing drumbeats, defiant vocals, and swaggering rhythms, one can hear the entirety of the pantheon of rock heroes channeled through each and every note: Chuck Berry, Duane Eddy, Gene Vincent & the Bluecaps, Eddie Cochran, Big Joe Turner, Jerry Lee Lewis, Little Richard, Roy Orbison, the Rolling Stones, the Who, Creedence Clearwater Revival,

Bob Seger, Bo Diddley, Johnny Burnette, Ike Turner, Arthur "Big Boy" Crudup, Doug Sahm, Link Wray, Mitch Ryder, Elmore James, the Yardbirds, the Band, Bob Dylan, and the almighty Elvis himself. The song is three minutes and twenty-two seconds of pure, unvarnished rock 'n' roll cheap thrills, the likes of which come around far too infrequently these days for my tastes and, I'm betting, your tastes too...

There's more, much more to be heard on *Pure*, the album probably the best example you'll ever hear of three guys getting together and making music for the sheer joy of it all. Every note played, every word sung, every beat of the drum is the result of lives lived in thrall to the muse of rock 'n' roll, albeit with a distinctively Southern perspective. As a result, *Pure* lives up to its name, the album probably the purest expression of reckless country soul that's ever been carved into wax. (2012)

THE FEATURES
Some Kind of Salvation   (self-released)

Back in the earlier part of this decade, the Features were fated to be the "next big thing" in Nashville rock 'n' roll. Sure, they didn't have the curious, media-ready back story of their friends the Kings of Leon, but what they did have was years of hard-won experience on the Southeastern club circuit. After releasing a self-titled indie EP in '97, the band delivered a strong (and critically-acclaimed) debut album with *Exhibit A* for Universal in 2004, but a subsequent clash of wills with the evil media corporation found the Features back out on the street.

The loss of their label deal was a big blow to a young band, no doubt, but unlike many of their brethren, the Features had the steel to persevere. Their return to the rank-n-file of indie-rock resulted in *Contrast*, a fine five-song EP in 2006 and now, a half-a-decade since their fall-from-major-label-grace, a triumphant full-length effort in the self- released *Some Kind of Salvation*.

Some Kind of Salvation shows that not only has the band not lost its sense of humor after the whole U-music spectacle, but that they've

emerged with all of the musical elements that made them so special in the first place firmly intact. The Features' trademark sound is an odd blend of '60s psychedelia and pop, '70s guitar-rock, and '80s punk/ new wave with scraps of Britpop and singer-songwriter angst thrown in for good measure. Behind frontman Matt Pelham's keening voice and slashing fretwork, the sturdy rhythm section of bassist Roger Dabbs and drummer Rollum Haas build a surprisingly robust structure while keyboardist Mark Bond throws in a little rolling 88s whenever necessary.

Since the core of the Features has been together for better than a decade, the band's innate chemistry allows them to follow Pelham's lead and spin pure magic. For instance, "Wooden Heart" sports a strutting Memphis soul soundtrack within its timeless rock framework as the song's wall-of-instrumentation is punctuated with blasts of rhythmic guitar and piercing vocal harmonies. "The Temporary Blues" is a working-class coming-of-age tale with insightful lyrics, joyously clashing instrumentation, and Pelham's appropriately strained vocals.

The electro-pop rhythms of "Concrete" are matched by Pelham's whipsmart lyrics – "I'm the king of indecision, just sitting on my throne, and if you ask me my opinion, I'll tell you I don't know" is a delicious bit of wordplay, while the song's chorus – "nothing is complete, nothing is concrete, nothing is for certain, as far as I can see" – is pure genius, summing up perfectly both the band's experience and life overall. "Off Track" sounds like a melancholy version of the Strokes, minus the fog of faux NYC hipness, chiming rhythms and dashes of guitar paired with soulful vocals that are nearly lost in the depths of the mix.

The closest musical comparison that you could make for the Features would be to their Nashville neighbors Lambchop – both bands are talented, unpredictable, and seemingly without fear in their creation of music that is anything but cookie-cutter or trend-following. Whereas

Lambchop uses country music as its jumping off point, however, the Features are firmly set in a pop-rock tradition. Onto this musical foundation, Pelham and crew include the playful anarchism of Wayne Coyne and the Flaming Lips, the wry sense of humor of Ray Davies, and probably a 100 or so other influences that are thrown into the blender and come out imminently sounding like nothing other than the Features.

Maybe *Some Kind of Salvation* provides the band with exactly that – salvation in the wake of their stormy past – and it comes as no surprise that your new favorite rock band closes the album with the pleading "All I Ask," where Pelham implores "I won't give up on you, so don't give up on me." With this, the Features are well deserving of another shot at the brass ring. The Rev sez "check 'em out!" (2009)

THE GODZ
The Godz   (Rock Candy Records U.K.)

Back at the dawn of American hard rock – circa 1969 or so, 1970 at the latest – you had such eardrum-smackin' dino-stompers as Grand Funk Railroad, Blue Cheer, Dust, Sir Lord Baltimore, and other mono-browed Cro-Mags that roamed the dangerous rock 'n' roll backstreets. Most of these bands took the blues-derived, guitar-driven music of British dandies like Cream and Status Quo as a starting point, ratcheted up the amperage to cerebellum-shredding volume, threw in some fancy on-stage gymnastics like hair-whipping and broken-string flagellation, and subsequently had their choice of the least skanky of their distaff backstage admirers for a little extra-curricular activity once the spotlights were turned off.

While many of this first wave of hard rock heroes never made it to first base outside of their limited geographical popularity (future cult band status notwithstanding), the rare widespread success of a handful of like-minded chowderheads like Grand Funk was proof to a generation of bar-hopping teens that fame, fortune, and feminine charms were just three (loudly played) chords away.

Grand Funk Railroad was hated by college-educated critics with a passion not expressed in print again until the nerf-metal era of the mid-'80s; but while these egg-headed rockcrit types were grooving to their George Harrison and Crabby Appleton albums, the boys and girls were banging their heads in rhythm to the fab new sounds of bands like Alice Cooper, Kiss, Angel, and the favorite sons of Columbus, Ohio, the Godz.

Not to be confused with the hippie-dippie, psychedelic-folk noise terrorists of the same name from New York City that recorded for the ESP Records label, the Harley-humpin' long-haired hard rock thugs from Columbus pursued a blooze-n-booze swagger that was a universe away from the lysergic fever-dreams of their namesakes.

Formed by bassist/vocalist Eric Moore and guitarist Bob Hill from the ashes of the L.A. by way of Ohio band Capital City Rockets (who recorded one ill-fated LP for Elektra that is often considered one of the worst albums of '73), the Godz simplified hard rock into a white light blur of boogie-blues and feedback-drenched guitar chords. Although the band toured with labelmates Kiss and Angel, as well as folks like Cheap Trick and Judas Priest, the Godz never found much of an audience outside of their hometown, and all but disappeared after a pair of albums that have since achieved near-rabid cult status.

To be entirely honest, the Godz never hooked the earlobes of the young, gullible rock 'n' roll fan because, well…they just weren't really very good. Yeah, all the pieces fit together like the well-oiled rock 'n' roll machine they brag about being on "Gotta Keep Runnin';" guitarists Hill and Mark Chatfield (who would go on to play with Bob Seger) hit some smokin' notes; and in Moore they had a gravel-throated grease-n-grits vocalist to mangle their too-often misogynist lyrics. And, as they say somewhere, therein lies the rub…while the band's hearty, Vikingesque four-part harmonies were years ahead of their time, their shitty songwriting could suck a bowling ball through a vacuum-cleaner hose.

Nope, there wasn't a decent word-wrangler in the bunch, the six original tunes on their self-titled 1978 debut split evenly among three of the four band members, Bob Hill effectively frozen out of the mix after penning the bulk of the mind-numbing tripe that made the Capital City Rockets album the critically-reviled diaper-candy that it was. Booze, bikes, broads, and "rawkin roll" are the primary subjects found in the lyrics on *The Godz*, and while such lofty intellectual fare strikes a chord with a bar/club audience jacked up on bottles of Old Crankcase lager (4.1% alcohol by volume) and pheromones, it loses quite a bit of gravitas when played at home on the crappy BSR turntable in your bedroom...not a great selling point with a record-buying teenaged audience trying to figure out whether disco or booger-rock is going to get them laid faster.

Still, you gotta give these Godz boys their props...by the late 1970s, when the band had its coming out party, Southern rock had pretty much begun giving up the ghost in favor of punk, funk, disco, and the heartland-bred arena-rock sounds of Seger and Springsteen. The Godz managed to create a near-perfect musical fusion of north-meets-south, combining the reckless hard rock energy of the Motor City with the bluesy vibe of Southern rock, kind of a cross between Ted Nugent and Molly Hatchet, with a healthy dose of Midwest rustbelt biker aesthetic thrown in for kicks.

The Godz starts off with the riff-happy "Go Away," a rollicking booger-rocker that sounds like a less-distinctive Jo Jo Gunne, with squalls of ringing guitars, a neck-breaking backbeat, and a solid tho' unspectacular bass line. Played live, the song probably kicked serious ass, and it sounds OK on the stereo today if you down a shot or two of rotgut and let the guitars carry you away on a cloud of alcohol-inspired bliss.

By contrast, "Baby I Love You" is a real fart in the cookie jar, songwriter Moore ripping off about half-a-dozen tunes from better artists, not limited to Chuck Berry, Bob Seger, and the Rockets, the chorus alone pinching the infamous "rock me baby" line that was chiseled in stone sometime during the hieroglyphic era of rock 'n' roll, delivered here like a flaccid reminder to move your clothes from the washer to the dryer.

The next couple of tunes salvage the remainder of what was originally side one of the album, the first of 'em, "Guaranteed," rocking like a cross between Status Quo and Lynyrd Skynyrd, machine-gun drumbeats matched by twangy vocals and high-flying, razor-sharp guitars. The proto-metal jam "Gotta Keep Runnin'" borrows a bit of the cowbell intro from Grand Funk's "We're An American Band," and pairs it with the locomotive redneck rock of Blackfoot in the creation of a pud-pounding, steel-toed, junkyard brawl of epic proportions. Moore's spoken word bit in the middle about how we're all "rock 'n' roll godz" was ridiculous even by 1970s standards but, once again, if you drop enough Quaaludes and chase 'em down with enough rye whiskey, Moore's absurd ramblings hit your ears like a Shakespearean soliloquy.

Side two of *The Godz* is a mercifully short, albeit athletic three songs long, jumping off the turntable with the raucous "Under The Table." Opening with some sort of industrial drone intro more suited to a Joy Division single, the song blasts your senses with a pyrotechnic display of twin guitars that sound like BTO but smack your medulla oblongata like Judas Priest. From the chaotic peak, the song devolves into an ear-pleasing Southern rock jam with all four instruments intertwining to great effect. "Cross Country" is a standard-issue, country-flavored rocker with screaming guitar solos and a choogling rhythm that plays well to Harley-Davidson enthusiasts on either side of the Mason-Dixon line.

The undeniable highlight of *The Godz*, though, is the album-closing cover of Golden Earring's "Candy's Going Bad." An unlikely choice in material (every *other* bar band at the time was playing "Radar Love"), "Candy's Going Bad" showcases the band's instrumental skills while removing the "ick" factor of their self-written lyrical turds.

Starting slowly with a blast-oven intro that is more industrial than anything Einstürzende Neubauten ever thought of, the song unrolls in ways both predictable and otherwise, with plenty of scorched-earth fretwork, an unusual and somewhat syncopated arrangement, a blizzard of drumbeats-and-cymbals crashing down in the back of the mix, and gangfight vocals reminiscent of the Dictators. The song rocks harder and faster and with more energy than anything else on the album, and shows what these lunkheads may have achieved if they'd had a half-decent (and literate) songwriter on the payroll.

The question, then, would be "are the Godz worth their cult band status with hard rock and heavy metal fans?" The short answer: I dunno!? The Reverend saw 'em perform once, way back in the day, and I remember being pretty damned entertained at the time. Given my nutritious daily diet of psilocybin, pizza, Stroh's beer, and Jack Daniels during that era, however, I couldn't reliably bet my rockcrit reputation on the Godz' onstage prowess.

The band's self-titled debut, produced by Grand Funk drummer Don Brewer, shows moments of hard-rockin' brilliance surrounded by trite period clichés that would be repeated ad nauseum a decade later by a younger generation of similarly shaggy-headed, Marshall-stacked cretins. That the Godz proved to be influential far beyond their meager album sales is undeniable, and while they may have rocked many a stage at the time, their trademark biker boogie-rock sound would be pursued with greater success by bands like Badlands, Jackyl, and the Black Label Society years down the road. Still, not a bad musical legacy for a bunch of guys from Columbus... (2011)

THE GROUNDHOGS
Live At The Astoria **DVD**   (Eagle Rock Entertainment)

The Groundhogs, who hail from mid-'60s England, hardly even rate as a cult band on U.S. shores. A pair of critically-acclaimed releases during the dawn of the '70s – *Thank Christ For The Bomb* (1970) and *Who Will Save The World?* (1972) – were hits in the U.K. but flew beneath the radar on this side of the pond. The band's track record speaks for itself, however: working with blues legend John Lee Hooker, kibitzing with John Mayall, better than four decades of recording and performing...but outside of a few red, white, and blues diehards, the Groundhogs have always been invisible in America, and are thus ripe for rediscovery by music lovers seeking a new flavor.

Groundhogs vocalist and guitarist Tony (T.S.) McPhee has been fronting the band seemingly since kindergarten. An old-school Brit blooze-rocker...one of the oldest, in fact...through the years he's lead revolving line-ups through a variation of blues, hard rock, and psychedelic styles, sometimes with progressive overtones, but usually playing it straight down the (party) line. The Groundhogs' *Live At The Astoria* DVD represents the band's first full-length concert taping, the cameras capturing a 1998 show in support of their Howlin' Wolf tribute CD, *Hogs In Wolves' Clothing*. The double-disc set includes a CD of the concert as well, so you can take the 'Hogs with you in the car, or slap it in your stereo for an instant good time.

McPhee leads a classic power trio into battle, the exciting guitarist backed by bassist Eric Chipulina and drummer Pete Correa. Putting on a display of good ole-fashioned six-string strangulation in front of an enthusiastic audience, McPhee pulls every stunt at his command out of his decades-old bag o' tricks.

Although sometimes lapsing into the clichés of the blues-rock form, McPhee's talent and on-stage charm manage to transform even the most pedestrian of songs into a boozy party. Brick-by-brick, *Live At The Astoria* delivers plenty of down-n-dirty cheap thrills that you'll happily take a shower after hearing to wash off the grime, then cue it up on the box again.

"Eccentric Man" hits the listener between the ears like Cream on steroids, a heartbeat bass line and powderkeg drums ignited by McPhee's six-string pyrotechnics. Longtime fan favorite "Split Part 1," from the band's 1971 album of the same, is a vintage rocker with randomly-injected riffs, shifting time signatures, and surprisingly fluid fretwork balanced by screaming eagle solos. A blobby, lava-lamplike tapestry is projected on the wall behind the band, so that when McPhee launches into a whammy-bar-crazed solo, he sounds like a cross between Hendrix and Buckethead, with a Hawkwind chaser.

McPhee tries out his finest falsetto on an abbreviated reading of "Cherry Red," swarming guitar notes blistering like the stings of an entire beehive, while "Still A Fool" is a greasy, slow-burning blues tune with plenty of built-up frustration and denial, and a bottom-heavy solo with notes as thick as a rhino's hide. The band encores with its signature "Groundhog Blues," a throbbing slice o' Delta-inspired booger-rock that would do John Lee proud. With a heavy walking riff and salt-cured vocals, McPhee happily casts his lot with the long-gone ghosts at the Mississippi crossroads.

A merry band of musical luddites, the Groundhogs crank out the type of dino-stomp that went out-of-fashion with the loom, and doesn't exist these days outside of the British Museum, on display beside the Rosetta Stone. McPhee and the lads seem to be more the pub type, though, and *Live At The Astoria* is a fine representation of the band's timeless – and out-of-time – sound. (2008)

THE POGUES
Red Roses For Me / Rum, Sodomy & The Lash   (Rhino Records)

Top o' the morning' to ya, matey! The Reverend K here to engage in discourse about the Pogues, as motley a crew of drunken, swaggering, fun-loving musicians as ever took up an instrument. No AOR aesthetics or middle-of-the-road mindlessness in these grooves, you betcha, 'cause the Pogues perform a unique mix of traditional Irish and English folk melodies thrown in with their own appropriately antiquated originals. They present it with a spirit and vitality that out-rocks any half-o'-dozen heavy metal or hardcore bands you'd care to mention, and with the recent re-release of the band's glorious first two albums, we citizens of the colonies can refamiliarize ourselves with the Pogues.

Red Roses For Me was originally released in the UK in 1984 by the legendary Stiff Records, and made it to these shores a year or so later courtesy of the long-lost Enigma imprint. One is tempted to call this a dance record, *Red Roses For Me* offering up a baker's dozen of rollicking, never-miss-a-beat sea chants and stories that are guaranteed to get those lumbering toes of yours tingling and tapping in no time. The music is rich and hearty, with the basic guitar-bass-drums trio turned on its head by the Pogues, their trademark sound created with the addition of fiddles, accordion and concertinas (not to mention tin whistle).

Frontman Shane MacGowan's vocals are rowdy and hoarse, shouted or croaked in the mix above the instrumentation. As for the

lyrics…well, they mostly concern themselves with drinking, women, great battles at sea, more drinking, and even more women. In other words, the sort of thing that all of us of Gaelic descent have hidden deep within our ancestral blood, to be brought out when the beat is right and the rhythm rocking.

Among the highlights of *Red Roses For Me* are "The Battle Of Brisbane," "Streams Of Whiskey," and the wonderful "Down In The Ground Where The Dead Men Go." This Rhino reissue adds six good "bonus" tracks, including "Whiskey You're The Devil" and "The Wild Rover." A sixteen-page booklet includes a lot of pics and extensive liner notes, tho' they fail to mention where any of the bonus tracks come from.

If *Red Roses For Me* was dismissed by many at the time of its release as a mere Celtic folk novelty, then *Rum, Sodomy & The Lash* – produced by Elvis Costello and released in 1985 – is a steely-edged saber, an aural cannonball waxing your cranium. Under Costello's strong hand, the music on this sophomore effort is richer and brighter than on the band's debut, MacGowan's vocals cruder though more intelligible, and the lyrics wordier and more fanciful.

The result of the pairing of the Pogues and Costello is a bone-rattling, senses-shaking, hell-raising record album that has easily withstood the test of time based, as it is, on timeless traditional music and raw punk attitude.

The pace varies a bit on *Rum, Sodomy & The Lash*, Costello mixing the faster-moving pieces in between several coarse ballads. The spirit and the verve exhibited on the Pogues' first album can be found here in abundance, albeit tempered with a slight maturity. Tunes like "The Old Main Drag" and "Jesse James" are rowdy fun while instrumental cuts like "Wild Cats of Kilkenny" are every bit as energetic and out-of-control as the rollicking lyrical tunes.

The result is an inspired, well-balanced mix of sober reflection and drunken lunacy. Of course, the finest anti-war song ever written, the traditional "The Band Played Waltzing Matilda," is provided a weary reading by MacGowan, which serves to only strengthen its powerful sorrow. The Rhino reissue includes another batch of fine liner notes, song lyrics, and six cool "bonus" tracks, including "A Pistol For Paddy Garcia" and "Body of An American."

Picture in your mind a weather-beaten old ship, its sun-discolored sails lowered onto its salty, wooden deck, anchored in Galway or Cork. Its pirate crew holds forth in the local tavern, guzzling rum and whiskey and, late in the drunken evening, they break into a rambling, lusty song of life on the sea, or the lassie that they left far behind. That's the sound and spirit of these first two albums from the Pogues. The band's immense legacy has long since been writ large in the big book of rock 'n' roll, and their long musical shadow has influenced everybody from Billy Bragg and Flogging Molly to the Dropkick Murphys and the Tossers. To many – this humble scribe included – the Pogues remain the Emerald Isle's best musical import, and any that would disagree can "pogue mahone." (2007)

THE STRAWBERRY ALARM CLOCK
Wake Up Where You Are   (Global Recording Artists)

The Strawberry Alarm Clock is in the unenviable position of being both 1960s-era psychedelic legends *and* a rock 'n' roll trivia question. The band is remembered largely for their unexpected 1967 hit "Incense and Peppermints," the song originally the B-side of a long-forgotten single, its authorship shrouded in controversy, just another musical footnote to the decade. Truth is, however, that among their peers – bands like the Chocolate Watchband and the Electric Prunes – the Strawberry Alarm Clock were arguably the most talented and musically forward-thinking of the lot.

True, most of these arguments over the relative status of a slew of obscure mid-to-late '60s bands take place among rabid record collectors, fanatical psych-rock aficionados, and poorly-paid rock critics, but dammit, they still count for something! The Strawberry Alarm Clock recorded four albums of varying quality with an ever-changing line-up, the best of which included vocalist Lee Freeman, keyboardist Mark Weitz, guitarist Ed King, bassist George Bunnell, and drummers Randy Seol and Gene Gunnels. The band's first two albums, 1967's *Incense and Peppermints* and the following year's *Wake Up...It's Tomorrow*, are both bona fide psychedelic classics, the former re-issued on CD in 2011 by archive label Sundazed Records.

Spurred on, no doubt, by renewed interest in the band prompted by their inclusion as part of the *Nuggets* garage-rock compilation, the Strawberry Alarm Clock re-united in the mid-'80s and have been around, in one form or another ever since, usually sans Ed King, who went on to fame and fortune as part of Lynyrd Skynyrd (but who has still found time to sit in with his boys now and then). With *Wake Up Where You Are*, Strawberry Alarm Clock has delivered its first new album in nearly 40 years, a strong collection of buried gems and new material that contemporize the band's psych-rock sound while still displaying the same playful sense of musical experimentation that characterized the band's first two albums.

Wake Up Where You Are is no mere cash-grab rehash of old glories – you won't find "Incense and Peppermints" here – but rather a creative bridge between the band's sound as it is now and as it was then. With a current line-up of Mark Weitz, George Bunnell, Randy Seol, and Gene Gunnels from back in the old days, as well as long-time collaborator Steve Bartek (guitar) and guitarist Howie Anderson (who joined in 1986), Strawberry Alarm Clock has managed to bring their trademark psychedelic sound into the 21st century without losing an iota of the energy and vision that thrived on their 1960s-era recordings, mixing old tunes with new, and even throwing in a couple of choice cover songs.

Strangely enough, *Wake Up Where You Are* cranks up with one of the aforementioned covers, the band offering their take on fellow garage/psych-rockers the Seeds' "Mr. Farmer," an acid-rock cult classic taken from an upcoming Sky Saxon tribute album. SAC does Mr. Saxon's musical eccentricity proud, delivering the curious tune with a claustrophobic wash of instrumentation and a wild, buzzing electricity that perfectly captures the zeitgeist of the '60s. A longer version of the song, with more psychedelicized instrumentation, is tacked on near the end of the album. Of the new material, "World Citizen" stands out, the band seamlessly welding syncopated world music rhythms to socially-conscious lyrics, the sort of song that wouldn't sound out of place on a vintage '80s Talking Heads or Oingo Boingo album.

Another new song, Howie Anderson's "Wake Up," is a muscular rocker with strident vocals and chiming guitars and keyboards that could easily pass for a 1990s-styled alt-rock number if afforded noisier production. The band's cover of the Fuzztones' "Charlotte's Remains" is oddly disconcerting, a mind-bending trip both forwards and backwards in time, SAC an authentic '60s psych-rock band performing a song by a gang of 1980s-era '60s revivalists…the sort of M.C. Escher dichotomy that would have even Timothy Leary's head spinning around in circles. The band delivers the goods, though, making "Charlotte's Remains" sound even trippier and period-perfect than the original version.

Of the vintage Strawberry Alarm Clock material reinterpreted for *Wake Up Where You Are*, although the band passed by the chance to remake its biggest hit, they still take a stab at a couple of their other charting singles. "Sit With The Guru" sounds just as good as it did in 1968 when it hit #65 on the charts; here it benefits from a new perspective, with gorgeous backing harmonies joined by exotic, Eastern-flavored stringed instrumentation and busy percussion. The band's second biggest hit, the Weitz/King song "Tomorrow," peaked at #23 back in 1968, but it sounds just as lively and vigorous in 2012. Again benefitting from luscious harmony vocals and thick instrumentation, it's a welcome slice of psych-pop sunshine driven by joyous keyboards and rolling drumbeats.

Strawberry Alarm Clock walk a fine line on *Wake Up Where You Are*, managing to combine the youthful enthusiasm they shared in the late 1960s with the experience and chemistry they've developed as a live band through the years. The band's first new album in nearly four decades doesn't disappoint, SAC delivering a strong set of performances that display a luster provided by maturity, but tempered by a musical legacy that is as strong as any of their contemporaries. (2012)

THE ZOMBIES
Recorded Live In Concert At Metropolis Studios, London
(Convexe Entertainment)

The Zombies offer up a textbook example of the magic of rock 'n' roll to create legend out of obscurity. Formed in the U.K. in 1961 by singer Colin Blunstone, guitarist Paul Atkinson, bassist Chris White, keyboardist Rod Argent, and drummer Hugh Grundy, the band was signed by Decca Records after winning a local music competition. They scored a hit single right out of the gate when the Argent-penned "She's Not There" charted in both the U.K. and the U.S. in August 1964. The Zombies rode the British Invasion wave into the U.S. Top Ten with Argent's "Tell Her No" later in '64, but half a dozen or so subsequent single releases failed to match the band's earlier chart success, and Decca dropped the band in early 1967.

The Zombies had spent a couple years of hard touring across the United States, performing alongside folks like Dusty Springfield and the Searchers when they signed a last-gasp deal with CBS Records which resulted in what has since become known as the band's magnum opus, the wonderful *Odessey and Oracle*. An inspired mix of the band's British R&B roots and contemporary late 1960s psychedelic pop/rock with symphonic overtones, support by the label for the making of *Odessey and Oracle* was virtually non-existent. This forced the band to use a then-novel Mellotron to mimic orchestral passages because they couldn't afford studio musicians on the miniscule recording budget provided by CBS. When the label demanded a stereo mix of the album (which was recorded in mono), Argent and White footed the cost themselves.

The album sank like a stone in the band's homeland, and was only released in the U.S. because of support from Columbia Records A&R man Al Kooper, a talented musician and songwriter in his own right, who had bought a copy of *Odessey and Oracle* during a trip to

London and recognized its brilliance. By the time of the album's late 1968 U.S. release, the Zombies had already broken up and Rod Argent had begun forming his self-named hard rock band with Zombies bandmate Chris White...all of which made the unexpected success of "Time of The Season," which would rise to #3 on the U.S. charts in late 1969, all the more awkward. The band members declined to tour in support of the album and hit single, resulting in at least three counterfeit versions of the band touring the states as "the Zombies" well into the 1980s.

Somewhere along the line, though, that ol' rock 'n' roll magic kicked in, and as new audiences discovered *Odessey and Oracle*, the album became a bona fide record collectors' dream, a holy grail of 1960s-era psychedelic pop that commanded hundreds of dollars for an original vinyl copy. Music historians connected the dots between the Zombies and like-minded "sunshine pop" bands like Left Banke and the Millennium, while musicians like Paul Weller and Dave Grohl confessed their admiration for the band and its landmark album. In the wake of renewed enthusiasm for their work, three of the five original members reunited briefly during the 1990s to record a new studio album, mostly to retain their rights to the Zombies name.

In 2008, Blunstone and Argent got back together and re-formed the band with White and Grundy to celebrate the 40th anniversary of *Odessey and Oracle* with a series of live shows. The duo has been at it ever since, touring annually as the Zombies featuring Colin Blunstone and Rod Argent, the two joined by former Argent/Kinks bassist Jim Rodford and his son, drummer Steve Rodford, along with guitarist Keith Airey, who would be replaced by Tom Toomey by the time the re-vamped Zombies recorded their critically-acclaimed 2010 album *Breathe In, Breath Out*.

In January 2011 the Zombies were invited to perform in front of a small, albeit enthusiastic "invitation only" audience in London's Metropolis Studios, an intimate concert that was documented for the subsequent release of *Recorded Live In Concert At Metropolis Studios, London*, a two-disc audio/visual extravaganza certain to thrill the pants off of any longtime fans of the band. The CD and DVD offer up 19 tunes, most of 'em bona fide classics, including six from *Odessey and Oracle* as well as the earlier hits, and even a couple of cuts from the Zombies' most recent, *Breathe In, Breath Out.*

The show starts out with "I Love You," a popular but failed 1965 single that features a distinctive riff and forceful melody. How can a "failed single" be popular, you ask? Well, it was originally released as the B-side to a meager U.S. single, "Whenever You're Ready." But the song would become a hit when it was later recorded by the California pop band People! in 1968, rising to #14 in the U.S. and working its way into the top ten in Japan (twice!), Mexico, Israel, the Philippines, and elsewhere. Decca reissued the Zombies' original as a single in late '68 but it sank like a stone. Still, it's remained one of the band's more popular live songs, and here it's provided a strong performance, with solid vocal harmonies, psychedelic fretwork, and plenty of Argent's manic keyboard-pounding.

The band acquits itself nicely on the Jimmy Ruffin smash "What Becomes of the Broken Hearted," which was a U.K. hit for Blunstone and keyboardist Dave Stewart (not the Eurythmics guy) back in 1981. With the band providing Motown-styled backing harmonies, Blunstone imbues the song with a longing and wistfulness that falls just short of Ruffin's original. An odd instrumental interlude mid-song detracts somewhat from the performance, but Argent's soulful keyboard riffing hits just the right note. Toomey's guitar solo near the end is elegant and tasteful, extending the song to its short, discordant ending. "A Rose For Emily" is the first of a half-dozen songs pulled from *Odessey and Oracle*, a wan pastoral ballad that displays moments of Beatlesque melodic brilliance and interesting vocal harmonies.

The audience is preternaturally patient waiting for the hits, and they get the first in the form of "Time of the Season," an uncharacteristic song in light of the rest of the band's more sedate psych-pop milieu. With its familiar riff, unusual melody, chiming keyboards, and oblique lyrics it's an instantly accessible tune and while it originally flopped as a 1968 single in the U.K. it would hit #3 in the U.S. and top the charts in Canada a year later. "Tell Her No" suffered a similar fate previously when released in 1964, hitting big in North America while the band's hometown audience largely yawned. "Tell Her No" offers a similar syncopated melody and chorus, and the 21st century Zombies do it well, Blunstone's soft lead vocals providing a counterpoint to the band's almost overwhelming backing harmonies. It's an engaging moment that thrills the audience.

The last of the Zombies' hit U.S. singles to be performed this night was also the band's first, "She's Not There" hitting #2 in the U.S. and Canada while charting at #12 in the U.K. In many ways, it would set the standard by which subsequent releases would be measured, which is why, perhaps, "Tell Her No" and "Time of the Season" rose above the band's other singles in that they all share a distinctive harmonic vibe that stood out as different and innovative at the time.

Performed here, the song lends itself to a lively Argent keyboard solo, with great vocal harmonies lending to the larger-than-life sound of the song. The classic rock radio standard "Hold Your Head Up" was Rod Argent's biggest hit with his self-named band, the 1972 single hitting #5 in the U.S. and receiving constant radio airplay ever since.

The Zombies' version here of "Hold Your Head Up" is stretched out and definitely over-the-top, allowing Argent to bang away at the keyboards with reckless abandon, his vocals assisted by the band's harmonies on the chorus while Toomey delivers the song's timeless guitar lick. Although the audience came to hear the hits, the Zombies had a lot of good-to-great songs that never received their due.

"I Don't Believe In Miracles," from the band's 1991 reunion album, is a bittersweet ballad that features a strong vocal turn, beautiful harmonies, a melancholy melody, and finely-crafted lyrics. "Care of Cell 44" is a deceptively catchy slice of sunshine pop with a uniquely British ambience and instrumentation similar to colleagues the Kinks while "Beechwood Park," at times, reminds of Procol Harum with classical-tinged baroque instrumentation and somber yet effective vocals.

While some 1960s-era bands touring the oldies circuit these days are living entirely on past glories, you can't say the same of the Zombies. Sure, *Recorded Live In Concert At Metropolis Studios, London* strikes all the highlights of the band's career for an appreciative audience, but the hits are a small part of the 19 inspired performances caught on audio and video that night. There's a reason why *Odessey and Oracle* is considered a rock 'n' roll classic, and it has a lot to do with the depth of the band's songwriting chops, their instrumental prowess, and their often whimsical imagination, all of which are on full display on both the CD and DVD of *Recorded Live In Concert At Metropolis Studios, London.* (2012)

TODD RUNDGREN
Todd   (Rock Beat Records)

Save for a loyal but rapidly-graying audience, Todd Rundgren is in danger of being lost amidst a sea of cookie-cutter indie-rockers that don't possess an ounce of his individuality, innovative nature, or sheer musical "chutzpah." As close to a true renaissance man as rock 'n' roll has created, Rundgren – a talented multi-instrumentalist, songwriter, producer, video and multi-media artist, and tech wizard – has pretty much always done it his way, often with interesting results, exploring the outer limits of pop, rock, prog, and electronic music both as a solo artist and with his band Utopia.

Although he's been making music for better than 40 years now, the anything-goes 1970s were Rundgren's era, the prolific musician cranking out eleven critically-acclaimed albums that hit the charts with varying commercial returns over the ten year period. The 1972 double LP *Something/Anything?* provided Rundgren with a modicum of pop stardom, a not entirely-welcome status that the artist quickly denied with the following year's difficult, albeit exciting album *A Wizard, a True Star*. Featuring nearly 56-minutes of music crammed onto two sides of vinyl…a technological marvel in and of itself for the time…side one of the album featured a Beatlesque extended medley of proggish rock, side two a few pop/rock songs surrounding a ten-minute medley of R&B hits.

Against this backdrop, the release of the double-album *Todd* in February 1974 found the artist's fans wondering which Todd Rundgren would show up in the grooves. While *Todd* ventured further into the musical experimentation that Rundgren began with *A Wizard, a True Star*, especially considering the artist's growing fascination with synthesizers and other technological means to shape music, in truth the album also crossed paths with Todd's *Something/Anything?* era pop-rock cheap thrills and Utopia's just-over-the-horizon electronic adventures.

Although *Todd* didn't set the woods on fire commercially, the pricey double-album did climb to #54 on the *Billboard* Top 200 LP chart, and yielded a minor hit (#69) in the lofty, ethereal-pop tune "A Dream Goes On Forever." Undaunted, Rundgren moved onward and upward with 1975's aggressive *Initiation*, a reckless synthfest that further pushed the boundaries of vinyl capabilities with better than 30 minutes of music squeezed onto each side, the album's electronic-rock soundscape furthering the artistic sojourn that Rundgren had begun with the release of the *Todd Rundgren's Utopia* album a few months after *Todd*.

Whereas *Todd Rundgren's Utopia* would initially best *Todd* in sales, rising to #34 on the album chart without the benefit of a hit single, through the years the equally-difficult *Todd* has taken on an aura of its own, the album's reputation often preceding the actual listening, with gems like the aforementioned "A Dream Goes On Forever," rocker "Heavy Metal Kids," and Rundgren's flirtations with Gilbert & Sullivan satisfying the curious and influencing a generation of like-minded fellow-travelers to follow in Rundgren's considerable wake.

In 2010, Rundgren put together a band of various friends, including bassist Kasim Sultan from Utopia, guitarist Jesse Gress, keyboardist Greg Hawkes (The Cars), drummer Prairie Prince (The Tubes), and saxophonist Bobby Strickland to perform *Todd* live, for the first time ever, in its entirety. The Philadelphia show of the special, limited six-date sold-out mini-tour – which also included a performance of Rundgren's 1981 album *Healing* – was recorded and videotaped for subsequent release on CD and DVD. While *Healing* will be released at a later date, the live performance of *Todd* is more or less a re-creation of that classic album, in spirit if not exactly musically, minus one song – "In and Out the Chakras We Go."

While some of the more technologically-created fantasia from the original album has been stripped from this live performance, modern electronics allow a lot of the factory showroom sheen to rise out of songs like "I Think You Know," a discordant albeit lovely mid-tempo ballad with shimmering fretwork and squalls of electronic snowfall. Rundgren's operatic satire of the music biz, "An Elpee's Worth of Toons," mixes Gilbert & Sullivan with a dash of Utopia-styled electronica and a pop/rock vibe to deliver its devastating lyrical message amidst a cacophony of instrumentation and Todd's best bent vocals. Changing directions so rapidly that it could give the listener whiplash, Rundgren and crew slide effortlessly into the ethereal "A Dream Goes On Forever," this live version slightly less busy than the studio reading, but lacking none of the bittersweet melancholy of the original.

Rundgren further indulges in his Gilbert & Sullivan obsession with a spry cover of "Lord Chancellor's Nightmare Song," evoking memories of Sideshow Bob from *The Simpsons*. This performance is pure delight, Rundgren's unabashed enthusiasm dripping from his nimble vocals as Greg Hawkes' provides the rhythmic backdrop with his chopping piano play. One of the overlooked gems from the original *Todd* was the hard rocking "Everybody's Going to Heaven/King Kong Reggae" mash-up, the live version pounding at the pavement with jackhammer ferocity, guitar-drums-bass-keyboards slam-dancing behind Todd's strained vocals, the man finally cutting loose with a fire-and-brimstone guitar solo before breaking down into the monster jam that is "King Kong Reggae."

Another overlooked cut from *Todd* was the smooth-as-silk pop song "Izzat Love?" With an undeniable melodic hook and harmony vocals rising about the swirl of low-key instrumentation, the song sounds like something from Todd's early band Runt, updated with a few modern flourishes but otherwise a lofty example of Rundgren's 1960s-styled pop/rock chops. The song ends abruptly, descending into madness in an electronic storm, leading into the muscular, blustery "Heavy Metal Kids," an up-tempo rocker with malevolent intentions, crashing drumbeats, and tortured guitarplay. *Todd* ends with the gospel-tinged pop of "Songs of 1984," a perfect showcase for both Rundgren's songwriting skills and his immensely diverse musical sense, the mid-tempo verses brought up a notch by the uplifting, choir-like choruses.

While it's unlikely that this live *Todd* will gain Rundgren many new fans, it's certain to appeal to his horde of longtime followers…but if a couple of young pups are curious after hearing the live versions of these songs and decide to check out the originals, or other equally-exciting entries in Rundgren's large early catalog – many of which have been repackaged by British archival label Edsel Records as reasonably-priced double CD sets – all the better! (2012)

URIAH HEEP
Celebration   (Ear Music)

Back in the early '70s, British progressive hard rock band Uriah Heep enjoyed an unprecedented string of hit albums in the U.S. Beginning with 1972's *Demons & Wizards*, and running through 1973's *The Magician's Birthday* and *Sweet Freedom* and 1974's *Wonderworld*, Uriah Heep albums would consistently place in the *Billboard* Top 40. The band's original musical mix of operatic vocals, bludgeoning rhythms, Goth-tinged keyboards, and scorching fretwork found an eager audience among (largely male) teenage ne'er-do-wells even as it was scorned by the critical intelligentsia in the music press.

With the benefit of the ensuing years, however, it's not beyond reason to consider Heep as important an artistic precursor to heavy metal as Black Sabbath, Blue Cheer, Deep Purple, and Led Zeppelin. Singer David Byron's over-the-top vocal style would inspire a legion of imitators, from Bruce Dickinson and Ronnie James Dio, to just about every European power metal band of note through the modern day. Keyboardist Ken Hensley's dark riffs and chiming notes would bring the "prog" edge to the band's sound, while guitarist Mick Box's solid-but-spectacular fretwork would forge the blueprint for bands like Judas Priest and Iron Maiden to follow.

By the end of the decade, however, Uriah Heep had all but fallen apart. Vocalist Byron was asked to leave in 1977 due to his excessive drinking, while bassist Gary Thain died of an overdose in 1975. Hensley left in 1978 to pick up on the solo career that he began with 1973's *Proud Words On A Dusty Shelf*. Box soldiered on throughout the 1980s and '90s and well into the new century as Uriah Heep toured constantly and released scads of new music – some good, some not so much – with a line-up that has remained pretty much the same for 25 years. In the process, Mick Box and Uriah Heep managed to cement their legacy as one of the important heavy metal bands of the era.

In recognition of the band's 40th anniversary in 2009, Uriah Heep released *Celebration* in England, with the album recently receiving a belated release in the United States. A collection of the band's "golden oldies," if you will, *Celebration*'s song selection skews heavily towards the aforementioned early '70s albums that still represent the high water point of Heep's extensive catalog.

While singer Bernie Shaw is no David Byron, his vocals are nevertheless perfectly suited for this sort of lofty hard rock/metal, and his familiarity with the material – he's sung many of these songs hundreds of times during his two decades of fronting Heep – provides an invaluable perspective to the performances.

While the hardcore Heep fan may question the need for *Celebration*, the truth is that the song selection here provides a great mix of beloved songs like "The Wizard," "Easy Livin'," and "Stealin'" as well as lesser-known Heep gems like "Free 'n' Easy" and "July Morning." The band delivers the proper amount of bottom-heavy ballast on tunes like "Bird of Prey" and "Gypsy" while Shaw's slightly different vision for "Stealin'" brings a greater gravitas to the song.

Box's fretwork on "The Wizard" is still amazing, and if this modern version doesn't quite have the magic of the original, it still treads that fine line between folk-fantasy and balls-out rock 'n' roll. A new version of "Free 'n' Easy" actually trumps the original (from *Innocent Victim*), Shaw's raw, powerful vox out-manning John Lawton's more considered efforts as they rise above a suitable rape-n-pillage soundtrack.

Mick Box's guitar still crunches and devours every note in its path like a snaggle-toothed predator, and Shaw's vocals are second only to Byron's primal howl in the Heep canon; Phil Lanzon's keyboards, while adequate, still pale in dark malevolence to Hensley's groundbreaking 88-key torture rack. Russell Gilbrook's drums are a suitably explosive replacement for retired pyro expert Lee Kerslake

and, coupled with bassist Trevor Bolder's weapon-of-destruction approach to the instrument, create a rhythm section that can beat the listener into submission as brutally as any gang of hard rock/heavy metal punters. As a result, the modern-day Heep may lag a step or two behind the band's glory-day roster, but as shown by *Celebration*, they still put the pine to the ol' cranium when the occasion calls for it. (2010)

URIAH HEEP

Wake The Sleeper   (Noise/Hip-O Records)

Back during the early-to-mid 1970s, Uriah Heep was the band that the critics hated, but the little boys understood. One of the crucial artistic building blocks – along with Black Sabbath and Deep Purple – of what would later become known as "heavy metal," Uriah Heep's brief commercial peak pales in comparison to the band's enormous influence and amazing longevity…these guys are the "Energizer Bunny" of rock music, and nearly 40 years after their first recording, Uriah Heep stands as loud and proud as ever.

A lot of the credit for the Heep's death-defying lifespan must go to guitarist Mick Box, a genuinely nice guy and rock 'n' roll true believer that has kept the band going long after even its most fervent followers had given up on 'em. With the release of *Wake The Sleeper*, the first Uriah Heep album in a decade (since 1998's *Sonic Origami*), the band has hungry metal fans climbing the barricades once again as critics begrudgingly give the band their (past) due props.

Wake The Sleeper follows the tried-n-true Heep formula: equal parts vocal histrionics, blistering torch guitar, explosive rhythms, and prog-rock-tinged keyboard riffing. Whereas often-maligned vocalist David Byron and talented keyboard wizard/songwriter Ken Hensley once manned the castle walls, Box has since put together a virtual doppelganger of that '70s-era band with big-lunged singer Bernie Shaw, keyboardist Phil Lanzon, and former Bowie bassist Trevor Bolder.

Wake The Sleeper has been receiving a modicum of acclaim, hailed by many as a "return to form" for the band. Considering that the classic Uriah Heep sound has varied little through the years, maybe metal tastes have simply circled around and caught up with the band. "Tears of The World," is a perfect example of the sort of melodic power metal that Heep wrote the blueprint for three-anna-half decades ago, guidelines that have since been used by everybody from Iron Maiden to Stratovarius to build their own musical dynasties.

With a circular keyboard riff nicked straight from *Sweet Freedom*, the song's unrelenting rhythm and soaring vocals are matched by ethereal harmonies and Box's cutting six-string slash. "Ghost of the Ocean" is afforded a wiry, psychedelic guitar intro before launching into a galloping gangfight of crashing drumbeats, stabbing keyboard licks and scorched-earth guitar mangling.

Truth is, if you enjoyed any of Heep's best albums in the past – industrial strength wrecking-balls like *Return To Fantasy* (1975), *Abominog* (1982), or *Sea of Light* (1995) – then you'll most likely groove to *Wake The Sleeper* as well. The album is not so much a "return to form" as it is a continuation of that which Uriah Heep has done so well through all these years… (2008)

WARREN ZEVON
Warren Zevon
(Rhino Records)

Forget all about *Wanted Dead Or Alive*, Warren Zevon's uncharacteristic 1969 debut LP. The album shows none of the wit or caustic wordplay that Zevon would become known for, and is clearly an attempt by a young artist to make a play for success long before he's ready to do so. The album deserves neither your time nor a place in your collection. Opt instead for Zevon's self-titled 1976 follow-up, his true debut and, perhaps, one of the finest sophomore efforts in rock music.

Warren Zevon, the album, also represents the beginning of an amazing rock 'n' roll success story. By 1975, Zevon had spent nearly a decade in Los Angeles, doing session work, writing advertising jingles, performing behind the Everly Brothers, and occasionally writing songs for folks like the Turtles. What Zevon didn't have was a record deal, or even the promise of one.Fearing that his career would never take off, he fled to Spain with his wife, taking up musical residency in a local bar owned by an American soldier of fortune. A postcard from his friend, singer/songwriter Jackson Browne, hinting of the possibility of a record deal lured the ex-pat musician back to the United States and California.

The eventual result would be the brilliant *Warren Zevon* album. With an additional six-plus years spent honing both his songwriting craft and performing chops, Zevon entered the studio with seasoned veterans like multi-instrumentalist David Lindley, guitarist Waddy Wachtel, and saxophonist Bobby Keys. Friends like Browne, Bonnie Raitt, Phil Everly, and Lindsey Buckingham and Stevie Nicks of Fleetwood Mac provided vocal harmonies behind Zevon's incredibly designed songs.

Displaying the same sort of gonzo sensibilities as author Hunter S. Thompson's best work, Zevon's songs are filled with brightly-colored and finely-crafted characters from the seedier fringes of society. "Frank and Jesse James" is a finely-detailed tale of the Civil War vets turned outlaw gunfighters, Zevon's fully mature vocals matched by spry, vaguely Western piano (think San Fran gold rush) and shotgun drumbeats.

The beautiful "Hasten Down The Wind" was covered wonderfully by Linda Ronstadt, but Zevon's original version is equally considerate, with Phil Everly's harmony vocals adding depth to Zevon's deep purr as David Lindley's slide guitar weeps openly. The boisterous "Poor Poor Pitiful Me" was also later covered by Ronstadt, but not like this. On Zevon's version, Wachtel's guitar rips-and-snorts and tears at the reins while honky-tonk piano blasts out beneath the singer's half-mocking, self-effacing vocals.

The Dylanesque "Mohammed's Radio" sounds a little like Jackson Browne, too, but the song's contorted, colorful personalities and gospel fervor belie its anthemic nature. In many ways "I'll Sleep When I'm Dead" presages Zevon's notorious hard-partying lifestyle, while "Desperados Under The Eaves," perhaps the best song ever written about Los Angeles, is haunted by the reckless spirits of Charles Bukowski and Hubert Selby, Jr. (yes, both were alive and well when the song was written, thank you, but they still had their otherworldly stank all over the song).

A bonus disc provided this reissue of *Warren Zevon* is chockfull o' demos and other goodies for the fanatical completist. A solo piano arrangement of "Frank and Jesse James" is fine, but lacks the powerful drumwork of the final version, but the sparse arrangement given the alternative take of the junkie's tale "Carmelita" enhances the song's inherent loneliness and hopelessness. The second take of "Join Me In L.A." evinces a looser, funkier vision of the song while a live radio performance of "Mama Couldn't Be Persuaded" is a rollicking, joyful reading of the song that places the spotlight firmly on Zevon's lyrics. Taken altogether, the second disc's rarities provide some insight into Zevon's early creative process.

Zevon would follow-up his self-titled sophomore effort a couple of years later, 1978's *Excitable Boy* yielding the hit "Werewolves Of

London" and making the singer/songwriter a rock star. Over the following 25 years and a dozen albums, until his tragic death in 2003, Zevon would cement a legacy fueled by his unique talent and personality…and it all started with *Warren Zevon*. (2008)

WILLIE NILE
House of A Thousand Guitars   (River House Records)

Long ago freed from the commercial and critical expectations that painted Buffalo NY native/New York City transplant Willie Nile as the "next Springsteen," the talented wordsmith and blue-collar rocker with the fiery heart has had his share of ups-and-downs through the years. Lawsuits, illness, and industry indifference have often conspired to derail Nile's apparent breakthroughs, but none of the crap flung at him has ever drowned out his rock 'n' roll passions.

Nearly thirty years later, Nile is still banging 'em out with the best of them, and if he only has a handful of recordings to show for his blood, sweat, and tears well, they're damn fine records by any standards. Studio album number six comes courtesy of *House of A Thousand Guitars*, and to say that it represents Nile's best work yet would be an understatement of Biblical proportions. Much like Scott Kempner's *Saving Grace* last year, *House of A Thousand Guitars* is an incendiary shot-across-the-bow from a long-suffering industry veteran who has drawn a line in the sand.

Opening with the rockin' title cut, "House of A Thousand Guitars" pays tribute to Nile's forbears and idols, name-checking legends and giants like Jimi Hendrix, Hank Williams, Robert Johnson, Muddy Waters, John Lee Hooker, Bob Dylan, and John Lennon. With a Dylanesque twang and a Springsteen soundtrack drenched in admiration and jangly guitars, the song proves that the rock 'n' roll spirit is still strong in this one.

The rest of *House of A Thousand Guitars* does not disappoint. From the up-tempo escapist fantasy of "Run" and the guitar-driven, swamp-blues rockabilly boogie of "Doomsday Dance" to the melodious throwback garage-pop of "Magdalena," Nile's lyrics have never been

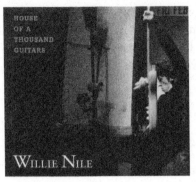

WILLIE NILE

sharper, his music more stunning. "Now That The War Is Over" is a brilliant, sing-song anti-war screed whose beguiling nature conceals the intelligent social commentary hidden within that bites with the ferocity of a drunken pitbull. The allegorical "The Midnight Rose" is a statement of faith and determination disguised as a hard-rocking romantic fantasy, with stinging guitars and driving rhythms that should be blasted out of your car windows *right now!*

Gently guiding the album's flow with a mix of folkish ballads and full-tilt rockers, Nile's particular brand of urban-Americana is the sound of a mature, battle-hardened, and maybe just a little saddened survivor of a thousand cuts. Backed by top-notch musicians like guitarists Andy York (Jason & the Scorchers, John Mellencamp) and Steuart Smith (Rodney Crowell), bassist Brad Albetta (Martha Wainwright) and drummers Rich Pagano (Rosanne Cash) and longtime friend/collaborator Frankie Lee, Nile brings his vision into sharp focus with laser-like intensity.

Almost three decades after being proclaimed the "next big thing," Willie Nile is living up to every promise he ever made, *House of A Thousand Guitars* delivering uncompromised and uncompromising rock 'n roll from one of the last true believers in the power and the majesty of the music…and he sounds like he's having a hell of a good time doing so… (2009)

ZZ TOP
La Futura   (American Recordings)

Over the past decade, ZZ Top – that little ol' band from Texas – has largely relied on their electrifying live show to push their career forward as it enters into its fifth decade. The trio of guitarist Billy Gibbons, bassist Dusty Hill, and drummer Frank Beard has been together since the beginning and the band's 1970 debut album, a raucous amalgam of blues and rock that took both genres into new territory. They would build on that sound with subsequent landmark releases like *Rio Grande Mud* and *Tres Hombres*, reaching their commercial peak with 1983's *Eliminator*.

The band has been absent from the studio for much of the 2000s, though, ZZ Top's last studio album also the fourth release under a reported $35 million deal with RCA Records. When 2003's *Mescalero* met with diminished commercial returns, however, the band was left in the hinterlands without a label deal, and save for a couple of well-received live releases – including *Live In Germany 1980* – ZZ Top has done much of their talking from the stage. Changes were afoot, however, and around 2008 the band broke with long-time manager Bill Ham and signed with producer Rick Rubin's American Recordings, the result being *La Futura*, the band's first studio effort in over nine years.

Four years in the making, *La Futura* takes ZZ Top recklessly into the future while unashamedly drawing upon the band's storied past. Gibbons and gang delve into a bit of what Chris Thomas King calls the "21st century hip-hop blues" for the album-opening "I Gotsta Get Paid." The song is based on a 1990s track by Houston rapper DJ DMD ("Lighters"), and the ZZ crew dirty it up a bit with some Rio Grande mud, drawing out the groove to a monolithic drone while Gibbons' guitar screams and stutters like James Blood Ulmer's Harmolodic blues. More of a greasy Texas blues-rock vamp than anything remotely hip-hop, it's an interesting and edgy direction for the aging greybeards in ZZ Top. By comparison, "Chartreuse" is a mid-tempo boogie-blues tune firmly in the band's wheelhouse, a rolling, rollicking beat punctuated by Gibbons' fuzzy, frenetic guitarplay.

La Futura also takes ZZ Top onto new musical turf with the emotionally-raw and darkly elegant ballad "Over You." Co-written with roots 'n' blues musician and songwriter Tom Hambridge, "Over

You" is a slow-paced, smouldering, and heartfelt ode that levels Gibbons' rough-throated, heartbroken vocals over a swelling crescendo of sound. His fretwork here evokes the best of every blues guitarist that comes to mind, but especially Albert King for its raw strength, and Otis Rush for its understated beauty.

Gibbons' shaky, slightly distorted tone adds to the mournful resonance of his solos. Revisiting the twelve-bar blues of their youth, "Heartache In Blue" is a torrid, mid-tempo rocker with Hound Dog Taylor roots, Gibbons' torn 'n' frayed vocals complimented by rolling blasts from James Harman's harmonica and his own switchblade guitar notes.

Another Hambridge co-write, "I Don't Want To Lose, Lose You," treads similar lyrical ground, but with a bigger, bolder sound, the double-tracked machine-gun guitars reminding of the band's *Tres Hombres* era, Gibbons' blustery vocals backed by a choogling rhythm (think "Beer Drinkers & Hell Raisers" on steroids) and sonic blasts of razor-sharp guitar licks. "Flyin' High" sounds more like the *Eliminator* '80s, but with less emphasis on synthesizer hum, the song copping a melody from a vaguely-remembered minor hit of the era and embroidering it with classic rock chops – soaring guitarplay, riffs that circle back around on you, a mean-as-hell backbeat, and a heavy bass line.

The trio visits Nashville for a cover of country-folk duo David Rawlings and Gillian Welch's "It's Too Easy Manana." Much as they did with the aforementioned rap song, ZZ slaps layers of bluesy grime and grit onto the song like cheap paint at Earl Scheib. Slowing down the pace to a dinosaur plod, texture is provided by Gibbons' electronically-enhanced guitar sound, a big drum blast, and world-weary vocals. It's a great performance that bears repeated listens. Ditto for "Big Shiny Nine," possibly the best…or at least the most fun…song on *La Futura*, a blues-rock romp from the 1970s with flamethrower guitar and driving rhythms.

Gibbons' guttural, growling vocals (think Howlin' Wolf with a cold) are matched only by his jagged git solos and the song's fluid groove. Down 'n' dirty in the pocket for "Have A Little Mercy," the band closes with another throwback to the early '70s, the song bringing to mind "Waitin' For The Bus" but with a slightly-funky, slow-boiling groove and shards of deep-cutting, raw-boned guitar.

Bringing a fresh perspective into the studio in the form of producer Rick Rubin – the first person not named "Gibbons" or "Ham" to sit in that chair since 1970 – has paid off in spades for ZZ Top, the band delivering its most inspired work since 1983's *Eliminator*, and possibly its most blues-oriented album since *Tres Hombres*, nearly 40 years ago.

The band has never strayed far from its Texas blues roots, but the synthesizer overkill that characterized its chart-topping tunes of the 1980s has been dialed back to a mild buzz, allowing Billy Gibbons' joyful guitar playing to dominate the performances and lead the band back into the blues-rock spotlight. (2012)

BOOK REVIEWS

BARNEY HOSKYNS
Waiting For The Sun   (Backbeat Books)

British-born rock writer Barney Hoskyns' *Waiting For The Sun* is subtitled "A Rock 'n' Roll History of Los Angeles," an ambitious conceit to be sure. Hoskyns does an admirable job of wrapping up 40+ years of L.A. music in nine neat chapters, condensing the complex and often-controversial music that has come from the City of the Angels into an insightful and entertaining tome.

Hoskyns' begins *Waiting For The Sun* with the thriving L.A. jazz and R&B scenes of the 1940s and '50s, mostly as a way of setting the stage for the rock 'n' roll fairy tales to come. In laying out the drugs, decadence, and artistic innovation that burned out its favorite sons in the '40s every bit as fast as those in the city's late '60s rock scene, Hoskyns creates a brilliant parallel that foreshadows the debauchery of the 1980s hair metal revolution.

Waiting For The Sun hits its stride with the burgeoning rock 'n' roll scene of the late 1950s that launched stars like Rick Nelson and Sam Cooke into the pop stratosphere. By including the founding of Burbank's powerful Warner Brothers, and independent labels thriving with the growing popularity of rock music, the book details the development of game-changing producers, managers, and characters like Kim Fowley, Phil Spector, Sonny Bono, and Lou Adler that could only have come from Los Angeles.

The meat of the book, though, may well be in Hoskyns' detailed overview of the creative decade 1964-1974, which saw the rise and fall of the Beach Boys and the trials and tribulations of future hall of famers like the Byrds, the Doors, and Frank Zappa and the Mothers of Invention.

Hoskyns positions Brian Wilson and the Beach Boys as the epitome of L.A.'s "sun and surf" culture, peeling back the thin veneer to reveal the city's inherent racism, as well as Wilson's tragic descent into mental illness. His recounting of the Byrds, threaded throughout several chapters, outlines the creative tensions that made the band great, but also broke them apart.

By the mid-'70s, the success of the L.A. rock scene had brought wealth and fame for businessmen and artists alike, and folks like David Crosby, Joni Mitchell, Randy Newman, and the members of the Mamas & the Papas all handled their newfound status differently. As the sound of the city further evolved into the singer-songwriter trend of the '70s, artists like Jackson Browne and Warren Zevon had their chance to grab the brass ring, while the calculated – and extremely successful – commercial country-rock sound of the Eagles enabled them to walk off with a treasure worthy of King Midas.

Hoskyns ends the book with the heady decade of the '80s, documenting the rise and subsequent commercial failure of the Sunset Strip scene that yielded mopes like Poison, Motley Crue, and Ratt, the era peaking, perhaps, with the incredibly over-the-top success of Guns N' Roses. As the fast-moving hair metal scene was laid to rest by the ascendance of Seattle's grunge scene in the early 1990s, Hoskyns paints a disturbing portrait of diehard sleaze-rockers roaming the strip, mere shadows of their influences, trying in vain to grab a record deal in the face of changing musical trends.

Unfortunately, *Waiting For The Sun*'s history of L.A. music ends at the dawn of the '90s, and although the book was originally published in 1996, the only addition Hoskyns made to this new edition was a postscript on Beck taken from a previously-published article on the artist. I would have liked to have seen a chapter on L.A.'s musical successes over the last decade. There are also a number of factual inaccuracies that should never have made their way into *Waiting For The Sun*, easily-verifiable statements such as Hoskyns' reference to Jimi Hendrix being stationed in San Pedro, California while serving in the Air Force when, in reality, Hendrix served in the Army and was stationed at the time in Fort Campbell, Kentucky.

Still, the true charm in *Waiting For The Sun* is in Hoskyns' uncanny ability to capture the charisma and personality of the artists and businessmen that helped put Los Angeles on the musical map. The history of rock 'n' roll in L.A. is peopled with madmen, junkies, egotists, fringe-dwellers, and musical geniuses, and *Waiting For The Sun* is their story. (2009)

BOB PROEHL
The Gilded Palace of Sin
(33 1/3 series - Continuum Books)

You'll get no argument from me about Gram Parsons' role as the forefather of the "alt-country" movement, as well as an incredible influence on both country and rock music from the '70s through the present day.

As an artist, Parsons' all-too-brief catalog has taken on a near-mythological status, the man himself deified with a fervor reserved for dead icons like Nick Drake and Tim Buckley that never achieved the fame and/or notoriety of a Hendrix or a Morrison.

As writer Bob Proehl shows in his excellent and insightful addition to Continuum's ongoing 33 1/3 series of books, as talented and visionary as Parsons was, he didn't do it all alone. Often overlooked as part of both Parsons' grand experiment in late 1960s country-rock after he hijacked Roger McGuinn's Byrds, and as a founding member of the much-lauded Flying Burrito Brothers, without multi-instrumental talent Chris Hillman, neither the *Sweetheart of the Rodeo* (1968) or *The Gilded Palace of Sin* (1969) albums would have been the same, and indeed might not have existed without Hillman's invaluable contributions.

Proehl tackles *The Gilded Palace of Sin* album for the 33 1/3 series with an approach that is part historical and part critical. In truth, this is a difficult musical masterpiece to dissect…although the album's mix of rock, country, and classic R&B was undeniably unique, and it would take decades for it to be fully digested and spit back out by bands like Uncle Tupelo, it's an album of dichotomies, as well. The songs penned by Parsons and Hillman are among the best the two men would ever create, the tense chemistry between the two artists resulting in lyrics that were topical and timeless.

However talented the assembled musicians, much of the music on *The Gilded Palace of Sin* sounds tentative, weakly produced, and often times it is Parsons himself who fails to deliver in measure with the status he has since been accorded.

Make no mistake – this is a classic album by any standards, but it is Hillman's voice that often soars in harmony with Parsons', and the impact of Sneaky Pete Kleinow's mournful steel guitar on the band's sound cannot be underestimated. In short, it was a true band effort, not just the GP show.

Proehl frames his book by quickly touching on Parsons' brief, but tumultuous membership in the Byrds, an artistic invasion if you will as Parson attempted to bring the vision of country music that he tried to create with his previous outfit, the International Submarine Band, to McGuinn's folk-rock hitmakers.

Under Parsons' influence, *Sweetheart of the Rodeo* would become a different album than McGuinn originally envisioned but, in the end, one of the band's worst-selling albums would become, perhaps, its best-known based entirely on Parsons' meager presence in the final product.

Proehl offers up just enough biographical information on Parsons to explain his Southern heritage and country music inclinations, quickly plunging his protagonist into late 1960s Southern California and the formation of the Flying Burrito Brothers with former Byrds bandmate Chris Hillman. Proehl divvies up each chapter according to Biblical sins, using "vanity," "envy," "sloth," "avarice," etc to frame the story of the band, and of key songs on *The Gilded Palace of Sin* album.

There's a lot drama here for Proehl to draw from…Parsons, a trust fund baby from a well-off Southern family had the money to ensure comfort and plenty of drugs to feed his growing habit, while the rest of the band struggled as the stereotypical "starving artists" they were. A cross-country tour by train (Parsons was notoriously afraid of flying unless "doped up to his eyeballs") was a financial and artistic disaster, the barely-practiced band's performances outside of Los Angeles drawing meager audiences.

The album, although receiving glowing endorsements from *Rolling Stone* magazine and counter-culture icon Bob Dylan, sold sluggishly and was mostly misunderstood by its target audience.

Proehl's descriptions of the culture, environment, and aspirations behind the album are lively, while his use of quotes from musicians and hangers-on alike helps put the story in proper context, fleshing out the story. Surprisingly, although Proehl included *Hickory Wind*, writer Ben Fong-Torres' biography of Parsons, in his research he seems to have neglected musician Sid Griffin's excellent biography of the artist, as well as John Einarson's acclaimed *Hot Burritos* book on the band, although he does include Einarson's *Desperados: The Roots of Country Music* in his bibliography.

In the end, the same creative and economic tensions that helped make *The Gilded Palace of Sin* a classic album also forced Hillman to fire Parsons shortly after the release of the band's sophomore effort, *Burrito Deluxe*. Hillman would later play musical matchmaker, pairing his former songwriting partner with singer EmmyLou Harris, thus providing the spark that would launch Parsons' widely acclaimed (and equally influential), albeit brief solo career. Proehl ends his telling of the tale with Parsons' tragic, but not entirely unforeseen death in 1973.

Proehl does a fine job of describing the musical dynamic in the band, Parsons' and Hillman's creative process, and both the triumphs and obstacles experienced by the Flying Burrito Brothers. Proehl's prose is entertaining and informative, providing the casual fan or newcomer to the Burritos' mythos an easy-to-use guide to the band's most important album, while still providing plenty of meat on the bone for longtime fans to gnaw upon.

More importantly, whether he set out to do so or not, Proehl places *The Gilded Palace of Sin* in its proper historical context, his emphasis on Hillman's role with the band in no way diminishing Parsons' importance. His work doesn't deflate the still-growing Parsons' mythology as much as it humanizes it and grounds Parsons' enormous musical contributions in reality, where they belong. (2009)

BRYAN CHARLES
Wowee Zowee   (33 1/3 series - Continuum Books)

Pavement was, without a doubt, one of the most interesting and influential bands of the 1990s. The band's so-called "slacker aesthetic," distinctive lo-fi sound, and the songwriting genius of frontman/guitarist Stephen Malkmus made Pavement the flag-bearers for the decade's indie-rock revolution. The band released five brilliant albums over the course of a decade, each experiencing varying encouraging levels of sales, but with their 1995 album *Wowee Zowee*, Pavement created the kind of classic album that often outshines a band's legacy.

At the time of its release, *Wowee Zowee* confused and infuriated fans and critics alike. Although the album's material didn't veer far from the musical blueprint that Pavement had written with *Slanted and Enchanted*, the band's phenomenal 1992 debut, or 1994's *Crooked Rain, Crooked Rain*, the 1995 album's expanded number of songs and shotgun-blast style of incorporating disparate elements of folk, country, and jazz music into Pavement's typical rock 'n' roll chaos was met with tentative elation by the band's hardcore fans.

Count writer Bryan Charles among those who were initially underwhelmed by the charms of *Wowee Zowee*. As he outlines in his insightful, highly personal account of the album – one of Continuum's wonderfully entertaining 33 1/3 book series – it was a couple of years after the album's release before he really gave *Wowee Zowee* a fair listen, at which time it "went through me like a blast of pure light." It became Charles' favorite album, its complex and textured musical and lyrical construction revealing new secrets with each hearing.

As such, Charles approaches his book on the album with the serious intent of the music journalist and the gleeful abandon of the adoring fanboy. In creating his narrative on the album, Charles rounded up interviews with all of the major players, from band members Stephan Malkmus, Scott Kannberg (a/k/a "Spiral Stairs"), Mark Ibold, Bob Nastanovich, and Steve West to Chris Lombardi of Matador Records, Warner Music exec Danny Goldberg, Memphis studio engineer Doug Easley, and album cover artist Steve Keene. In lively prose, Charles manages to paint a detailed portrait of the making of this classic album that juxtaposes his own ruminations on the work with the memories and opinions of those involved in its making.

True to form, the notoriously curmudgeonly Gerard Cosloy of Matador provided Charles a non-interview, answering his considered questions by email with nonsensical non sequiturs and unnerving hipster bullshit. In retrospect, Charles would have been better off holding a séance with the hellbound spirit of Cosloy's old buddy G.G. Allin to ask him his opinion of *Wowee Zowee*. Cosloy's insulting lack of effort rattled Charles' confidence and almost derailed the project; luckily Charles carried on and managed to pull an engaging story out of his other interviewees, even if some of the band members seem bemused that anybody cares after a decade and a half.

Then again, that's been the story with *Wowee Zowee* all along...underrated and misunderstood at the time of its release; the album's reputation has only grown during the ensuing years. While it remains the lowest-selling of Pavement's first four (*Crooked Rain, Crooked Rain* being the band's best-selling), *Wowee Zowee* remains the album of choice for the band's enduring faithful. With his entertaining and informative look behind the scenes, Bryan Charles has enhanced the album's status as one of the landmark releases of the 1990s. (2010)

CHUCK EDDY
Rock And Roll Always Forgets   (Duke University Press)

Over the past 15 or 20 years, music criticism has become both ubiquitous and mostly disposable. The evolution of this once-hallowed literary endeavor can arguably be traced to the criticism of classical composer George Handel by his contemporary Charles

Avison in 1752, although it would be modern scribes like Dave Marsh, Lester Bangs, Paul Williams, and Greg Shaw, among others, that would define and develop the dubious art form known as "rock criticism" during the 1960s and '70s.

As writing about music evolved beyond the milieu of handmade zines and poorly-distributed magazines, it would eventually become known as "music journalism," and album reviews and artist interviews could be read everywhere from syndicated columns and glossy mainstream publications to small-town newspapers. Until recently, many big city newspapers usually had one, if not two writers working the "entertainment beat," talking about music and such. Not coincidently, the downfall of music criticism can be traced somewhat to the advent of the Worldwide Web, which allowed anybody to be a publisher, and everybody to be a critic, albeit without editors and whether or not they had writing chops, or even a faint knowledge of music history whatsoever.

Now the Reverend has a vested interest in this unfortunate evolution of music criticism, what with being an old-school rockcrit who teethed on Marsh and Bangs and Metzger, and who mentored under, perhaps, the greatest of the early rock 'n' roll wordsmiths – the one and only Rick Johnson. But the Rev is no aging luddite blaming all the publishing industry's ills on the gosh danged Internet. While the web has definitely upset the traditional applecart as far as music magazines go, it has also enabled low-budget, high-quality media outlets like *Blurt* magazine to exist.

But even among the glut of online music zines and personal blogs, a few intelligent voices have managed to rise to the top like cream, writers like Jim DeRogatis, Martin Popoff, Fred Mills, and Chuck Eddy managing to bring new insight and perspective to an increasingly noisy critical realm too often overwhelmed by static and poorly-formed opinions expressed in too-brief reviews. Eddy, in particular, has distinguished himself as a critic to be reckoned with, both as music editor at the *Village Voice* and as a contributor to such publications as *Creem*, *Rolling Stone*, and *Spin*, among others. Eddy has also penned a couple of highly-entertaining tomes of music criticism and theory – *The Accidental Evolution of Rock 'n' Roll*, and the controversial and often hilarious *Stairway to Hell: The 500 Best Heavy Metal Albums in the Universe*, which made a strong argument for the inclusion of recordings by funk-soul diva Teena Marie.

Eddy's latest book, *Rock And Roll Always Forgets*, is sub-titled "a quarter century of music criticism" and, as such, it collects essays and reviews chosen from throughout Eddy's 25 years as one of America's most entertaining and annoying music critics. While it suffers slightly from a lack of an overall concept afforded his previous books, Eddy has broken everything down to thematic chapters, such as "Predicting The Future," in which he illustrates the futility of predicting where music is going by using his own past statements, and "Alternative To What," where Eddy questions the often-mindless pigeonholing of music through reviews/essays on the Ramones, Big Black, SST Records, Nirvana, Marilyn Manson, and others.

Much of *Rock And Roll Always Forgets* is entertaining and thought-provoking as only Eddy can achieve. Chapters tackle heavy metal (Metallica, AC/DC, Def Leppard); hip-hop (Sir Mix-A-Lot, Just-Ice, Spoonie Gee); and pop music (Debbie Gibson, Pet Shop Boys) as well as offering perspective on the racial aspects of soul and rap music with fascinating pieces on Eminem, Kid Rock, and the aforementioned Teena Marie. Most of this stuff is well-written and insightful, offering a unique perspective and personality that few music critics are wont to reveal these days. Eddy's willingness to champion genres often ignored or outright disdained by the typical rock critic, such as metal and rap, is legendary, but he also displays a deft hand at writing about pop and even vintage music.

Still, it's easy to find evidence of middle-age dementia creeping into Eddy's work. His complimentary reviews of contemporary Nashville floss like Mindy McCready, Toby Keith, and the horrible Big & Rich, among others, may read well, but they also provide cause to suspect Eddy's critical credentials. Sure, Eddy has covered glossy pop like Michael Jackson and the Spice Girls before – and done so without a hint of irony or patronizing opinions – but his dismissal of "pseudo-traditionalist hypocrisy" as the "country party line toed by most rock critics" as an excuse to wax ecstatically about Montgomery Gentry is pure D bullshit.

Like whatever music that you wanna like, Chuck, but the Reverend is old enough to remember when Jon Rich was trying (in vein) to become a rock star in Nashville and Toby Keith was the punchline to a Music Row joke. Country music *really was* better back in the days of Johnny Cash and Waylon Jennings and David Allen Coe, and its current persona as 1970s-era singer/songwriter lite-rock with twang is a slap in the face to those that came before. That's not a party line to be drawn in the sand, that's just reality. Coe might be one ugly sumbitch, but he can sing circles around today's crop of country stars relying on Pro Tools and image consultants to get over with the suburban housewives that buy their records. Don't try and sell us sour milk and claim that it's aged whiskey…

Eddy's critical flights of fancy notwithstanding, he's a solid writer of no little wit and humor, and if we readers (such as yours truly) can agree to disagree on some of the dreck that he immortalizes in *Rock And Roll Always Forgets*, we can all find middle ground. As music critics go, Chuck Eddy has always been a bit of a provocateur, and his tendency to risk ridicule with absurdist or unpopular critical stances is what has always made him an engaging and intelligent writer. *Rock And Roll Always Forgets* certainly includes its share of those questionable moments, but it's also an entertaining and informative look back at the past quarter-century of popular music. (2011)

DREW DANIEL
20 Jazz Funk Greats
(33 1/3 series - Continuum Books)

Just about any aging hipster or backwards-gazing youngster with an interest in '70s-era underground culture is familiar with the British band Throbbing Gristle, but few of 'em have actually ever really *heard* the band. Part of the reason for this is that TG were, well, somewhat loud and noisy in the pursuit of their particular artistic vision. The progenitors of what would later become known as "industrial music," the four muckrakers that made up Throbbing Gristle – Genesis P-Orridge, Cosey Fanni Tutti, Chris Carter, and Peter "Sleazy" Christopherson – spun the fledgling genre out of their genuine anger at English society, tempered with a sound that was pure aural terrorism.

Throbbing Gristle's third album, 1979's *20 Jazz Funk Greats*, eschewed the band's previous alchemical brew of clanky metallic factory noise, found vocals, tape loops, and aggressively distorted sound to go in an almost completely different creative direction. As explained by writer Drew Daniel in his 33 1/3 series book on the album, *20 Jazz Funk Greats* was both a departure from the band's standard modus operandi, as well as a grand artistic statement. Lyrically, the album strays ... albeit not far ... from TG's poetic obsessions with death, mayhem, and the perverse, dancing coyly into the battleground of interpersonal relationships (including their own), adding their unsubtle social commentary on the era to the mix.

Daniel points out that *20 Jazz Funk Greats* actually includes none, and plenty of both, the album representing TG's unique tongue-in-cheek perspective on jazz music *and* funk, in addition to their normal industrial-strength Sturm und Drang. From the off-putting album cover, where the four members look like anything but the "wreckers of civilization" that they'd been referred to by the British tabloids, to the relatively accessible sounds created by the band for the album, *20 Jazz Funk Greats* is admittedly the creative high point of Throbbing Gristle's brief, but notorious career.

Unlike those aforementioned listeners, Daniel *has* delved deep into the album, and dissects it here, song-by-song, with acute insight, and with some thought in providing the context and meaning of each track. Daniel had access to all four band members for the book, garnering valuable information in his conversations with each, also drawing upon the band's historical record as documented in print (much of it in the British press, some through the excellent RE/Search *Industrial Culture* book).

Although Daniel comes across as a fanboy one moment, and a dry academic the next, overall his commentary on the album fits well within the 33 1/3 series' purview. Although Daniel readily admits that *20 Jazz Funk Greats* is not widely considered a classic album, he treats it as such in his exploration of both the album, and the band's lasting importance and influence. In the end, he convinces the reader that, perhaps, this little-heard work by an obscure band is nevertheless deserving of another spin on the turntable. (2008)

ERIC DAVIDSON
We Never Learn   (Backbeat Books)

(Dateline: *the Future*) Gather 'round, young 'uns, 'cause Grandpa has a story to tell ya snot-nosed little miscreants! Take those earbuds outta those pincushion lobes for a minute, sit back in your officially-licensed Misfits™ beanbag chairs, and listen to what the doddering old fool has to say…

Now, I know that you kids these days don't have any proper musical culture of your own to speak of, just that dreadful, droning muzak that Sony Universal Music downloads to your sound implants at $20 a pop…which is probably why y'all have become obsessive nostalgists genuflecting at the mention of St. Cobain's name and eagerly buying all that "collectible" grunge crapola on the Sony Universal eBay auction website.

Lemme fill you drooling cretins in on a dirty lil' secret, though…there was more to rock music in the 1990s than Nirvana, Sir Edward and Pearl Jam, and those Soundgarden fellows (yeah, years before they were android superstars, they were real flesh-n-blood musicians).

Bubbling under the mainstream during the decade of the '90s was an entire shadow scene of honest-to-dog rock 'n' roll bands that had nothing at all to do with Seattle, Athens, or Austin. Bands like the New Bomb Turks, the Supersuckers, the Lazy Cowgirls, the Dwarves and others were too reckless, too raucous, too filled with the spirit of St. Iggy to appeal to the hype-jaded ears of the flannel-clad, unwashed masses.

While *Ruling Stooge* and other middlin' mainstream music rags featured St. Cobain and his evil transvestite bride on the cover, and a generation of dim-bulb record-buyers fell for the hype, some of us oldsters were groovin' to madcap tunes like "Born Toulouse-Lautrec."

Little Suzie Q, pull down that book with the orange spine from the shelf…yeah, *We Never Learn* by author Eric Davidson. Yes, I know that only canines and old geezers like the Reverend still keep these wood-fiber antiques around anymore, but *We Never Learn* is an important tome, ya know! Davidson, ya see, was a rocker, and a member of one of the underground scene's best bands, the New Bomb Turks. From his rare viewpoint at the forefront of what we rockcrit types called "garage-punk," and Davidson terms the "gunk punk undergut," the book documents the musical achievements and failures of the era, roughly 1988 to 2001, in brilliant (and, often sordid) detail.

We Never Learn works 'cause Davidson was there, riding the ramshackle rollercoaster that was underground rock during the 1990s, and the words here are written in his blood, sweat, and tears, and more than a little spilt beer. Wearing his most erudite rock-writer hat, Davidson interviewed dozens of musical fellow travelers from like-minded guitar-wielding gangs, folks like Eddie Spaghetti from the Supersuckers, Mick Collins from the Gories, Blag Dahlia from the Dwarves, and too many more to tell you bloody test-tube babies about in one short sitting. He also talked to deal-makers and scene-breakers like Crypt Records' Tim Warren and Long John of the Sympathy For The Record Industry record labels, as well as show promoters and zinesters and other satellites that orbited the gunk punk planet.

While you black leather-brained perpetual teens may deem your senile ol' grandpa a relic from another age, back in the day the one true spirit of rock 'n' roll continued to thrive decades after its "sell by" date. Davidson's *We Never Learn* chronicles the wild-n-wooly era of a fragmented and marginally-popular music scene that was never going to challenge *Nevermind* for chart hegemony, much less make even more than a slight imprint on an increasingly corporate-dominated decade of music that would come to a crashing close with clowns like the Backstreet Boys and Britney topping the charts.

Still, for a short while, cold-blooded rock 'n' roll dinosaurs stomped across America, Europe, and even Asia with a disdain for the popular music of the day, and a penchant for the absurdly reckless and self-destructive sort of behavior that killed off the reptilian age in the first place (meteors my tired old ass!). It was bands like the aforementioned that breathed new life and fire into a moribund musical scene that, thanks to their efforts, managed to keep rock music inspired well into the 21st century or, at least...ahem...until President-for-Life Palin outlawed music.

Davidson does a fine job of collecting these dodgy stories from the scene's participants, and weaves them into an informative narrative that accurately sketches a portrait of the grime and grit that personified the "gunk punk undergut." That Davidson downplays his own band's experiences in favor of those stories from other bands is admirable, but it is his firsthand knowledge of the scene and its players, and his own stories that help shape the book into more than a mere personal memoir.

So, the lesson that Grandpa is trying to teach you too-young pinheads is this: instead of pining for long gone and tired '90s music scene that was over-hyped and under-criticized, take a damn nanosecond to check out Eric Davidson's *We Never Learn* and bring a little white light to your cerebellums. You'll discover a lost world of great rock 'n' roll that, if you give it a chance, will have all of you strutting down the cyber-hallways of your virtual high school like streetwalkin' cheetahs with hearts fulla napalm! (2010)

GLENN HUGHES w/JOEL MCIVER
Glenn Hughes: The Autobiography
(Jawbone Press)

Glenn Hughes is a contradiction – the talented singer, songwriter, and musician remains a relatively obscure figure in America, in spite of his status as a bona fide rock 'n' roll legend. Although you may not have heard of Hughes, or maybe remember his name only vaguely, chances are that if you're a fan of ye olde "classic rock," you've probably heard the "voice of rock" upon a time.

Hughes' tenure with bands such as Trapeze, Deep Purple, and Black Sabbath during the 1970s and '80s has long been the stuff of myth, while collaborations with like-minded musicians like Sabbath's Tony Iommi, singer Joe Lynn Turner, and guitarist Pat Thrall have only added to his legacy. Throw in a moderately successful solo career (especially in Europe) that has yielded almost two-dozen recordings, and add Hughes' role as an integral part of the classic rock supergroup Black Country Communion, and the question becomes not "who is Glenn Hughes" but, rather, "why haven't you heard of Glenn Hughes?"

With better than 40 years of rock 'n' roll history behind him, Hughes has some stories to tell, and tell them he does in *Glenn Hughes: The Autobiography*. Unlike similar celebrity rock bios that either shovel mud on somebody else (Keith, I'm thinking of you) or mindlessly revel in behavioral excesses (ahem, Mutley Crew…), the punches that Hughes throws are almost exclusively thrown at himself. Glenn *has* been a bad boy through the years, and the decades of soul-seeking and struggling with addiction he reveals in these pages

aren't shared as thinly-veiled boasts but rather as cautionary tales.

Although Hughes' longtime struggle with cocaine is certainly no secret to many in the industry, the extent to which it threatened to derail his career is shocking in its extremity. That Hughes managed to come out the other side of decades of abuse with his musical gifts and sense of humor intact is not only amazing, but downright encouraging. Aside from the obvious sincerity that shines from the pages of *Glenn Hughes: The Autobiography*, Hughes' conversational style and the way he frames his story conveys a friendliness and down-to-earth personality that the average reader can relate with. Personally, I've spoken with Hughes on occasion, and have always been struck by the ease in which he engages you…it's like meeting an old friend on the street and coming away thinking "what a hell of a guy!"

As for the dirt in *Glenn Hughes: The Autobiography*, there's little of it, really, although Hughes comes embarrassingly clean on a number of high-profile sexual and romantic liaisons, and offers the truth, from his perspective, of a number of high and low points throughout his storied career, most of the self-professed lows involving drugs of one sort or another. The bio begins with a brief overview of his childhood and teen years, and touches upon his early musical efforts. Hughes' first band of note, the vastly-underrated Trapeze, is covered to some extent, leading up to the unexpected break that would launch his career into the stratosphere – his recruitment as a member of Deep Purple.

Joining Deep Purple in 1973 was a huge advance for the young singer and bass player's career. Purple were already one of a handful of jet-setting, globe-spanning superstar rock bands at the time, and Purple's choice to bring in Hughes and vocalist David Coverdale to replace Ian Gillan and Roger Glover had the band's longtime fans wondering. Hughes contributed bass and vocals to three of the band's mid-to-late 1970s studio albums, and a handful of live discs, and he goes into detail on his time with the band, his relationships with both old members like Jon Lord and Ian Paice as well as newcomers like Coverdale and, later, Tommy Bolin. For a Purple fan, Hughes' memories of his time with the band – positive *and* negative – provide priceless inside info.

After the break-up of Deep Purple, Hughes would be involved with a number of various projects, some more successful, creatively and/or commercially, than others. There would be a short-lived Trapeze reunion, a pair of well-regarded albums made with former Pat Travers guitarist Pat Thrall (Hughes/Thrall); an unsatisfying collaboration with blues-rock guitarist Gary Moore; and a number of projects with Tony Iommi, some better than others, that would culminate in the ill-conceived Iommi solo work cum Black Sabbath album-in-name-only *Seventh Star*. Some of these projects Hughes touched upon only fleetingly, others he offers more detail, but often they are just presented as an interesting aspect of the overall narrative flow.

Also only briefly addressed is Hughes' seemingly secret career as a studio gun for hire. Although Hughes' career is indelibly marked by high-profile band memberships and musical collaborations, he has also often lent his talents to a lengthy list of other artists' recordings. Among Hughes' session credits are those one would expect – guest appearances on albums by Purple alumni like Roger Glover, Jon Lord, and Tommy Bolin – the not entirely unexpected, such as singing with Pat Travers or Ken Hensley (Uriah Heep), and the surprisingly diverse, including sessions with the KLF, Motley Crue, Ryo Okumoto, and Quiet Riot, among many others. One gets the sense that Hughes brought his unique voice to many of these sessions not for monetary gain (although there probably was some) but rather because of the immense joy he has in the music.

Given short-shrift by *Glenn Hughes: The Autobiography* is the artist's lengthy and, at times, brilliant solo career, which began in 1977 has since resulted in a number of solid albums of Hughes' trademark funk-infused rock 'n' soul music. Although Hughes touches upon a few of the milestones of his solo work, including his 1977 debut *Play Me Out*, he concentrates mostly on his post-sobriety recordings of the 21st century, which include such gems as 2003's *Songs In The Key Of Rock*, 2005's *Soul Mover*, and 2006's *Music For The Divine*.

A little more insight is provided Hughes' role in the formation of Black Country Communion with blues-rock guitarist Joe Bonamassa, drummer Jason Bonham, and keyboardist Derek Sherinian. Hughes has seemingly found a new creative spark playing alongside these three talented musicians, and the overwhelming European acceptance of the band's blues, rock, and soul hybrid sound has added another interesting chapter to Hughes' still-ongoing story. Two studio albums and a live CD and DVD into the career of a band that's only a couple of years old, only stateside dominance as eluded Black Country Communion so far.

Glenn Hughes: The Autobiography is constructed as a sort of oral history, with Hughes' recollections punctuated by commentary from family (including his wife and parents), friends like Rob Halford (Judas Priest) and Tom Morello, and former band mates like Coverdale, Thrall, and Iommi.

Woven throughout Hughes' tales of famous musicians and various girlfriends, however, is that of his struggle in the face of overwhelming addiction, including the self-deceit, the rationalized relapses, and the final moment of clarity where Hughes heard the voice of God (not literally, tho' maybe…I'm not revealing any spoilers!) that led to his current sobriety and obvious joy of life.

Overall, *Glenn Hughes: The Autobiography* tells an amazing and engaging story – that of the rock star brought down to earth and subsequently resurrected to enjoy a second (third?) chapter of his career. One aspect of the book seemingly overlooked by others who have reviewed it is the perspective of the various people who have offered their comments on Hughes. Without exception, they all seem genuinely relieved that Hughes has found peace with himself, their comments displaying a fondness for the man and an appreciation of his talents...for Glenn Hughes is living proof that a nice guy *can* finish first... (2011)

HAYDEN CHILDS
Shoot Out The Lights   (33 1/3 series - Continuum Books)

Richard & Linda Thompson's *Shoot Out The Lights* is undeniably one of the most harrowing albums in the canon of rock music. Long interpreted as documenting the break-up of the Thompson's marriage, the reality – as presented by Hayden Childs in his interesting 33 1/3 series book on the album – is something else entirely.

As Childs explains, much of *Shoot Out The Lights* had been written before the couple's divorce, and better than a year before the album was released in its familiar form...which, perhaps, requires an explanation of its own. An earlier version of *Shoot Out The Lights* had been recorded at the expense of producer Gerry Rafferty, he of the saccharine folk-pop hit "Stuck In The Middle With You," in 1981. Overproduced and lacking the sparking emotions of the later recording, the Rafferty sessions remain unreleased, tho' available to Thompson fans as various bootleg recordings.

In 1982, producer Joe Boyd, who Richard Thompson had worked with during his Fairport Convention days, launched the Hannibal Records label. Boyd was interested in recording the couple, and with his steady hand behind the board, the Thompsons created the critically-acclaimed version of *Shoot Out The Lights* we all know and love.

By this time, the Thompson's relationship was in complete shambles. Linda was pregnant and Richard's affections had turned elsewhere. The palatable tension between the two artists translated into a unique dynamic in the studio, breathing new life and fire into the established songs while driving the newer material to greater heights.

This, in a nutshell, is the story behind *Shoot Out The Lights*, but Childs provides both more information and a larger context for the album. Using an unusual literary construct in his interpretation of the album, Childs creates a fictional narrator whose make-believe life parallels that of Richard Thompson's – his doppelganger, as it were.

Comparing Thompson's "descent into hell" with Dante's *Inferno*, Childs' protagonist recounts his own spiral into the underworld's lower circles as he travels from Florida to New York to claim his recently deceased ex-wife's body. Obsessed with the Thompson's *Shoot Out The Lights* album, Childs' downtrodden character Virgil (also the name of Dante's guide into hell), compares the aspects of his life to that of Richard Thompson's.

If all this sounds confusing, well, it is…Childs provides a completely different way of looking at an album from the couple dozen previous 33 1/3 series books that I've read, and the first three or four chapters are difficult to slog through. By the end of the sixth chapter, though, the damn thing begins to make sense, and if you stay on the ride through the end, the insight proffered by Childs is rewarding as well as eye-opening.

Hayden Childs has definitely broken beyond the normal form of rock criticism with his take on *Shoot Out The Lights*, creating a review of some depth and intelligence, his critique as layered and textured as the album it explores. Whether you're a longtime fan of the Thompsons, or a listener just discovering the brilliant and disturbing *Shoot Out The Lights*, Childs' book provides the perfect guide to this difficult album. (2008)

JIM DEROGATIS
Staring At Sound   (Broadway Books)

It's no secret 'round these parts that the Reverend is a big fan of the big man from Chi-town. Jim DeRogatis is the author of *Let It Blurt*, a fine biography of Lester Bangs, perhaps the most cherished Godfather of music criticism, and *Milk It!*, an entertaining and informative collection of his columns and music reviews from the *Chicago Sun Times* that both reminisces about and dissects the roller-coaster decade of the '90s. The most enjoyable of mainstream music writers, DeRogatis is erudite, knowledgeable and, most importantly, has never lost his fanboy love of rock 'n' roll.

With an intro like that, you'd expect *Staring At Sound*, DeRogatis' biography of the Flaming Lips, to be a slam-dunk…and it is. A longtime fan of the best-known rock band to come out of Oklahoma, DeRogatis had full access to the band and surrounding characters, drawing on his own professional relationship with Lips' frontman Wayne Coyne to craft an enormously entertaining story of the band.

From the Coyne family's 1961 relocation from Pittsburgh to Oklahoma and the influence that the tight-knit family's trials and tribulations had on the future rock star to Coyne's initial musical experiments and the subsequent early '80s formation of the Flaming Lips, DeRogatis presents an honest and loving recounting of the years.

The most important story in *Staring At Sound* is that of Coyne's longstanding friendship with musical brother-in-arms Michael Ivins, and, after many personnel changes, the addition of multi-instrumental talent Steven Drozd to the band. Throughout the many ups-and-downs and close calls since 1983, Coyne and Ivins have collaborated on some of the most inventive and interesting music of the past two decades.

Bringing Drozd into the band completed the musical chemistry that would eventually launch the band, if not to the top of the charts, at least to a sustainable middle-rung of mainstream acceptability. Through it all, the admirable work ethic and commitment to their artistic vision has seen Coyne, Ivins, and Drozd through the tough times to a point where they have achieved the freedom to create some of the best music of their lengthy career.

Staring At Sound pulls no punches, and DeRogatis presents the band warts and all throughout his narrative. Interestingly enough, for a band with a strong rep for strangeness, what is striking about the Flaming Lips is the trio's normality. Coyne's enormous charisma and belief in hard work drives the band, Ivins' solid presence and tinkerer's curiosity adds an essential element to the Lips' sound while Drozd's innate talent enables the experimentation that is the hallmark of the band's creative legacy.

DeRogatis spins it all together into a mesmerizing story, that of the band's success against all odds and the wonderful dynamic that drives their unique sound. *Staring At Sound* is recommended, not only for the Flaming Lips' growing legion of fans, but also for anybody who loves rock music. It is an essential read for young musicians, if only to point out what is possible to achieve if you are willing to work hard and stand by your vision, which, in the end, is what the Flaming Lips have always represented. (2006)

JOHN KRUTH
To Live's To Fly   (Da Capo Press)

There are two things that everybody seemingly agrees on in the pages of *To Live's To Fly*, John Kruth's excellent biography of Townes Van Zandt: 1) TVZ was one of the greatest songwriters that country music has ever known; and 2) TVZ was one messed up dude.

For those unfamiliar with the man that many consider country music's poet laureate, Townes Van Zandt was born to a wealthy Fort Worth, Texas family whose roots reach back to the city's founding. Like most musicians of his generation, a twelve-year-old Townes was mesmerized by Elvis Presley's 1956 appearance on *The Ed Sullivan Show*. Afterwards, Kruth writes that "overnight, Van Zandt became completely obsessed with rock and roll."

Having grown up on the country sounds of Lefty Frizzell and Hank Williams, Townes' new favorites were Ricky Nelson, Jerry Lee Lewis, and the Everly Brothers. It was his father, however, who suggested that he begin writing his own songs, pointing the young Van Zandt towards his eventual destiny.

Van Zandt went to college, but he really wasn't one to attend classes, instead preferring to lock himself in his room, drink, listen to records, and play the guitar. The education he received wasn't what his parents believed it would be. Concerned about his drinking and wild ways, his parents had TVZ committed to a mental hospital in Galveston, Texas where he was diagnosed as "manic depressive" and received three months of electric-and-insulin-shock therapy. The impact this treatment had on Van Zandt is arguable, but it most likely contributed to his ongoing adult depression, alcoholism, and mental instability.

Townes got married, went back to college for a while, finally dropping out in 1964, ending up in Houston doing the only thing he had ever really wanted to do: sing and write songs. Van Zandt fell in with a like-minded crowd of singer/songwriters that included life-long friend Guy Clark, Mickey Newbury, and Jerry Jeff Walker. It was here that Van Zandt honed his performance skills and began displaying the songwriting skills that have made him a legend.

Over the next 30 years, Van Zandt would go on to record some two-dozen albums for a number of independent labels, and write scores of songs, some like "Pancho & Lefty" or "If I Needed You" becoming significant hits for other artists. He moved to Nashville in 1976, but headed back to Texas in '78 and didn't record again for almost a decade. He landed back in the "Music City" just when his songwriting fortunes began to rise and it was in Nashville that he died on New Year's Day, 1997.

The mystery of Van Zandt's appeal is easy to solve. A charismatic personality and performer, Townes possessed a great charm and intelligence. By any standards, Van Zandt wasn't really a country artist…influenced greatly by bluesman Lightning Hopkins, his music is more a mix of twangy folk and country blues. His skill with the language, however, is pure poetry, his lyrics expressing intricate thoughts and emotions but flowing casually. His influence on songwriters crosses all musical genres, however, and it comes as no surprise that artists as disparate as Willie Nelson, Emmylou Harris, Mudhoney, and the Cowboy Junkies, among others, have recorded his songs.

To Live's To Fly offers an in-depth and, at times, depressingly exhaustive overview of Van Zandt's life, from childhood through his death. Kruth interviewed hundreds of Townes' friends, family and fellow artists and paints a detailed portrait of both the man and the demons that plagued him for most of his life. Most of all, Kruth provides an understanding of the man through both his actions and his songs. I'd recommend reading *To Live's To Fly* while listening to one of Van Zandt's classic early albums, preferably *Live At The Old Quarter*. It will definitely enhance your appreciation of Townes Van Zandt to experience the music along with reading the tales of this great artist's life. (2008)

KIM COOPER
In The Aeroplane Over The Sea   (33 1/3 series - Continuum Books)

Writer Kim Cooper, editor and publisher of the charming and informative pop culture zine *Scram*, has made a career out of championing the underrated and ill-fated musicians of days past. Both with her zine, and in wonderful books like *Lost In The Grooves* or *Bubblegum Music Is The Naked Truth*, Cooper evinces a great deal of affection for, and insight into, the music and musicians she writes about. Thus it should come as no surprise that Cooper has hooked up with Continuum to write one of the better books in the company's esteemed 33 1/3 series about one of the more obscure, yet deserving albums in rock 'n' roll.

In The Aeroplane Over The Sea offers more than just Cooper's take on the landmark 1998 album by cult faves Neutral Milk Hotel. Cooper delves into the band's roots, setting up the relationships between all of the musicians that made up the Elephant 6 collective and bands like Apples In Stereo and the Olivia Tremor Control. She outlines the collaborative efforts of the players, the travels necessary to bring them all to certain points (and places) in time, and the work behind the loose-knit collective's various projects. Finally, she focuses in on Jeff Mangrum, the multi-talented musician and songwriter who is the spark behind Neutral Milk Hotel and the man mostly responsible for the short-lived band's two excellent albums.

With her easy-going narrative, Cooper achieves one of the hardest things to do when introducing readers to perfect strangers: she infuses each of the main players with a personality. When finishing *In The Aeroplane Over The Sea* – a quick read at a too-short 104 pages, a hallmark of the 33 1/3 series – the reader not only has a sense of who Jeff Mangrum and friends are, but also what they were trying to accomplish with their music.

Although both the album *In The Aeroplane Over The Sea* and its 1996 predecessor *On Avery Island* are dense, textured, and maddeningly obtuse works, Cooper manages to shine a new light on both albums.

Although I must admit to no more than a passing familiarity with either Neutral Milk Hotel album, Cooper's book made me go out and buy both CDs, dammit! A perfect companion piece to the album that it dissects, Cooper's *In The Aeroplane Over The Sea* explains why the album's audience and importance grows with each passing year while doing a fine job of also relating the music's immense charm and…dare I say it…magic. Both the book and the album are highly recommended for anybody searching for meaningful music beyond this week's trends. (2006)

MARTIN POPOFF
Fighting My Way Back: Thin Lizzy 69-76
(Power Chord Press)

Canadian music journalist Martin Popoff has been writing about hard rock and heavy metal music for almost as long as the Reverend has been listening to the stuff, which is to say a long, loooong time. Popoff shows a commitment to the genre that's impressive even to a confirmed lifer such as yours truly, co-founding the respected metal magazine *Brave Words & Bloody Knuckles* in 1994 and penning nearly 8,000 album reviews, most of which have been compiled into four volumes of Popoff's *The Collectors Guide to Heavy Metal* series of books.

Often overlooked are Popoff's contributions in documenting rock 'n' roll history, which he has achieved with the five books in his *Ye Olde Metal* series as well as around two-dozen band biographies covering everybody from Black Sabbath and Deep Purple to Rush and Blue Oyster Cult, among others.

Admittedly, few of these tomes published by Popoff's Power Chord Press sell on the level of, say, some sordid celebrity sleaze tell-all or that new Steve Jobs bio that lucked its way onto the top of the best-seller list when, by happenstance and circumstance, the author benefiting from the Apple CEO's untimely death. No, Popoff writes these things 'cause he *wants* to, not because he thinks he's going to find a pot of gold at the end of the rainbow.

Popoff's latest labor of love is his in-depth biography of classic rock titans Thin Lizzy, titled *Fighting My Way Back: Thin Lizzy 69-76*. The first of a pair of books covering every aspect of the band's too-brief, albeit influential lifespan, it has been compiled from numerous interviews Popoff conducted with former Lizzy guitarists Scott Gorham, Eric Bell, Gary Moore, and Brian Robertson, as well as drummer and original member Brian Downey. Interviews with associates like artist Jim Fitzpatrick, who created a number of the band's memorable album covers, or Brendan "Brush" Shiels, who played with Lizzy's Phil Lynott in the band Skid Row, bring additional perspective to the band's history. Since he never had the opportunity to speak with Lynott, the late, great creative force behind Thin Lizzy, here Popoff draws upon previously-published articles and interviews to flesh out the story...

And what a story it is, a trio of young Irish lads making a name for themselves (originally as "Tin Lizzy") in the band's hometown of

Dublin, the band formed by Lynott and Downey with guitarist Eric Bell and keyboardist Erix Wrixon, who would leave after recording the band's first single. Actually, Popoff delves deeper than that, coaxing memories from Brush Shiels about Lynott's time in Skid Row with him and guitarist Gary Moore, setting the stage and defining the important relationships that would be threaded throughout Lizzy's timeline. The band's signing with Decca Records, its re-location to London, the recording of their self-titled 1971 debut album, and Lizzy's subsequent struggles, both artistically and commercially, are all covered in depth.

Popoff follows the band through the making of its sophomore effort, 1972's *Shades of a Blue Orphanage* and even delves into the story behind the long-lost album of Deep Purple cover songs recorded by Lynott and crew for quick cash that year. He outlines the band's reaction to their unexpected hit single "Whiskey In The Jar" and the subsequent fall-out when their third album, 1973's *Vagabonds of the Western World* failed to chart, or even produce a minor hit.

When Bell left the band in 1973, to be temporarily replaced by Gary Moore, Lynott chose to reboot the band's sound with the addition of twin lead guitarists. After a failed experiment with guitarists Andy Gee and former Atomic Rooster member John Cann, what is now known as the classic Thin Lizzy line-up formed with guitarists Brian Robertson and Scott Gorham joining Lynott and Downey.

A new label deal with Phonogram was nearly scuttled by the lackluster performance of Lizzy's first albums for the label, 1974's *Nightlife* and the following year's *Fighting* failing to produce much in the way of sales, although the latter album's development of the twin-guitar sound would set the stage for Thin Lizzy's breakthrough album, 1976's *Jailbreak* and the monster hit "The Boys Are Back In Town." Success breeds its own problems, and Popoff's chapter on the album looks deep inside the band's ups-and-downs in the wake of their sudden worldwide fame. It's here that Popoff ends the first part of the story, setting up the reader for the forthcoming second book.

While Popoff's engaging manner of storytelling should appeal to both Thin Lizzy fanatics as well as classic rock fans, *Fighting My Way*

Back is also profusely illustrated with B&W artwork, from band photos and miscellaneous memorabilia to album covers, photos of rare singles, gig flyers, and much more. The resulting effort provides a solid literary and visual document of the band's early career, as important a slice of rock 'n' roll history as exists and a tale well-told by Popoff. (2012)

MICHAEL WALKER
Laurel Canyon   (Faber & Faber)

Book sub-titles are often rife with hyperbole, but in the case of Michael Walker's excellent *Laurel Canyon*, "The Inside Story of Rock And Roll's Legendary Neighborhood" is a somewhat subdued description. From the fabled canyon's humble beginnings as a mid-'60s hippie enclave to its eventual late 1970s disintegration and literal incineration, Walker captures the magic and the moments that made Laurel Canyon a virtual Mecca for a generation of musicians.

Located to the north of West Hollywood, and just minutes away from the notorious Sunset Strip and legendary clubs like the Troubadour, The Whiskey A Go-Go, and The Roxy, Laurel Canyon was the perfect place for the musical wunderkinds of the sixties to put down roots. Walker begins his tale around 1965, when the Byrds discovered folk-rock and the power of a creative Dylan cover, and the burgeoning L.A. rock music scene was about to explode into the nation's consciousness and the top of the *Billboard* charts. From Frank Zappa and Cass Elliot to Joni Mitchell and Graham Nash, Walker explores the contributions and importance of the canyon's high-profile residents.

Through dozens of interviews as well as published articles and, importantly, the music created by the canyon's residents, Walker captures the memories and the vibe of Laurel Canyon. The influence and emergence of young artist managers and label executives like David Geffen and Elliot Roberts is integral to the story, as is the impact of the almost-instant wealth enjoyed by these young musicians, and the drugs that would eventually change the canyon's persona for the worse. Walker offers up a picture of Hollywood nightlife during the period, complete with groupies, cocaine and the clubs where deals were made and careers created, as well as exploring the antics of well-known visitors like John Lennon and members of Led Zeppelin.

With *Laurel Canyon*, Michael Walker has not only done a wonderful job of documenting the cultural currents that still influence popular music today, but he manages to put a human face on the canyon's legendary status, imbuing the participants – both well-known and otherwise – with distinctive personalities, desires and emotions. Doing so, he has managed to legitimize the often-told tales of Laurel Canyon and put them in proper perspective. A mesmerizing story, *Laurel Canyon* is an entertaining and informative history of one of rock music's most fabled eras, a once-in-a-generation alignment of talent, fate and circumstance that may never again be seen. (2006)

PETE FRAME
Even More Rock Family Trees   (Omnibus Press U.K.)

Music Journalist Pete Frame has enjoyed the sort of career that any music fan would give his or her eye teeth to experience. Frame was the founder of the British music magazine *ZigZag*, acting as the publication's editor from 1969 through 1973, and again later from 1976 through 1978. He managed the English cult band Starry Eyed & Laughing, worked as an A&R man for the Charisma Records label, and as press officer (publicist) for the legendary Stiff Records label.

Since 1979, Frame has made his living directly as a writer, contributing to publications like *New Music Express*, *Melody Maker*, *Rolling Stone*, and others. He has also been a producer on several documentaries for BBC radio, including tributes to Buddy Holly, Leonard Cohen, Elvis Presley, and Frank Zappa. Frame is best-known, however, not for his pen but rather for his penmanship, as the creator of intricate, detailed, and fascinating "rock family trees" that provide a genealogical history of various bands, right down to the names of individual members and what instrument they play.

Frame first began creating his rock family trees for *ZigZag*, putting together a chart on the Byrds for an issue in 1970, following it with a chart for British blues pioneer John Mayall a couple of issues later. By the magazine's 21st issue, published in July 1971, Frame landed on the "family tree" format that he's followed ever since, putting together a complex Al Kooper genealogy. These rock family trees have been used in the packaging of recordings by folks like Eric Clapton, Iron Maiden, Talking Heads, and many more, and were the basis for two six-part BBC television series during the 1990s that were narrated by the late John Peel.

Frame's work has also been published in a number of books. The first *Rock Family Trees* collection was published in 1979, and a second book, *Rock Family Trees, Vol. 2*, in 1983; the two volumes later combined in 1993 as a single book, *The Complete Rock Family Trees*. Frame took the series in a different direction with 1997's *The Beatles & Some Other Guys*, which covered in no little detail the British rock music scene of the 1960s, and followed it up a year later with the *More Rock Family Trees* collection.

After taking some time to put together the exhausting and entertaining *The Restless Generation*, a 500-page history of British rock in the 1950s, a decade of Frame's work has culminated in the recently-published *Even More Rock Family Trees*. Since that first chart in *ZigZag*, Frame has created some 140 family trees tying together over 2,000 bands and artists. Today, as they were 40 years ago, Frame's rock family trees are hand-drawn and notated on large 4' x 3' sheets of paper that are then scanned and reduced in size for publication. Sometimes a particular family tree is so crammed with details that a reader has to reach for a magnifying glass (or, for us old geezers, magnified reading glasses) to take it all in.

Even More Rock Family Trees features 33 absurdly-annotated genealogical charts of various bands that were created by Frame from the 1980s through the 2000s, and while there is some overlap with previous collections, there really is precious little duplication between volumes. The over-sized book begins with a bare-bones history of England's famed Creation Records label, outlining the connections between bands like My Bloody Valentine, Teenage Fan Club, the Boo Radleys, and Oasis, among others. Another quite detailed tree examines the 15 different Jesus & Mary Chain line-ups, including information on the band's recordings during the 1980s and '90s.

Frame doesn't restrict his work to just British rock history. His "Grunge: The Sound of Seattle" digs deep into the roots of popular bands like Pearl Jam, Nirvana, and Soundgarden, outlining the evolution of grunge from the early 1980s through the current superstardom of the Foo Fighters. Frame reaches back to his own youth for a chart on American R&B legends the Drifters, following the troubled band from its formation by singer Clyde McPhatter in 1953 to the hit-making, late '50s Ben E. King years, through the final shadow of the band that gave up the ghost during the mid-'80s.

While Frame has a taste for the classic rock of the 1960s and 1970s, he's not afraid to jump in and chronicle more recent bands like Suede or the Lyres. He's at his most comfortable with the oldies, though, and his four-page extended Allman Brothers Band family tree is a thing of beauty for the hardcore fan. "Surf City Here We Come!" outlines the history of the Beach Boys, Dick Dale, the Surfaris, and other like-minded bands while his detailed outline of Fleetwood Mac ties together John Mayall's Bluesbreakers, Rod Stewart, Chicken Shack, and Savoy Brown in a tree of many branches.

The careers of Elton John, Steve Winwood, Roger McGuinn, and Eric Clapton benefit from Frame's keen eye and steady hand; ditto for Roxy Music, Rainbow, Fairport Convention, and Emerson, Lake & Palmer, while Frame's history of the Boston folk scene, augmented by quotes from artists like Geoff Muldaur and Amos Garrett, shines a light on a wealth of often overlooked musical talent. Only one chart in *Even More Rock Family Trees* wasn't created by Frame, his acolyte Paul Barber putting together a fantastic timeline of jazz great Miles Davis's live bands from 1955 to 1975.

Admittedly, Frame's rock family trees books are for the diehard rock 'n' roll geek or OCD-inflicted music historian, but they're also a heck of a lot of fun. For those of us who have spent untold hours peering through the cryptic credits of the albums and CDs that we've spent a lifetime collecting, trying to piece together the minutiae of our favorite bands and artists, Frame's efforts seem downright Herculean.

Even More Rock Family Trees carries on the tradition of excellence begun by artist Pete Frame – and these rock family trees are, indeed, works of art – over 40 years ago. Be careful, though, 'cause once you dig into one of these books, you're going to lose hours at a time peering through the pages. (2012)

SUZY SHAW & MIKE STAX
Bomp 2: Born In The Garage
(Bomp!/Ugly Things Publishing)

OK, listen up kiddies! Back in the dark days before the electron-pushers moved all the even remotely interesting content to websites and blogs, we old folks used to have something known as a "fanzine," kind of like a magazine but usually published by an individual or small group of friends. Grandpa won't bore you all with the lengthy history of these "zines," as we called 'em, but they began circulating back in the 1930s among science-fiction fans, and were instrumental in underwriting the homegrown, hardcore punk rock movement of the '80s once photocopying technology made the damn things ubiquitous.

One of, if not the first music zine publisher was an elfin rock 'n' roll fanatic by the name of Greg Shaw. A rabid record collector, and a pretty darn good writer for somebody that considered himself an amateur, Shaw brought an insight to his work honed by thousands of hours listening to the *right* kind of music – 1960s-era garage-rock, three-chord punk (think the Seeds, not the Sex Pistols), British Invasion bands, classic soul, and R&B.

Shaw was also nothing if not a prolific publisher of various zines, and little was beyond his bourgeoning publishing empire and seemingly pathological need to put some words in print (an obsession shared by many of us of a similar bent). A familiar figure among science-fiction circles, one of Shaw's earliest publishing efforts was a *Lord of the*

Rings fanzine, and by the time that he graduated high school he had cranked out over 200 issues of various zines on the trusty mimeograph machine he had bought for just that purpose.

In 1966, however, influenced by the exploding San Francisco Bay area music scene, Shaw began publishing the zine that would arguably launch this entire "music journalism" thing. *Mojo-Navigator Rock & Roll News* began as a mere two-page mimeographed gossip rag, but quickly grew into a respectable full-color tabloid. *Mojo-Navigator* served a valuable purpose, documenting a vital music scene and writing the rules for music criticism.

Shaw's friend Jann Wenner would "borrow" heavily in style and substance from *Mojo-Navigator* when launching *Rolling Stone* magazine in 1967, and all sorts of out-of-the-mainstream music rags like *Creem*, *Rock Magazine*, and others would follow shortly. Meanwhile, Shaw pulled the plug on *Mojo-Navigator* after a couple of years when it became too big to manage, but this was really just the first step towards creating what would become the writer and publisher's lasting legacy – *Bomp!* magazine.

All of this, of course, is merely back story, a way of letting you young 'uns know that something **IMPORTANT** and **EXCITING** was happening long before your dag-nabbed Internet, and the Jonas Brothers reaching puberty, and all that Perez Hilton-approved rubbish. Greg Shaw moved from SF to L.A. around 1970 or so, and with that familiar itch rising up again like the black cat moan that it is, he began publishing a new mimeo zine called *Who Put The Bomp*.

By this time, mind you, Shaw had become an in-demand rockcrit writing for esteemed publications like *Creem* and *Fusion* and others, as well as editing the beloved corporate music zine *Phonograph Record Magazine*, which was published under the aegis, and with the checkbook of United Artists Records (yes, sometimes major record labels have gotten it right).

Shaw still managed to publish two or three issues of *Who Put The Bomp* annually during the early 1970s, featuring writers like Ken Barnes and the legendary Lester Bangs.

Who Put The Bomp evolved into *Bomp!* and grew, albeit slowly, throughout the 1970s until it became a full-fledged music magazine on the newsstand alongside relative latecomers like *Trouser Press*. Exhibiting Shaw's record-collecting interests, *Bomp!* often included full discographies alongside artist interviews and album reviews, and the one-time fanzine spun off a record label and a successful mail order business, both of which still maintain a healthy existence today.

As for the magazine itself, it became a victim of its own success, growing too large and popular and outgrowing Shaw's fanzine roots, so he pulled the plug on it in 1979. It was a wild ride while it lasted, however, and for those of us who were loyal readers, much of what we knew of British punk, new wave, American power pop, 1960s garage-rock, and lots of other music came from the pages of *Bomp!*.

All of which brings us around to the fine tome *Bomp! 2: Born In The Garage*, the second collection of material culled from Greg Shaw's many publications. The first volume, *Bomp! Saving The World One Record At A Time*, was published in 2007, edited by Mick Farren and overseen by Shaw's wife Suzy. A beautiful hardback collection, it included reproductions of pages from *Mojo-Navigator Rock & Roll News* and *Who Put The Bomp* mixed in with a lot of photos and commentary and such, all laid out rather artfully edgy, a design befitting a coffee table book meant to be seen and admired, but seldom read.

For *Bomp! 2*, Suzy Shaw has enlisted the help of editor Mike Stax, publisher of the obviously *Bomp!*-influenced music zine *Ugly Things*. The differences between this second, paperback collection and the abovementioned hardback tome are like those between a favorite indie-label rock album and a slick, overproduced major label release.

Befitting its garage-rock roots, the pages of *Bomp! 2* are untarnished by artifice and pretension, instead presenting pages and articles from Shaw's various zines in all their lo-fi glory! This is a book meant to be pored over, read and re-read until the wheels fall off.

The core of the book is, naturally, bits and pieces of issues of *Who Put The Bomp* and the wealth of material that Shaw published during the zine's tenure. Guided by the acronym "R.I.A.W.O.L." (rock is a way of life), Shaw offered commentary on favored bands, often assisted by readers like future Patti Smith Band guitarist and rock historian Lenny Kaye, and many others. *Bomp! 2* also includes segments of zines like Shaw's personalized *Karnis Bottle's Metanoia* and zines within zines like *Liquid Love* and *Alligator Wine*.

The importance of *Bomp!* was in its early, prescient musical coverage of artists now considered as important touchstones in the evolution of rock music. Shaw was the consummate fan, and his writing brims over with enthusiasm, while long-time contributor Ken Barnes offers a perspective and insight in his contributions that was too often missing from his more recent work for the *USA Today* newspaper.

Folks like Dave Marsh, Nick Tosches, Greil Marcus, Richard Meltzer, and Lester Bangs – the first generation of honest-to-god rock critics – often wrote interesting and sometimes lengthy letters that appeared in the zine's "Feedback" section, while articles like "Ahead of his Time: Gene Vincent's Influence in Rock & Roll" and "The British Invasion," featuring bands like the Pretty Things, the Dave Clark Five, and the Nashville Teens, helped readers get a handle on the music in this pre-Internet era.

As the fanzine evolved into a bona-fide music magazine, *Who Put The Bomp* expanded its coverage of bands like the Kinks, the Standells, Sky Saxon & the Seeds, the Easybeats, the Flamin' Groovies (which Shaw briefly managed during this time), and many others, all of which can be found in *Bomp! 2*. Articles providing comprehensive overviews of city-specific "scenes" in places like San Francisco, Chicago, Detroit, and Boston not only offered invaluable glimpses into young local bands (many of which would go "national"), but were also accompanied by lengthy discographies. Surf music (Dick Dale, etc),

"Girl Groups" (The Shangri-Las), power pop (Dwight Twilley), even Abba and Mexican punk music were all grist for Shaw and company's diverse and far-reaching musical tastes.

The many bands covered by the publication are timeless, and Greg Shaw's biggest strengths were his recognition of talents that were often unheralded at the time, and his unyielding belief in the music. Shaw was never trying to sell ads on his blog, nor was he angling for an appearance on a reality TV show. He never lost sight of the music he revered, collected, and fretted over for decades. This unbridled passion infects both his writing and that of his contributors through the years which, freed from the expectations of their journalistic "day jobs" at typical music magazines and newspapers, allowed them to pursue their own musical passions in *Bomp!*.

Bottom line: if you care a whit about rock 'n' roll music prior to 1980, *Bomp! 2* belongs on your bookshelf. This is vital, exciting music writing for the rock 'n' roll fan in all of us, and hopefully a modest success for *Bomp! 2* will lead to the publication of a third book offering more great stuff from the Greg Shaw archives. (2009)

Note: A word should be said about Suzy Shaw, Greg's wife and long-time friend and the person responsible for keeping the Bomp! legacy alive. Suzy took the reins of Greg's early record mail order business when he lost interest in the late 1960s, and it has been her commitment and business sense that supported the magazine, and kept the Bomp! family of record labels and the accompanying mail order business going strong all these years. If not for Ms. Shaw, Bomp! zine might have been lost to the ages. Thanks, Suzy!

CPSIA information can be obtained at www.ICGtesting.com
Printed in the USA
BVOW06s0057270916

463239BV00006B/22/P